BLACK MOTHERS AND ATTACHMENT PARENTING

Sociology of Children and Families series

Series editors: **Esther Dermott** and **Debbie Watson**
University of Bristol, UK

The *Sociology of Children and Families* series brings together the latest international research on children, childhood and families and pushes forward theory in the sociology of childhood and family life. Books in the series cover major global issues affecting children and families.

Out now in the series:

Sharing Care
Rachel Brooks and **Paul Hodkinson**

A Child's Day:
A Comprehensive Analysis of Change in Children's Time Use in the UK
Killian Mullan

Designing Parental Leave Policy:
The Norway Model and the Changing Face of Fatherhood
Elin Kvande and **Berit Brandth**

Social Research Matters:
A Life in Family Social Science
Julia Brannen

Nanny Families
Sara Eldén and **Terese Anving**

Find out more at
bristoluniversitypress.co.uk/sociology-of-children-and-families

Sociology of Children and Families series

Series editors: **Esther Dermott** and **Debbie Watson**
University of Bristol, UK

The *Sociology of Children and Families* series brings together the latest international research on children, childhood and families and pushes forward theory in the sociology of childhood and family life. Books in the series cover major global issues affecting children and families.

International advisory board:

Harry Brighouse, University of Wisconsin-Madison, US
Sara Eldén, University of Lund, Sweden
Mary Jane Kehily, The Open University, UK
Zsuzsa Millei, University of Tampere, Finland
Tina Miller, Oxford Brookes University, UK
Meredith Nash, University of Tasmania, Australia
Emiko Ochiai, Kyoto University, Japan
Gillian Ranson, University of Calgary, Canada
Anna Sparrman, Linköping University, Sweden
Ulrike Zartler, University of Vienna, Austria

Find out more at
bristoluniversitypress.co.uk/sociology-of-children-and-families

BLACK MOTHERS AND ATTACHMENT PARENTING

A Black Feminist Analysis of Intensive Mothering in Britain and Canada

Patricia Hamilton

B BRISTOL
UNIVERSITY
PRESS

First published in Great Britain in 2022 by

Bristol University Press
University of Bristol
1-9 Old Park Hill
Bristol
BS2 8BB
UK
t: +44 (0)117 374 6645
e: bup-info@bristol.ac.uk

Details of international sales and distribution partners are available at bristoluniversitypress.co.uk

British Library Cataloguing in Publication Data
A catalogue record for this book is available from the British Library

ISBN 978-1-5292-0793-4 hardcover
ISBN 978-1-5292-0794-1 paperback
ISBN 978-1-5292-0797-2 ePub
ISBN 978-1-5292-0796-5 ePdf

Cover design: blu inc, Bristol
Front cover image: Stocksy / Léa Jones

Contents

List of Figures and Tables

Figure

Tables

Acknowledgements

I've called three countries home in my life and each of these countries has contributed a great deal to the writing of this book. The idea of examining attachment parenting (AP) from the perspective of black mothers first germinated in South Africa, where I watched my sister wrestle with first-time motherhood. I gained new insight into something called 'parenting culture' when I did my Master's in Gender Studies at the University of Sussex in the UK and again, a few years later, when I returned to interview ten black mothers about their experiences with AP. And I did my doctoral work in Canada, interviewing a further nine women and where my status as a budding black feminist scholar was honed and shaped by the most skilful of supervisors. This book would not be possible without each of these three places that in different ways allowed me the intellectual and emotional space to work out my ideas and supported my growth as a scholar. More importantly, it would not be possible without the people who have travelled this journey with me.

I must begin with the mothers, the women who invited me into their homes, gave up their days off and lunch hours, introduced me to their children and told me their stories. I thank them for their generosity, their honesty and their passion (whether fervently dismissing AP or singing its praises). I only hope that I have done their narratives justice.

Thanks are also due to Erica Lawson, whose always insightful comments made my work that much stronger. Thank you also to Kristin Lozanski, Jessica Polzer, Andrea O'Reilly, Lorraine Davies and Pam McKenzie, for their thoughtful and invaluable feedback. I also appreciate the feedback and support offered by the team at Bristol University Press, particularly Esther Dermott, Shannon Kneis, and all of the peer reviewers. All errors remain my own.

Research isn't just reading, writing and pulling one's hair out. It's interspersed with (and made better by) barbeques, tarot readings and mid-week dinners. I wouldn't be able to do this work without the support and friendship of my peers. I'd like to thank colleagues in the Department of Women's Studies and Feminist Research at the University of Western Ontario, where I did my doctoral work. Special thanks are due to the 2013–14 MA and PhD cohort, Alicia McIntyre (she knows what she did!) and Jacqueline Potvin (thank you for the tarot reading, and everything else). Thank you also to colleagues in the Department of Sociology and Social Anthropology at Stellenbosch University, where I was given a warm welcome, kind advice and time to write. Thank you especially to Efua Prah, Ilana van Wyk, Khayaat Fakier, Lindy Heinecken and Rob Pattman. I must also thank Maud Perrier, Alison Phipps, Charlotte Faircloth and Tracey Reynolds for their advice and support along the way.

Thank you to the Ontario Trillium Scholarship for funding my doctoral work and to Health Canada for granting permission to reprint the Visible & Kissable poster.

And last, but certainly not least, I must thank my always supportive friends and my ever-patient family. Thank you to my mother, Eunice Maputle Hamilton, for your support and unwavering belief in me. Thank you to my father, Weizmann Hamilton, for reading almost every draft and bringing Marx into every political conversation we've ever had. Thank you to my sister, Shuia Hamilton Baloyi, for showing me the feminist light and for answering my inane questions about motherhood. Thank you to my niblings, Luka, Tiisetso, Isobel, Evie and Joseph for being absolute delights. Special thanks to Luka, whose birth inspired my fascination with mothering. And thanks, finally, to Jonny White, light of my life. Thank you for believing when I don't and putting up with my beautiful contradictions.

Introduction

Are you 'mom enough'?

In May 2012, *TIME* magazine chose a provocative image to capture its cover story on a new and increasingly popular parenting philosophy called attachment parenting (or AP). The image showed Jamie Lyn Grumet, a young white woman, breastfeeding her three-year-old son, Aram. Both Grumet and her son are standing, with Aram needing a stool to reach his mother's breast. If this pose and its subject matter were not challenging enough, the accompanying headline pushed further. 'Are you mom enough?', *TIME* asked, immediately evoking popular and particularly gendered debates about the kinds of parenting practices deemed 'enough'. Unsurprisingly, the cover resulted in an explosion of interest in the story, generating an abundance of thinkpieces, parodies and criticism.

In this single image, *TIME* skilfully (and perhaps, unintentionally) captured three of the central tensions at the heart of AP and the philosophy's rise to attention. First, the cover depicted breastfeeding, a simultaneously revered and reviled practice that embodies the contradictions of mothering discourse. Breastfeeding is encouraged and promoted by national governments and global health organizations but with seemingly little effect. Breastfeeding initiation and duration rates remain 'low'[1] and breastfeeding in public continues to attract angst and debate (Boyer, 2011; Tomori, 2014).

Second, the headline expressed the increasingly competitive nature of modern childrearing and its particularly gendered effects. Mothers are framed as individually responsible for their children's wellbeing and are measured by the level of energy, resources and attention they exert to achieve the goal of optimal child development (Hays, 1996). The range of tasks and duties for which mothers are responsible is increasingly specific and onerous, especially in the early years of a child's life (Edwards and Gillies, 2011). Mothers' heightened responsibility also reflects the contemporary neoliberal socioeconomic moment in which the wellbeing of children (and therefore society, according to some narratives) rests wholly on individual mothers' ability to successfully perform the duties of parenting.

Finally, the cover reveals the racial politics of contemporary mothering discourse and AP, in particular. Since the industrialization-era emergence of 'parenting' as an essential and socially significant obligation that requires expert intervention (Hays, 1996; Lee, 2014), race (as well as gender, class, ability, sexual orientation, citizenship, age and other social locations) has functioned to distinguish between those who are capable of 'good' motherhood and those who are not (Litt, 2000). AP's rise in popularity reflects this racialization of good motherhood. The philosophy draws inspiration from the parenting practices of so-called 'primitive' cultures for the purposes of delineating and affirming white, middle-class motherhood (Blum, 1999; Shome, 2011).

In this book, I examine the AP phenomenon from the perspectives of black mothers. What insights can their narratives offer about the contemporary experience of motherhood and the specific experiences of black mothers? As AP journeys from 'extreme' practice of privileged white hippies to an increasingly accepted and influential dogma in the policies of the state and medical professionals (Faircloth, 2013; Freeman, 2016; Hamilton, 2016), its equation with good mothering demands greater critical scrutiny. By measuring women by the extent to which they dedicate themselves to this kind of mothering, AP philosophy, and the ideologies it upholds, disciplines mothers, bolstering the status of white, middle-class mothers while constructing black, poor and other marginalized women as the sources of failed citizens. This book responds to this construction by turning to the experiences of black mothers.

By focusing on black mothers' engagements with AP, this book aims to disrupt the dominant construction of good mothering as the province of only white, middle-class women. The book documents the diverse ways black women use AP to assert themselves as good mothers. AP is a tool, differently taken up by the women interviewed for this book, but nonetheless central to understanding contemporary black motherhood. Through interviews with these mothers, the book develops a critical examination of AP, paying attention to both its emergence as a uniquely beneficial, state-endorsed style of parenting, as well as the philosophy's raced, classed and gendered dimensions. Attention to these aspects is a much-needed intervention in neoliberal contexts that disavow race, social class and gender as informing contemporary experiences and institutions of oppression.

AP is well suited to these contexts. It emphasizes individual childrearing decisions as a solution to the 'social and emotional diseases that plague our society' (Sears and Sears, 2001, p. ix). It mobilizes the parenting practices of 'traditional' cultures as a measure of white, middle-class motherhood, depriving 'traditional' women of expert status and disciplining all mothers. However, that does not preclude the possibility or space for alternative or unexpected interpretations of AP. The black mothers interviewed for this book engaged with AP in a myriad of ways, both embracing its reverence for 'nature' and rejecting its tendency towards the 'extreme'.

The analysis in this book focuses on the mothering experiences of 19 black women living in the United Kingdom (UK) and Canada, and AP's appearance in the state-produced parenting advice and policies of these countries. The book uncovers the complexity at the centre of societal definitions of good motherhood. It examines how mothers' understandings of how to be 'good' are shaped not only by dominant ideas that emphasize individual responsibility and intense dedication of physical, emotional, social and financial resources, but also by broader structural concerns such as racism, particularly its current neoliberal articulation. Who a good mother is and how she manages to maintain that status is a far more complicated picture than previous scholarship on motherhood, which has largely focused on white, middle-class experiences, has revealed. Tracey, one of the mothers interviewed, pointed to this complexity:

> '[W]hen it comes to black mothers, I think we want our voice to be heard about this. I think for a long time society kinda spoke for us and now that I think we're getting a little bit more educated in a lot of, just our own ... in our own experiences, I think now we want people to know that "Hey, we do this too."' (Tracey, 31, one daughter aged five months, interviewed in Canada)

Tracey's assertion that black mothers "do this too" counters the whiteness of AP as presented in the *TIME* cover story, which featured photographs of four AP mothers, all seemingly white. In this quote, she both accepts and rejects the dominant construction of AP (and, by implication, good mothering) as the preserve of white, middle-class women. She also signals black women's agency: in their claim on AP, the women in this study illuminate a vision of mothering that negotiates the individualizing, responsibilizing impulses of neoliberal ideology while centring their children's survival. Focus on their narratives facilitates a critical and complex view of mothering as both inherently informed by oppressive structures such as racism and sexism, as well as shaped by women's creative resistance to these oppressions. Through the lens of their experiences, this book sets out to explore two crucial and related questions: first, how do black mothers engage with AP, and second, what do those engagements tell us about AP, its inconsistent association with good mothering and the contemporary realities of black motherhood?

These questions cannot be answered without examining the context in which AP emerges. This book will consider the philosophy's alignment with neoliberal values while attending to the specific ways AP can be used to resist such values. Although the women profiled in this book express quite different opinions about the value of AP, sometimes rejecting the philosophy altogether, common themes weave through their narratives, each requiring a re-estimation of contemporary parenting discourses and cultures.

Structure of the book

Before turning to the women's experiences, Part I describes the context in which AP emerges and mothers engage with the philosophy. Comprising two chapters, Part I begins by considering AP's place in the broader ideological history of good mothering, indicating where the philosophy aligns with rather than rejects popular ideas about what constitutes a good mother. Chapter 2 examines the contemporary political context and pays special attention to how AP accords with neoliberal politics and the notion that society is 'post' race. In particular, it highlights both the specificities and similarities in Britain and Canada. With their similarly sized black populations and comparable histories of migration, these two countries offer unique and thus far underexplored insights about contemporary blackness and motherhood. Chapter 2 is also where readers are first introduced to the women interviewed in this study and some of the shared characteristics that inform the analysis of their experiences.

The chapters in Parts II and III focus on black mothers' lived engagements with AP. In Part II, the focus is on their negotiation of state-produced parenting advice that concerns the three Bs of AP: bedsharing, breastfeeding and babywearing. How does a focus on black mothers both reflect and shift normative practices of infant care in contemporary parenting culture? Part III considers how the mothers negotiate maternity and parental leave, whether using existing policies to fulfil their own idea of good mothering or criticizing policy gaps for failing working mothers. For some mothers, AP provides a useful tool to explain and justify their management of the demands of work and family.

Finally, Part IV explains the unexpected and resistive ways that AP may be deployed by black mothers and the potential this may hold in transforming how we examine and understand mothering. Here, the focus is on those mothers who identify most strongly with AP philosophy to tease out what possibilities (and limitations) AP offers as the women strive for good motherhood.

Examining AP through the lens of black mothers' experiences draws attention to the philosophy's place in neoliberal parenting culture. Specifically, this examination highlights how ideas about good parenting deploy or elide race, class and gender at different moments and for different, sometimes contradictory, purposes. Ideologies of good parenting purport to be free of gender, class and race but identify women as uniquely responsible for children's wellbeing, assume the practices of the middle classes (and the resources required for them) as the ideal and frame some children as more valuable and worthy of 'cultivation' (Lareau, 2011) than others.

AP offers a unique constellation of these raced, classed and gendered effects as it draws from monolithic 'primitive' cultures and rests on a taken-for-granted family form in which mothers are financially supported to stay at home, raising children, by well-earning fathers. The narratives of the black women presented in this study bring these realities into view, demanding an analysis of parenting that addresses the differential effects of racism and unequal access to resources. This does not mean that this book is the definitive explanation of contemporary black motherhood; instead my analysis offers *insights* into what it means to be a black mother today. This book is concerned not only with the experiences of mothers but also their ideas about appropriate maternal practice, the 'frames of meaning' (Silva, 2019, p. 4) through which mothers make sense of their parenting. Through their experiences, and the meanings mothers assign to them, this book suggests something as yet unexamined about the nature of mothering in a neoliberal, apparently postracial world.

This is the work of intersectionality: to point to the similarities and the differences in the experiences of marginalized groups and the structures (institutions, policies, ideologies) that govern these experiences; to dwell in the complexity of black mothers' experiences rather than offer simplified platitudes about what black mothers do.

The aim of this book is to find race, class and gender (where they have been sometimes overlooked) in contemporary parenting culture and AP, and black mothers' engagements with the philosophy provide a fruitful exemplar.

This book offers a rare focus on race (and black mothers in particular) in the growing field of parenting culture studies. Deploying an intersectional feminist perspective through which to consider these mothers' experiences allows for a re-examination of how we understand mothering, parenting and citizenship. The aim is to convey not only the ways that dominant ideologies restrict black women's experiences but also the opportunities for agency and resistance. Although this book may not be the promotional celebration of AP some of the profiled women may have wanted it to be, I hope that it offers not only a critique of AP but the potential for something more, a way to respond to the tensions generated by the current socioeconomic moment *and* suggest possibilities for alternative futures (McKittrick, 2006) of mothering.

PART I

Contextualizing Attachment Parenting: AP's Rise to Prominence (and Infamy)

From Scientific Motherhood to Intensive Mothering

The rich and complex history of childrearing practices most often coalesces around women's behaviour. Because women are imagined as best suited to perform the work of childrearing, maternal behaviour has long been the subject of state, public and academic scrutiny. Although the definitions and expectations of motherhood change with the times and advancements characteristic of a particular era, one consistency has been the construction of mothers as primarily responsible for preparing children as future citizens, ensuring that they grow up to be responsible, contributing members of society. This construction is particularly salient as transformations in the way we view childhood shift the way we understand childrearing (Faircloth, 2014a). Parenting is now a task, 'a form of learned interaction' that determines children's success or failure (Lee, 2014, p. 8). In this recent history of the emergence of parenting as a task, there are two key ideologies that help to contextualize the rise of AP. The first is scientific motherhood, the dominant framing for 'good' motherhood in the late 19th and early 20th centuries in the UK and Canada, and the second is intensive mothering, the cultural contradictions of which define contemporary parenting culture.

Scientific motherhood

Scientific motherhood is 'the idea that mothering should be guided by scientific supervision and principles' (Litt, 2000, p. 21). Although the ideology first emerged in the late 19th and early 20th centuries, the notion that science is best suited to inform parenting has continued to define what we call 'good' motherhood, evident for example, in the current reliance on neuroscience to shape parenting (Lowe et al, 2015). The emergence of scientific motherhood coincided with the arrival of 'scientism' (Wilkie, 2003, p. 177) in European and North American societies, during which major scientific innovations such as the discovery of germ theory completely transformed the way everyday people, particularly mothers, lived their lives. This discovery, and scientism in general, enabled the emergence of preventative medicine and thus began the first indication of medical interest in the behaviour and habits of mothers.

Physicians' newfound interest in mothering behaviour reflected a larger cultural phenomenon that emerged alongside and as a result of scientism: medicalization. Medicalization is 'the process through which medical interpretations have acquired cultural legitimacy' (Litt, 2000, p. 4) to the exclusion of other explanations. This process is most clearly evident in the shifts in the customs of childbirth over the past 300 years (Stone, 2009). Medical involvement in childbirth transformed the process from a woman–centred activity that took place in the home to a thoroughly medical exercise located in a hospital and attended by a (male) physician. Medical interest in motherhood was not limited to the location and functions of childbirth, in keeping with the principles of the newly discovered notion of preventative medicine; physicians were also interested in the behaviour of mothers after they had left the labour ward. Thus, scientific motherhood was born.

Although scientific motherhood may have first appeared as a legitimate route through which women might access science (Wilkie, 2003; Apple, 2006), in practice it became a way for physicians to promote their expertise as superior to that of mothers and extant birth attendants (Carter, 1995). Scientific motherhood required a good mother who listened dutifully to the instruction provided by physicians and required no explanations. It was in this guise that the gendered, raced and classed values that scientific motherhood espoused became clear, as the following two brief examples from each of the study sites in this book demonstrate: the marginalization of midwifery in Canada and the promotion of bottle feeding in the UK.

The marginalization of midwifery in Canada

In the late 19th and early 20th centuries, childbirth was a crucial site at which the superiority of science and medicine could be asserted. Given the high rates of infant and maternal mortality (for example, in Canada, between 1921 and 1925 the infant mortality rate was 99 per every 1,000 live births), this line of reasoning was effective, despite the fact that these mortality rates were largely the consequence of poverty and urbanization. These rates were particularly alarming for Canada and other Western nations as they experienced the upheaval of world wars, immigration and industrialization. Physicians positioned themselves as a solution to these problems and, supported by newly established public health bodies (Arnup, 1990), endorsed an effective campaign to delegitimize the people responsible for overseeing childbirth in the home at the time: midwives.

The marginalization of midwives in Canada was definitively shaped by racism, sexism and classism and echoed similar attempts to displace midwifery in the United States (US) and Europe in this same period. Male physicians were able to use the strength of their newly established professional organizations and the prevailing sexist ideology of the time to not only speak out against women's co-education, including their entry into medicine (Burke, 2007), but to condemn the practice of midwifery overall. Relying on the credibility garnered from societal appreciation of the wonders of science, physicians asserted themselves as the superior alternative to midwives. Myths about midwives as 'unsanitary, superstitious and dangerous' (Wilkie, 2003, p. 197) bolstered this process, alongside the association between midwifery and immigrant women (Plumming, 2000). Indeed, the racialization of midwives' inferiority (Nestel, 2006) was a particularly effective strategy to dismiss midwives' experience and expertise, especially in the broader historical context of majority white nations worried about the diluting effects of immigration.

Midwifery's 'alegal' status (Plumming, 2000, p. 169) also contributed to its decline. Lacking legal recognition, midwives were denied the use of life-saving innovations such as forceps. Their legal status also had financial effects. As a result, in some provinces, midwifery care could not be paid for using provincial health insurance. Physicians had a vested economic interest in laying claim to childbirth care and its ability to secure patients 'for life' (Baillargeon, 2009). The displacement of midwives had particular raced and classed effects on marginalized populations. The advice to seek out the care of a physician rather than a midwife was part of a broader medicalization of motherhood in which working-class and immigrant women's motherhood was redrawn 'in terms of white, middle-class values and attitudes' (Baillargeon, 2009, p. 5). For Indigenous communities, the derogation of midwifery was yet another apparatus of colonization (Jasen, 1997). The shift to physician-attended births disrupted cultural practices around pregnancy and childbirth and affected the transmission of cultural traditions associated with midwifery (Jasen, 1997). For immigrant and racialized communities, the realities of poverty and the limited number of physicians meant that many women were unable to pursue the scientific advancements offered by a physician-led birth but were forced to use the services of midwives in increasingly precarious positions, thanks to changes in legislation governing midwifery.

In almost every avenue, midwifery was reimagined as a dangerous pseudo profession that ought to be done away with for the good of individual women and babies, as well as for the good of the nation. The raced and classed elements of this reconstruction reflect the popularity of eugenics as an explanatory tool. Although midwifery is currently undergoing a resurgence in Canada (Nestel, 2006), the legacy of the dismissal of midwifery as a legitimate, woman-centred profession continues to inform the way in which childbirth is framed today.

The promotion of bottle feeding in the UK

In the UK, scientific motherhood was shaped by the state's long-standing interest in policing women's behaviour, particularly that of working-class and poor women. The notion that scientific, expert intervention was necessary to alter maternal behaviour expressed itself in the emergence of the 'semi professions' of health visiting and midwifery (Carter, 1995, p. 49), with particular attention paid to infant feeding. This attention is evident in the building of milk depots and the establishment of free milk programmes and infant welfare centres during the early 20th century and the often contradictory advice offered to women about how best to feed their babies. Although breastfeeding was identified as the key to solving high infant mortality rates and, more generally, the attainment of good motherhood, state authorities relied on the provision of artificial milk to maintain their interest in the control and surveillance of women's behaviour (Carter, 1995). This is best demonstrated in the establishment of milk depots in which sterilized milk was made available to mothers in exchange for consenting to having their babies weighed and monitored, sometimes in their own homes. These depots underlined the importance of expert intervention both in the form of provision of scientifically sterilized milk and in the guidance (and surveillance) provided by 'lady visitors' (Carter, 1995, p. 45) to ensure that infants were being fed hygienically. The wider context of the increased medicalization of childbirth also contributed to the discrepancy between claiming the superiority of breastfeeding while tacitly encouraging the use of artificial milk. The transfer of birth from the home to the hospital, which involved the practice of keeping newly born infants in a separate nursery, away from their mothers, significantly undermined any attempt to establish and maintain a viable breastfeeding relationship (Nathoo and Ostry,

2009). The ideology that required mothers to cede authority to medical experts meant that, while mothers were in the hospital, it was often nurses who were responsible for childrearing in the first days of an infant's life and, in these circumstances, bottle feeding was the most convenient method (Carter, 1995; Faircloth, 2013).

During this period, much of the scientifically motivated state intervention in childrearing was entangled with an attempt to discourage women from working outside of the home (Hardyment, 1983; Carter, 1995). Encouraging breastfeeding was one way to combine these two goals, emphasizing each child's need to be fed and nurtured by its mother. However, an entrenched class hierarchy that stressed working-class women's inferiority and ignorance, combined with a strong belief in the power of science, meant that the state preferred to rely on ' "scientific" solutions' (Carter, 1995, p. 47) to maximize infants' wellbeing. Even the minority of women who continued breastfeeding could not escape these scientific instructions. For example, the advice to feed to a schedule shaped breastfeeding mothers' experiences and, because routine feeding is so unsuited to breastfeeding, often resulted in women switching to the bottle (Hardyment, 1983). Whether choosing to breastfeed or bottle feed their children, women found that their experience of motherhood was constrained by the expectation that mothering 'required expert advice and intervention to be successful' (Faircloth, 2013, p. 40).

A fair exchange?

This is not to suggest that the rise of scientific motherhood was experienced as wholly oppressive by all women. In both the examples described in the previous sections, it is important to recognize that scientific motherhood was not merely an ideology forcibly imposed on women (Carter, 1995; Litt, 2000; Apple, 2006). For some working-class women, the demand for hospitalization during birth or the preference for bottle feeding over breastfeeding allowed them access to pain relief or the opportunity to have a break from the burden of housework and work outside of the home (Carter, 1995; Faircloth, 2013). Middle-class women could be similarly enthusiastic about the ideology of scientific motherhood, especially the professional status it granted motherhood. Some middle-class women were complicit in the displacement of midwives and actively encouraged the medicalization of childbirth as it offered reprieve from the pain associated with birth (Baker, 2010; Phipps, 2014). However, overall, women exchanged access to scientific expertise for surveillance and intensified attempts to control their behaviour (Arnup, 1990). Scientific motherhood also rested on and reinforced a construction of mothers as responsible for their children's and therefore wider society's failures, ranging from high infant mortality rates to the lack of proficiency among men who signed up to fight as soldiers in the First World War (Apple, 2006).

Although the examples of the marginalization of midwifery and the promotion of breastfeeding are described in country-specific terms here, they are not unique to Canada and the UK, respectively. While it is true that midwifery in the UK was able to survive the increased medicalization of birth that marks the turn of the 20th century, the ideologies that lauded physicians' superiority over that of midwives are still recognizable in Britain (Carter, 1995). Similarly, Canadian policy about infant feeding named breastfeeding as the best option but nonetheless promoted practices that undermined it. In particular, the growth of paediatrics resulted in a fascination with developing artificial alternatives to breastmilk, grounded in financial incentives involving mutually beneficial relationships between doctors and infant-milk manufacturers as well as physicians' suspicion of the quality of breastmilk (Nathoo and Ostry, 2009).

These examples mark a long trajectory of medical attempts to undermine mothers' power and autonomy, and these attempts have affected the way breastfeeding and childbirth are understood today. For example, the movement that helped bring about the re-emergence of midwifery in Canada in the early 1990s could not escape the tacit racism that led to the marginalization of midwifery in the first place. The project of rehabilitating the image of the midwife in Canadian society required emphasis on the contemporary midwife as 'respectable ... knowledgeable, modern, educated, and Canadian/white' (Nestel, 2006, p. 7), resulting in the exclusion of immigrant and racialized midwives, especially those educated in the Global South. The promotion of midwifery and related practices of home and natural birth in North America remains dominated by white, middle-class women and has become implicated in the language of not only scientific expertise but also neoliberal notions of consumer citizenship (Craven, 2007).

With regard to breastfeeding, the 1956 founding of La Leche League, one of the most influential pro-breastfeeding organizations operating today, was spurred by seven American mothers' determination to disrupt the image of mothering that scientific motherhood promoted. The League sought to redefine good mothering by linking it to breastfeeding and other mothering practices framed by what it called 'naturalism' (Weiner, 1997, p. 363). This turn echoes our contemporary exaltation of nature in the face of growing anxieties about the 'uncertain effects of technological progress' (Wolf, 2011, p. 17; Faircloth, 2013). Regardless of these uncertainties, we continue to rely on science to govern ourselves and our societies (Faircloth, 2013), transforming our preference for the 'natural' into an evidence-based decision. The elevation of breastfeeding as the most 'natural' infant-feeding option is directly connected to its scientifically confirmed benefits. The promotion of 'natural' birth is justified through reference to the improved outcomes for babies and mothers. The science and expertise of scientific motherhood is draped in the language of 'nature' and reborn in parenting philosophies such as AP.

The intersection of nature and science in the promotion of certain ideals of mothering has clear racial dimensions. Scientific motherhood rested on the belief that women were 'naturally' suited to mothering but nonetheless required expert guidance to get it 'right'. Those understood as especially close to nature, particularly black women and working-class women, did not benefit from this construction (Carter, 1995) and often found that their 'natural' capacity for motherhood was used as a pretext to deny them adequate healthcare (Phoenix, 1990; Bridges, 2011) and state support. These women were also subject to more stringent forms of surveillance and policing or, as in the case of some African-American mothers, understood as incapable of reaching the standard required of scientific mothers and simply ignored altogether (Litt, 2000). Scientific motherhood embodied the norms of white, middle-class motherhood and while it sought to disperse those values among all mothers, there were limited opportunities to meet its prescripts for marginalized women. These realities are much the same in our contemporary era of intensive mothering, an ideology that retains scientific motherhood's expert guidance and emphasizes women's responsibility to respond to their children's needs ahead of their own. AP emerges as a representation of this ideology with an added focus on nature and its corresponding racial undertones.

Attachment parenting

Most commonly associated with paediatrician–nurse couple William and Martha Sears, AP is a child-centred philosophy that prioritizes 'learning to read the cues of your baby and responding appropriately to those cues' (Sears and Sears, 2001, p. 2; Dear-Healey, 2011; Liss and Erchull, 2012). AP purports *not* to be a 'strict set of rules' (Sears and Sears, 2001, p. 2), but nevertheless tends to involves particular childrearing techniques, specifically 'natural' birth, extended breastfeeding, babywearing and bedsharing. These techniques or tools, as the Sears' refer to them, are promoted as most likely to produce 'kind, affectionate, empathic, well disciplined ... bright and successful' children (Sears and Sears, 2001, p. ix). Although its popularity is growing (as increasing numbers of news reports, features and social media groups demonstrate), the philosophy is often met with derision and characterized as 'extreme'. Its appearance in the mainstream reflects a broader discourse of expertise, which AP happily exploits, purporting to return expertise to where it 'rightfully' belongs: the parent. As the Sears' (2001) explain, 'The first step in learning how to guide your child is to become an expert in your child' (p. ix). However, this process is supported by accessing the expertise offered by the Sears' themselves in any one of their over 30 parenting books (Faircloth, 2014b).

The Sears' claim that their expertise is drawn from the parenting practices of 'traditional societies' (Green and Groves, 2008, p. 523). The claim is that parents in the West have become distanced from the 'instinctual' (Sears and Sears, 2001, p. ix) behaviours of their ancestors and need to look to the biologically beneficial activities of 'primitive' societies for inspiration. This focus on the 'naturally superior' parenting capabilities of racialized women in the Global South puts their counterparts in the Global North in a precarious position: the culture of their 'homeland' should predispose them to AP philosophy and therefore locate them as good mothers. However, the historical and ongoing pathologization of mothers of colour, particularly black mothers (Roberts, 1997a; Collins, 2000), in the Global North forecloses the possibility of black women being read as good mothers and overlooks the particularities and complexities of mothering practices.

A word on attachment theory

From its name alone, it is clear that AP draws and builds on the foundation laid by attachment theory, a psychological and child development theory developed in the 1950s. Attachment theory posits that every child needs and should have 'committed caregiving' from one or a few adults (Bretherton, 1992, p. 770). Most commonly associated with John Bowlby, who coined the term, and Mary Ainsworth, who provided methodological insights and conducted one of the most well-known attachment studies, attachment theory argues that the relationship formed between parent and child in the early years of life is crucial for healthy mental development (Bretherton, 1992). Although there is much talk of 'primary caregivers' in more recent work on attachment theory, Bowlby prioritized the *mother*–child relationship, reflecting dominant cultural prescriptions that deem women the natural caregivers of children and develop models of good mothering based on middle-class norms (Contratto, 2002; Símonardóttir, 2016).

Extending this focus on the 'natural', attachment theory draws on Ainsworth's work in Uganda in which she first began to lay the foundations for her famous 'strange situation' methodology (Bretherton, 1992). The 'strange situation' enables the measurement of children's attachment to their mothers as either ambivalent, avoidant or secure and involves subjecting 12- to 18-month-old babies to a 20-minute experiment in which they are separated from their mothers and introduced to a stranger over a series of eight stages. A baby's response when the mother returns to the room in the final stage determines their level of attachment. Despite questions about cross-cultural applicability, the 'strange situation' remains one of the key measures of infant attachment today (Cox, 2006), just as a belief in the importance of mother–child attachment continues to inform modern parenting advice.

The same 'infant determinism' (Contratto, 2002, p. 31) that underlies attachment theory operates in AP, evident for example, in the Sears' claim that adopting AP will cause children to 'turn out better' (Sears and Sears, 2001, p. x). Further, the Sears' similarly and problematically draw on the parenting practices of 'traditional societies' as proof of the superiority of AP. The distinction between attachment theory and AP lies in the latter's emphasis on certain techniques that are said to aid the development of secure attachment (a phrase seemingly lifted from Ainsworth's measure of attachment). The explicit link between extended breastfeeding, bedsharing and babywearing and the building of a securely attached relationship between mother and child is drawn by the Sears', rather than Bowlby, Ainsworth or other attachment theorists (Cox, 2006; Faircloth, 2013) and it is increasingly this vision of attachment, one focused on specific parenting behaviours, that dominates popular culture.

Continued reference to Bowlby and Ainsworth, who are both very well-known developmental psychologists, serves to offer credibility to the Sears' project and is reflected in their decision to change the name of their parenting approach from 'immersion mothering' to 'attachment parenting'. As Martha Sears explains: "I realised we needed to change the term to something more positive, so we came up with AP, since the Attachment Theory literature was so well researched and documented" (Nicholson and Parker, nd). Invoking attachment theory lends AP an immediate legitimacy and trustworthiness that helps boost the Sears' claim that AP is supported by science, regardless of the numerous critiques of attachment theory itself (Eyer, 1992).

AP certainly owes a debt to attachment theory (Símonardóttir, 2016). Such a theoretical foundation bolsters AP's gendered approach to good parenting and contributes to the assertion of the Sears' expertise. However, there is a distinction between the two and this book is concerned with attachment *parenting* and the particular practices it engenders.

Intensive mothering

AP's focus on childrearing techniques is a reflection of the broader ideology of intensive mothering. Intensive mothering, a term coined by sociologist Sharon Hays in the mid-1990s, defines good parenting as the ability to invest significant levels of physical, emotional and financial resources into childrearing (Hays, 1996). As Hays (1996) argues, intensive mothering calls for 'professional-level skills' (p. 4) and access to 'all possible information on the latest childrearing techniques' (p. 6). In other words, like scientific motherhood, contemporary mothering ideology calls on mothers to seek expert advice about an endlessly long list of specific behaviours but also requires that women retain this information in order to exercise the 'right' parenting choices. Expanding the model laid out by scientific motherhood, intensive mothering emphasizes mothers' responsibilities not only to ensure their children's 'normal' development but to maximize it. Mothers' success in this endeavour can be measured against the standards of 'normal' child development, standards that were only possible to establish because of the routinization of childbirth and infancy care characteristic of scientific motherhood (Faircloth, 2013). As suggested earlier in this chapter, medical professionals were granted unprecedented access to large numbers of infants both at the time of birth and through repeated visits either to mothers' homes (in the UK) or well baby clinics (in Canada). Through these interactions, they established standards of 'proper' child development and afforded great significance to parents' abilities to meet these standards. In the contemporary context, these standards are translated into norms of good mothering that require the transformation of 'the everyday experience of mothering [into a] … set of skills to be honed and perfected' (Faircloth, 2013, p. 22).

Both the content of these skills and the capacity to acquire them is structured by race, class, dis/ability, sexuality and other socially produced categories. The norms that determine intensive mothering

18

are white and middle-class in origin (Hays, 1996) and thus implicitly exclude and exploit marginalized women (Bloch and Taylor, 2014) while continuing to judge their mothering by its standards (Ennis, 2014). However, marginalized women do not merely submit to this judgement. Black mothers, for example, have, in some cases, organized their parenting outside these boundaries, rejecting the individualism of intensive mothering in favour of a collective approach in which mothering is shared by extended family members and the community (Blum, 1999; Collins, 2000; Forna, 2000). However, the extent to which black mothers practise such a collective approach is the subject of much scholarly debate (McDonald, 1997; Blum, 1999). Marginalized mothers' ability to negotiate intensive mothering is further contextualized by the contradiction at the heart of intensive mothering: the elevation of a self-sacrificing, sacred mode of childrearing and self-interested, rational, capitalist logic.

This contradiction is evident in the rising numbers of women entering the workforce and the 'increasing emphasis on the importance of labour-intensive, emotionally absorbing mothering' (Faircloth, 2013, p. 24; Hays, 1996). It is arguably the result of competing visions of efficient, self-disciplining workers and a resolute belief in children's need for dedicated and committed parenting in order to achieve their full potential (and themselves become efficient, self-disciplining workers). Women respond to this contradiction in a variety of ways, including, for example, full-time commitment to mothering at the expense of paid work or attempting to maintain a balance between both. Whichever approach women choose, access to material and social resources such as family support play an important role in women's ability to manage the demands of intensive mothering. The necessity of this support demonstrates how unrealistic intensive mothering ideology is: it positions mothers as exclusively and individually responsible for the intensive rearing of their children, but, in reality, cannot be accomplished without a wider network of support. The success of intensive mothering lies in the ideological work it performs to assert the superiority of a more traditional division of labour in households and workplaces, requiring that women return their attention to childrearing and other associated duties of the home.

The contradictions created by intensive mothering are racialized and may be particularly acute for black women, who have higher rates of lone parenthood and higher labour participation rates than their white counterparts, but are also more likely to be working in low-status, poorly paid jobs. Black women's experiences of work are shaped by racism and sexism but also by their experiences of migration and its associated policies. Racially exclusive immigration policies in both the UK and Canada, for example, have recruited black women to work in poorly paid, exploitative positions and often explicitly prevented them from bringing or starting families in their new homes (Massaquoi, 2007; Lawson, 2013). Social class further complicates black women's experiences of work and migration. For example, the myth of the black superwoman, often portrayed in contrast to her 'feckless', working-class babymother counterpart, overstates black women's achievements in employment and education for the purposes of perpetuating the myth of meritocracy (Reynolds, 1997) and postracism.

Conclusion

In its creation of the 'information-seeking mother' who relies on a physician for expert guidance (Apple, 2006, p. 35), scientific motherhood lays the groundwork for the emergence of AP. Although AP makes claims about nature and the practices of 'ancient' and 'traditional' cultures, AP experts such as the Sears' also cite (questionable) scientific support to justify their promotion of attachment-promoting childrearing techniques. Scientific motherhood establishes the 'relationship between motherhood and expert knowledge' that characterizes contemporary mothering (Faircloth, 2013, p. 28) and on which AP's popularity is built.

Such a relationship also facilitates intensive mothering, which, while unrealistic, remains the dominant model of good motherhood, shaping the experiences of women located at different social locations (Hays, 1996; Romagnoli and Wall, 2012; Elliott et al, 2013). The ideology's dominance reflects shifts in social, political and economic understandings of how society *ought* to operate and proposes a return to the traditional division of gender roles in families (McRobbie, 2013) echoed in scientific motherhood. AP encapsulates these shifts, strategically deploying science and harkening back to an imagined natural past in which social problems can be resolved through decisions such as where a baby sleeps at night. As an example of intensive mothering, AP demonstrates the raced and classed fallouts of such nostalgia and that exploring the experiences of black mothers complicates the contradictions expressed by intensive mothering. Attempts to address conflicting definitions of good motherhood and good citizenship are informed by the context that produces these definitions in the first place. In particular, how we understand the former has become intertwined with a belief in the stability and superiority of nature, a comforting safe space in which to retreat from the uncertainties of our risky world. The next chapter explores the details of this risky world, especially as they are shaped by neoliberalism and a belief that we are living in a moment after race.

Why Now? AP in a Neoliberal, Postracial Context

Since it was first named in the late 1980s, AP has grown in popularity and has inspired a host of media and public attention. The establishment of organisations such as Attachment Parenting International reflect the global expansion of the philosophy's reach, with forums and support groups in locations such as Brazil, Norway and Turkey. This increased interest in AP is part of a broader intensification of parenting, captured in the ideology of intensive mothering (Hays, 1996; Faircloth, 2013). This chapter considers why AP has emerged at this particular socioeconomic moment, linking AP's heightened popularity to the dominance of neoliberalism in Britain and Canada (and, indeed, the world). Neoliberalism shapes and is shaped by race, especially the role it plays in distinguishing between 'good' and 'failing' citizens, and is inextricably tied to motherhood, which is understood as essential to the production of such citizens.

Everything is neoliberal and neoliberalism is everything

Neoliberalism is a 'peculiar form of reason that configures all aspects of existence in economic terms' (Brown, 2015, p. 17; see also Banet-Weiser and Mukherjee, 2012), centring the market as the organizing principle of all aspects of life (Giroux, 2008). Neoliberal reason redraws the lines of democracy, citizenship and subjectivity and frames them in the terms of the market (Larner, 2000). The economy is the focus in all avenues, with the state's sole purpose conceptualized as the protection and facilitation of economic growth (Brown, 2006, 2015). In such a scenario, governments might champion ostensibly social justice initiatives but only insofar as they contribute to economic growth. Relations between people and their government are similarly structured, with principles of individual responsibility, entrepreneurialism and self-investment taking centre stage (Rose, 1999; Brown, 2015). In a 2016 speech describing his government's approach to poverty alleviation, the then British Prime Minister David Cameron emphasized both the essential role he imagines the family playing in overcoming poverty and the importance of addressing such problems for the purposes of protecting national 'economic security' (Cameron, 2016a). The Canadian Prime Minister Justin Trudeau's 2015 Liberal election promises concentrated on 'investing in the future' and 'helping the middle-class'. Economic growth is understood as a taken-for-granted good that can improve the lives of all.

The ruling political parties in both Canada and the UK express neoliberal values in the way they centre economic growth in their policy agendas, each choosing different paths to achieve this goal. During the 2015 federal election in Canada, Trudeau's Liberal party framed itself as distinct from the divisive politics and 'austerity agenda' offered by Stephen Harper's Conservatives (Ruckert and Labonté, 2016, p. 212). The Liberals' 2015 campaign platform spotlighted helping 'middle-class' Canadians and committed to investing in public infrastructure even if such investment requires running at a deficit. However, despite these shifts, the emphasis on economic growth above all else has limited the progressive scope of Liberal policies (Ruckert and Labonté, 2016). In the UK, the Conservative government's commitment to an austerity agenda has remained (largely) unshaken despite the upheaval following the 2016 referendum on the UK's membership of the European Union and several changes in leadership. Since 2010, in coalition with the Liberal Democrats to the 2016–19 premiership of Theresa May, the Conservatives have committed to '£82 billion in cumulative tax changes and cuts in social security spending' (Women's Budget Group, 2016) in their pursuit of a balanced budget, a trend that has continued under the current Prime Minister Boris Johnson despite claims to the contrary (Wren-Lewis, 2019). The deleterious effects of these policies on women, poor people, refugees and people of colour have been obscured by the veneer of a 'compassionate' Conservative ideology that purports to reward those who 'play by the rules' (Page, 2015, pp. 118, 129).

Although proponents of neoliberalism might portray it as merely a 'neutral, technical' (Duggan, 2003, p. xiii; Spence, 2012) exercise in achieving the 'universally desirable' goals of 'economic expansion and democratic government' (Duggan, 2003, p. 10), the neoliberal project cannot be separated from the cultural and political context through which it has emerged and which it continues to shape. The explicit purpose of neoliberalism – 'upward redistribution' (Duggan, 2003,

p. x) – cannot be achieved without the construction and promotion of ideological justifications to enable it (Duggan, 2003; Giroux, 2008).

The depoliticization of race

The ideological justifications that affirm neoliberal reason are fundamentally raced, classed and gendered. Although these social categories are declared as irrelevant to the fulfilment of good citizenship, neoliberalism functions *through* them (Duggan, 2003), relying, for example, on entrenched racism to justify the gutting of the welfare state (Roberts, 1993; Roberts and Mahtani, 2010). With its emphasis on individual choice and freedom, neoliberalism rejects the notion that social class, race and gender present structural constraints that limit life chances. Ostensibly, individuals are 'free' to make the 'right' decisions to make the best and least burdensome contribution to society. In this new vision of self-sufficient citizens and subjects, thanks to the 'successes' of the civil rights and feminist movements, racism and sexism are no longer credible threats to the health, wealth and success of individual women and people of colour.

The belief that we are in a 'post' phase of identity discourses and politics (Dunn, 2016) is a crucial feature of neoliberal governance and is particularly the case for contemporary approaches to race. Race functions as a kind of 'absent presence' (Hamilton, 2016, p. 413); on the one hand, the 'problem' of racism is located in the past (or elsewhere), while blackness, in particular, remains an indicator of poor economic productivity and, therefore, failed citizenship (Roberts and Mahtani, 2010; Hamilton, 2016). Even as (and perhaps, *because*) discourses of diversity and inclusion gain prominence, race is recast in terms of cultural difference (Lentin and Titley, 2011) rather than as a structural and political obstacle to racialized people's ability to meet the standards of neoliberal citizenship.

The consequences of postracialism and other post–identity discourses (for example, postfeminism) hinder attempts to build solidarity and coalition politics by 're-articulating [intersectional oppressions] as independent oppressions that can be repudiated one at a time, and thereby ensuring neoliberalism's oppressions writ large are never fully or sufficiently confronted' (Dunn, 2016, p. 273). Recognition of interlocking forms of oppression and articulation of the precise and complex ways in which the interrelationships between race, gender and social class among others shape policy and lived experience is a crucial aspect of understanding and undermining the effects of neoliberal projects (Dillon, 2012).

The key contention underpinning the claim that we now live in a postracial society is that we have overcome a racially problematic past (Cho, 2009). While much of the scholarship on postracialism tends to be situated in the US (many cite the 2008 election of Barack Obama as the 'racially transcendent event' marking the disavowal of racism [Cho, 2009, p. 1597; see also Springer, 2007; Squires, 2010; Teasley and Ikard, 2010]), the postracial in the UK and Canada appears and operates in ways uniquely suited to these locations. For both countries, comparison with the US is made in order to claim political superiority on matters of race (McKittrick, 2006; Perry, 2015).

In Canada, geographical proximity as well as close political and economic relations make comparison inevitable and enables the construction of the Canadian nation as a liberal, multicultural haven from the open racism and bigotry firmly located south of the border. One of the most pronounced examples of this dichotomous construction is the emphasis often placed on the sanctuary Canada offered to enslaved African Americans, an emphasis that facilitates the erasure of Canada's own history of slavery and its practices of racial oppression (Walcott, 2003, p. 50; Abdi, 2005). This dichotomy facilitates emotional distance from any racist policies and practices contained in Canada's history. Even if such practices are identified and acknowledged, the twin narratives of 'Canada as a mosaic' (Bannerji, 2000) and 'the USA is much worse' (Abdi, 2005) operate to negate their impact. As race relations in the US attract increased scrutiny and attention thanks to the activism of groups such as Black Lives Matter and the policies and popular support of president Donald Trump, myths about Canada's friendly non-racism persist (Nelson, 2017).

In the UK, postracial discourses are underlined by a long-standing 'mystique of anti-racism' (Perry, 2015, p. 19). The widely held belief that British history, and therefore contemporary Britain, is free of any whiff of racial impropriety, especially legally entrenched racism, is key to Britain's view of itself as a nation of 'liberalism, tolerance, and ostensible benevolence toward racialized colonial subjects' (Perry, 2015, p. 92). For example, this mystique allowed the state to identify immigration restrictions as the most suitable solution to the 'race problem' posed by increased Caribbean migration in the 1950s and 60s. Following the terrorist attacks of 11 September 2001 in the US, it is this mystique that enabled the implementation of initiatives such as Prevent, which explain terrorism and radicalization as a consequence of Muslims' 'failure' to integrate (Kapoor, 2013). In both examples, race is constructed as separate from the state, a problem that comes from outside of the liberal, tolerant British nation (Fisher, 2012). More recently, the

British state's approach is underlined by an intensification of individual citizens' responsibility for themselves. In the few scenarios where racial discrimination is acknowledged as a problem (Cameron, 2016b), the solution is not an extension of state protections for racialized groups (on the contrary, people of colour are disproportionately affected by public spending cuts) but the proliferation of more 'opportunities' for individual success and self-improvement, for all. The language of 'respecting difference' associated with multiculturalism no longer meets new postracial demands for race neutrality (Cho, 2009) and is widely understood as having failed (Lentin and Titley, 2011), replaced with the need to champion apparently racially neutral 'British values' in order to ensure social cohesion. In both the UK and Canada, this emphasis on racial neutrality contributes to the construction of each country as racially innocent, particularly distanced from the more overtly racist histories (and present) of countries such as the US. From such a position of racial innocence, any effort to address racial inequity is inevitably sanitized by the belief that the 'problem' of race is not especially serious.

Neoliberal motherhood as management of risk

Following Loic Wacquant's (2012) contention that neoliberalism produces a new kind of state for the purposes of disciplining citizens according to values of self-sufficiency and responsibility, it is not enough to attend to the widespread and significant consequences of cuts to public spending but also to note the neoliberal state's strategic use of the state budget to fund particular programmes and initiatives that aim to cultivate particular values. For example, the Ontario Early Years centres were created in 2001 to deliver information and awareness to parents about appropriate childrearing approaches rather than provide childcare (Wall, 2004). Such spending is understood as a more efficient use of taxpayer revenue than increasing benefit payments (Field, 2010) or spending to address social housing or poverty (Wall, 2004).

The neoliberal state anchors a wider social policy context that, above all other objectives, seeks to encourage 'self-reliance' (Hicks, 2008) as the guiding principle of good citizenship. Neoliberal citizens are governed *through* freedom (Power, 2005), particularly the freedom to make the right choices. The good neoliberal citizen is therefore not only economically productive, s/he makes the 'right' choices to avoid placing undue burden on the state. This requirement to reduce the state's burden is particularly salient with regard to health, and to be healthy has become a civic duty, valued just as powerfully as economic productivity (Cheek, 2008). Women's potential to fulfil these tenets of good citizenship is read through their motherhood; the state evaluates women's citizenship based on their behaviour as good mothers, a status that is measured by adherence to expert discourse. By following professional advice, women can be situated as 'responsible citizens' (Murphy, 2003, p. 445). The principles of individualism, self-discipline, choice and freedom lead to a definition that equates good motherhood to the responsibility of ensuring the production and 'health of future generations' (Lee and Jackson, 2002, p. 125). The requirement to be economically productive, too, remains a responsibility of the good neoliberal mother, a requirement that is mediated by race, class, dis/ability and other social structures neoliberalism has imagined as overcome.

The navigation of risk is an essential feature of good neoliberal citizenship and especially motherhood, where the comprehension and avoidance of risk, especially health risks, consumes every aspect of individuals' lives. The ideal neoliberal citizen is expected to consume information about risk and alter their behaviour accordingly (Wolf, 2011, p. 50). For mothers, this expectation is heightened by the belief that they are entirely responsible for the optimal development of their children, as summed up in the ideology of intensive mothering. Linking motherhood to responsibility for children's development is achieved partly as the result of the emergence of medicalization, which requires that social processes and problems in society are understood through a medical lens. Medicalization necessitates that good citizenship is measured through health and its link to economic productivity, which, in turn, justifies the state's surveillance of and intervention in individual lives. Neoliberal ideology brings forth risk consciousness, 'where dangers are redefined as risk and individuals hold themselves ever more responsible for managing risk' (Faircloth, 2014a, p. 29).

This dominant narrative of choice and freedom informs mothers' experiences of every aspect of parenthood as ever smaller childrearing decisions attract increased significance and attention (Edwards and Gillies, 2011; Reich, 2014). Constructed as 'managers of risk' (Reich, 2014, p. 682; see also Knaak, 2010), mothers are increasingly expected to access scientific expertise provided by health professionals and the state (for example, public health) and arrange their mothering accordingly. In addition to this scientific expertise, mothers are expected to develop their own expertise (Reich, 2014), evaluating and assessing information from different sources and acting as 'informed consumers' (Murphy, 2003, p. 457) to justify their risk-avoidant parenting decisions. In assessing different and often competing sources of expertise, mothers are told that they ought to rely on their 'maternal' insight and instincts to make childrearing decisions and yet are subject to a vast array of advice and recommendations suggesting that that 'insight' is insufficient. The neoliberal ideology of motherhood constructs mothers as 'both responsible for their families and incapable of that responsibility' (Apple, 1995, p. 162).

In a context in which 'perfect choices' are imagined as available to all citizens (Wolf, 2011, p. xvi) and structural constraints such as racism are similarly pictured as relics of a bygone era, racialized people's management of risk is a site at which these ideological values may be reasserted. While the guidance offered to mothers[1] appears to be race-neutral, it relies on the concealment of the effects of structural racism to explain why some mothers appear more capable of (and therefore more deserving of the supports necessary to achieve) good mothering than others. Black women's mothering in particular has historically been identified as a source of pathology and burden (Roberts, 1993; Reynolds, 1997; Collins, 2000) but is still measured by the capacity to meet neoliberal standards of good motherhood even as these same standards also preclude recognition of the structural constraints that make good motherhood impossible.

Constructions of black motherhood

AP emerges as one possible 'choice' for mothers as they navigate these peculiar features of neoliberal motherhood. It offers up 'private solutions' by which individual mothers can make sense of and negotiate neoliberal risk culture (McRobbie, 2013, p. 128). But AP also rests on and deploys racial ideologies to promote its strategies, relying particularly on an imagined Africa defined by its 'natural' style of childrearing. Such tropes suggest an obvious affiliation with black motherhood and yet the experts who represent AP, the Sears', are a white, middle-aged professional couple from the Midwestern US. This contradiction between the 'naturally' capable attachment mother in Africa and her pathologized counterpart in the West is sharpened by attending to the ongoing and historically rooted devaluation of black motherhood.

Just as AP travels from an imagined Africa as an ancient, primitive practice and arrives in the US, Canada and the UK as a parenting style of the discerning Western mother (Green and Groves, 2008), so is the devaluation of black motherhood a sweeping phenomenon shaping and being shaped by global debates about what constitutes good motherhood. Take, for example, the story of Shanesha Taylor, an African-American woman who in 2014 was charged with felony child abuse for leaving her two children in her car while she attended a job interview (Walshe, 2014). While sympathetic reports of her story garnered international attention and an online fundraising effort that raised over $100,000, the courts responded by requiring her to attend parenting classes and invest the bulk of the donations in a trust for her children in exchange for having the charges dropped. When she failed to comply with these requirements, particularly the trust fund stipulation, media reports became much less sympathetic, detailing her various 'inappropriate' use of the funds on 'non-essential items such as cable TV, clothing and dining' (Associated Press, 2014).

Taylor's story reveals much about the contemporary construction of black motherhood, especially as it meets (or fails to meet) the standards of good mothering. First, one of the fundamental tenets of contemporary mothering ideology, that mothers are primarily and individually responsible for their children (Hays, 1996), is complicated by the equally fundamental belief that black mothers are incapable of that responsibility. Taylor's decision to leave her children in her car to attend a job interview is not contextualized within the absence of affordable childcare or the inflexibility of employers who fail to accommodate working parents but is instead understood as the result of her lack of parenting skills. The state is thus required to intervene by offering her parenting classes and ordering her to spend her money 'appropriately'.

Second, the collision of expectations between the injunction that women dedicate themselves entirely to childrearing and the economic productivity required of good neoliberal citizenship, what Sharon Hays (1996) calls the cultural contradiction of intensive mothering, is shown to be unresolvable by black women's mothering, which is dismissed as lazy or uncaring, whichever path they choose. While white middle-class women might experience it as a recent phenomenon (Shirani et al, 2012), the requirement to work *and* mother has been the defining feature of black womanhood in the West and is the source of a 'mythology that denies [black women] their womanhood' (Roberts, 1991, p. 1438). Despite the fact that Taylor's instance of 'child abuse' took place while she was attending a job interview, the focus on her inability to spend the donated money appropriately positions her as the lazy welfare mother, abusing the generosity of the taxpayer or, in this case, the donors.

Taylor is aware of the dangers of this figure, as she explains her decision to defy the judge's orders to invest in a trust fund: "I'm not some lazy bum, sitting on my butt, sitting on the couch every day, I'm not someone who's sitting up, you know, living off what was given to me" (Taylor, cited in Bieri, 2014). Taylor's children were both under the age of two at the time of her arrest and thus are both potential beneficiaries of an early years focus that emphasizes the first five years of a child's life as a crucial developmental period (McCain and Mustard, 1999; Jenson, 2004; Field, 2010; Edwards et al, 2016; Gillies et al, 2017). Within the logic of what constitutes good mothering, Taylor should be lauded for staying at home with her children. Instead, her decision is identified as a sign of poor citizenship, reinforcing the already established association between blackness and 'antimarket behaviors … [antithetical to] the ideal neoliberal citizen' (Roberts and Mahtani, 2010, p. 249). If both Taylor's mothering is incapable and her children disposable, the usual rules of appropriate childrearing for the purposes of producing good citizens do not apply but are instead deployed to discipline Taylor, to justify dictating how she ought to spend her money and how she ought to parent her children.

Shanesha Taylor's experiences are framed by dominant narratives of black womanhood that sustain both racial oppression and postracial explanations of inequities (Collins, 2000; Fassin, 2011). News stories like hers evoke histories of exploitation, marking the transition from when black women's productive and reproductive labour were directed towards the enrichment of their white owners and the US as a whole to contemporary exhortations to reduce the economic burden on crumbling neoliberal states. The production of neoliberalism *through* the disposability of racialized bodies (Duggan, 2003; Giroux, 2006) contributes to the construction of a punitive criminal justice system that prosecutes Taylor for her reproductive choices. Through neoliberal state policies, appropriate (read: white, middle-class) motherhood is rewarded with 'maternity leave and baby bonuses' (Harris, 2004, p. 73), while the inappropriate, burdensome motherhood of women like Taylor is met with 'punitive regulation' (Wacquant, 2012, p. 67).

Pres(ci)ent histories of black motherhood

The practice of excluding women of colour, particularly black women, from the possibility of good motherhood does not appear unannounced in the contemporary era. Its historical roots are present, for example, in the 19th-century expectation that mothers ought to be angels of their households, an option only available to women with particular race and class privileges. Indeed, it is through the exploitation of black women's labour that norms of white femininity and domesticity have been established (Glenn, 1992). The ethereal qualities expected of good (white) mothers in the 19th and early 20th centuries were only possible because the physical work required to maintain a good home was outsourced to racialized servants or migrants (Glenn, 1992; Webster, 1998; Kershaw, 2005).

Such exclusions continue into the present, where the dominant construction of ideal motherhood remains reliant on the assumption that a good mother is available to dedicate all of her time and energies to the task of preparing children for a 'successful adulthood' (Fox, 2006, p. 235; see also Hays, 1996). This ideal has, while purporting to be racially neutral, categorically excluded women of colour, particularly black women, from its prescripts (Elliott et al, 2013; Bloch and Taylor, 2014). Institutionalized racism, especially ubiquitous stereotypes about black womanhood (Roberts, 1997b; Jordan-Zachery, 2009; Reynolds, 2016), have long barred black women from accessing and performing the activities that are deemed to constitute good mothering.

The increasing influence of 'natural' forms of good parenting repeats this pattern. The Sears' recommend the employment of a housekeeper to ensure that mothers are free to dedicate undivided attention to their infants, attention understood as critical to their optimal development (Sears and Sears, 2001). Indeed, AP's claims to superiority are underlined by references to the instinctive parenting activities of 'traditional' and 'primitive' cultures whose insights are translated into rational, scientifically supported parenting advice by the likes of the Sears' (Sears and Sears, 1993; Green and Groves, 2008). More than performing the physical labour that enabled white middle-class women to maintain the clean home and well-raised children required of ideal white femininity, black women's purported failures, their sexual and reproductive excesses, are directly contrasted against the superior constraint possessed by white women.

The exploitation of black women's labour for the purposes of freeing white, middle-class women from the drudgery of domestic tasks has a long history. Women of colour were (and are) disproportionately employed to perform the domestic duties white middle-class women consider beneath them, thanks, partly, to racialized constructions of womanhood that deny women of colour's mothering and wifehood (Roberts, 1997b; Litt, 2000). The dismissal of black motherhood as unimportant enables the expectation that black women engage in paid employment, regardless of their mothering status, while at the same time attributing the failures of black people as a group to black mothers' inadequacies (Reynolds, 1997; Roberts, 1997b).

The racial division of reproductive labour that produces good (white) motherhood is expressed globally, captured, for example, in antiblack immigration legislation (Bashi, 2004). One such immigration programme that recruited black women into poorly paid, low-status service work was the West Indian Domestic Scheme (WIDS) in Canada. The 1955 programme sought to solve the domestic labour shortage in Canadian cities by recruiting 'suitable' Caribbean women to work as domestics. Although for many of the women the scheme was the only available method of migration to Canada, the state sought to place a check on the women's capacity to settle there (Henry, 1968), especially those who already had children. While the women's imagined maternal instincts were desirable when put into service for the benefit of wealthy, white Canadian children (Hochschild, 2009; Lawson, 2013), this same maternal care could not be directed towards their own children (Lawson, 2013).

In Britain, the ideological devaluation of black mothers is wrapped up in a national vision that both celebrates colonial enterprise and disavows the British subjects produced through colonization, particularly those that journey from the colony to the metropolis. For example, during the reconstruction period following the Second World War, Britain recruited workers to administer its growing welfare state and, like WIDS, took advantage of pre-existing colonial and postcolonial relationships with Caribbean nations, as well as recruiting from Africa, Asia and Europe. Migrant recruitment was racialized, with white Europeans preferred (Perry, 2015), but it also acknowledged the role to be played by black women as nurses and aides. In Britain, the invisibility of black motherhood was produced not through the direct subordination of black women's domestic labour to the maintenance of the white family; on the contrary, black women were not desirable as maids or nannies. The racial discourse of this period was marked by a fixation on the danger black men posed to white women's motherhood, thus obscuring black femininity altogether (Webster, 1998; Perry, 2015).

This invisibility made the exploitation of black women's labour that much simpler, concentrating the women in low-status, poorly paid work with little regard for the children they may have been supporting, whether those children were in the UK or elsewhere (Mama, 1997; Webster, 1998). The collapsing of all black women into the category of 'recent immigrants' (Mama, 1997), common in scholarship on this era and contemporary race relations in Britain, further aids this invisibility by conveniently locating their children beyond the nation's borders and therefore outside of the state's responsibility.

However, the curtain of invisibility was lifted as female migration surpassed men's in 1958 (Perry, 2015), and although black women's presence was initially read as a check against black male 'interference' with white women (Webster, 1998), British society soon came to treat black motherhood as a threat to the wellbeing of the nation. Black women (as well as men) were constructed as lacking the emotional depth and psychological capacity that had attracted increasing attention in the postwar period (Carter, 1995). Black people were excluded both from pre-war discourses of physical hygiene that defined them as 'dirty' and from the postwar focus on emotional and psychological development that considered them emotionally bereft (Webster, 1998), a focus that directly contributes to the emergence of AP as detailed in the previous chapter.

Appropriate childrearing strategies from both before and after the war were similarly classed and raced, whether the rigidity of scientific motherhood (Apple, 1995; Litt, 2000) or the child-centred, psychologically influenced style associated with experts such as John Bowlby (Webster, 1998). The construction of black women's inability to mother in this psychologically appropriate manner rendered black women's mothering practices particularly dangerous, made more so when fears about being 'overrun' by black children manifested in the construction of black mothers as a 'burden on the welfare state' (Webster, 1998, p. 127).

This concern with the imagined threat posed by black women's reproductive capacities is present in contemporary stereotypes attached to black mothering (Reynolds, 2005), particularly those that signal inappropriate dependence on the state such as the conflation between blackness and lone mothers, popularly depicted as reliant on public benefits (Phoenix, 1996). The anxiety about black mothers' burden on the welfare state is sharpened within the context of neoliberal austerity measures as citizens are implored to take greater responsibility for themselves in the midst of a public spending crisis. Contemporary immigration discourse is shaped by this context, expressed, for example, in the naming of health tourism as posing an as yet undetermined threat to the National Health Service (NHS) (see Jamieson, 2017 for an example). Echoing 1960s' concerns with black women's 'swarming' of the maternity wards, 21st-century fears are focused on keeping black women and their babies deprived of any legal or moral right to citizenship, regardless of where their children are born. These efforts are captured in the immigration detention system, now a common feature of European immigration and complicit in the gendered and raced denials of black women's humanity (Tyler, 2013).

Making sense of AP and black motherhood: black feminist theory

In order to understand how black mothers negotiate philosophies of good mothering as they are produced in neoliberal contexts that disavow all but 'appropriate' (read: white) motherhood while locating racism, sexism and other structural barriers as obstacles that have largely been overcome, this book attends to the historical foundations laid about the nature and value of black motherhood. The notions of good citizenship and good mothering popularized today are made possible *against* black mothers as failing citizens (Tyler, 2010) and the source of burden and disposability. Black feminist theory offers one possible tool to challenge these constructions of black womanhood.

A black feminist theoretical framework offers an important perspective through which to critically examine the historical conditions that continue to inform black women's contemporary experiences and social realities. One of the central tenets of black feminist theory is its identification of the relationship between 'personal biography [and] wider historical processes' (Alinia, 2015, p. 2334) as crucial to understanding lived experience and the matrix of domination (Collins, 2000) in which this experience occurs. I draw on black feminist theory because it centres black women's experiences and, through this process, offers insight into the complex, heterogeneous circumstances of black women's lives (Wane, 2002, 2009). In this connection between experience and broader social structures, I draw on a black feminist perspective to critically examine AP, which is promoted as a 'natural,' cost-effective way to address social problems and precludes recognizing gendered forms of racism that shape both the experiences of and discourses about motherhood. Looking at AP from black women's perspectives reveals that the 'nature' on which the philosophy relies is socially constructed, reflecting rather than challenging mainstream ideas about good parenting, and upholds a vision of motherhood that enhances the status of white, middle-class women (Blum, 1999), who are positioned as ideal mothers.

The principles of black feminist theory are best summed up by Ula Taylor who, drawing from Collins, identifies four themes:

1. Black women empower themselves by creating self-definitions and self-valuations that enable them to establish positive multiple images and to repel negative controlling representations of Black womanhood.

2. Black women confront and dismantle the 'overarching' and 'interlocking' structure of domination in terms of race, class, and gender oppression.
3. Black women intertwine intellectual thought and political activism.
4. Black women recognise a distinct cultural heritage that gives them the energy and skills to resist and transform daily discrimination. (Taylor, 1998, pp. 234–5)

Each of these themes is connected to the black women's standpoint that Collins proposes (Taylor, 1998). This standpoint argues that black women offer a unique insight into the structures that shape social experience, which can 'stimulate a distinctive Black feminist consciousness' (Collins, 1989, p. 748). Such a consciousness lays the groundwork for resisting oppression through the principles of black feminist theory. Resistance is a crucial component; it is concerned not just with providing an analytical framework with which to describe oppression but with providing the tools to support social change through 'activism and [a] politics of empowerment' (Alinia, 2015, p. 2334). Thus, black feminist theory provides an explicitly political lens through which to read and interpret black mothers' engagements with AP.

The central principles of black feminist thought emerge from black women's articulation of intersecting oppressions as well as the political strategies that they devise to resist and challenge oppressive systems of power. Black women have a long and rich history of engaging in these practices, complicating narrow summations of injustice and grounding their activism in this complexity. Sojourner Truth's oft-cited declaration "ain't I a woman?" is one example that both expresses an intersectional view of oppression and resists that oppression. In a speech at a women's rights convention in Ohio in 1851, Truth, an African-American abolitionist and women's rights activist, drew on her own lived reality, recalling her experiences as an enslaved woman to challenge singular and oppressive images of womanhood. This tradition is followed by the Combahee River Collective, a black feminist lesbian organization that in 1977 issued a statement that clearly linked historical racial and sexual violence to contemporary forms of domination rooted in white male supremacy and patriarchy. In particular, they articulated how black feminist thought draws from 'the seemingly personal experiences of individual Black women's lives' (Combahee River Collective, 1977, para. 6) to build a critique of the broader structures that oppress black women. In so doing, the women clarified how lived experience informs an epistemology that framed their political activism and their desire for social change. This is a central tenet within feminist standpoint epistemology, which argues that marginalized groups such as women offer a different and hitherto unheard perspective on society and how it is organized. As such, the Collective illuminated a view of black feminism both as theory and practice and both as explaining historical conditions and informing their present manifestations. Black feminist theory enables an analysis of how participants forge a specific, unique epistemology of AP as this is shaped by their locations as outliers within the imagined and public communities of who good mothers are and within the terrain of shifting demands imposed by neoliberal states.

Black women create self-definitions and self-valuations

In its identification of black women's capacity to develop 'self-defined, counter-hegemonic knowledge' (Alinia, 2015, p. 2335), black feminist theory makes explicit the dialectical relationship between oppression and resistance. Black feminist thought is borne of the interaction between the two, and is expressed in the positive images of black womanhood created by black women to counter the 'controlling images' that demean them (Taylor, 1998, p. 234; Collins, 2000, p. 72). Controlling images are dominant cultural representations that serve ideological purposes, namely, 'to make racism, sexism, poverty, and other forms of social injustice appear to be natural, normal, and inevitable parts of everyday life' (Collins, 2000, p. 69). One of black feminist theory's central tasks is to challenge these images (Norwood, 2013), an especially important task given that these images have been used to justify the enactment of public policies that are harmful to all marginalized people and to black women in particular, including welfare and criminal justice reform (Roberts, 1997a; Kandaswamy, 2008; Jordan-Zachery, 2009; Carter and Anthony, 2015).

The common thread in the creation and circulation of these stereotypes is the othering of black women, particularly with reference to their sexuality and morality (Jordan-Zachery, 2009). This long-standing process of othering contributes to the dominant construction of black womanhood as not quite belonging to the societies in which they live and therefore as unworthy of societal resources (Lawson, 2002), a particularly vulnerable position given the increased emphasis on individual responsibility characteristic of neoliberal rationality. The positioning of black women as outsiders to the nation (Tyler, 2013) informs their experience of parenthood and is embedded in the stereotypes of black motherhood that predominate today. In a 'postracial' context, these stereotypes are shaped by an emphasis on cultural differences, reflecting a reluctance to name race explicitly except in non-threatening terms of diversity (Lentin and Titley, 2011) and multiculturalism (Bannerji, 2000), and, specifically, a deliberate disinclination to identify racism as a meaningful explanation for inequities.

These 'cultural' differences have been expressed in both new and familiar stereotypes, from the welfare cheat, who is disinterested in the wellbeing of her children, to the trope of the African earth mother, both images articulated by participants in this study. Despite the obvious contradiction in these two images of black womanhood, the cultural explanation is used to account for both stereotypes. Whether it is a black woman's casual indifference to her children or her affinity for nature, these are commonly offered and understood in neoliberal contexts as an expression of an underlying and undeniable reality of black culture (Mullings, 2000). And it is in this same culture that (individual) solutions to inequities will be found (Spence, 2012). In response to these controlling images and the broader ideologies that inform them, black women respond, reshape and resist. They create 'self-definitions' that counter stereotypical constructions of black womanhood and, in this study, use AP in creative ways to reassert themselves as good mothers and good citizens.

Black women confront the interlocking structure of domination

Recognition that the oppressive structures that constrain society are shaped by race, gender and social class is a foundational element of black feminist theory. The history of black feminist theorizing in the US, for example, is centred on a rejection of the white feminist foregrounding of gender and the black nationalist emphasis on race to the exclusion of black women's (and similarly multiply located groups') experiences (Wane et al, 2002). Out of this rejection, the concept of intersectionality emerges and 'posits that approaching discrimination and oppression through a "single-axis framework" (Crenshaw, 1989, p. 39) not only erases those who experience more than one form of oppression, particularly black women, but also limits the theoretical potency of anti-oppressive politics' (Hamilton, 2019, p. 3).

Although there is some question of its applicability beyond the North American setting in which it was conceptualized (Collins, 2009), intersectionality in this book is used to examine in particular how race, gender and social class shape and constrain black women's experiences of mothering in British and Canadian contexts. This book builds on the theoretical interventions identified by Bonnie Thornton

Dill and Ruth Zambrana that call attention to how intersectionality 'centres the experiences of oppressed groups, focuses on both group and individual identity, considers different expressions of and relationships between "domains of power" and directs these insights towards social justice initiatives in order to make real change' (2009, p. 5; see also Collins and Bilge, 2016; Hamilton, 2019). These interventions motivate my concentration on black mothers and the decision to use their experiences as a lens through which to examine AP as both an expression of neoliberal notions of citizenship and subjectivity and a tool of resistance against forces that seek to disavow the value of care and interdependence by and among black mothers, among others.

As an analytical strategy, intersectionality facilitates an analysis of black motherhood that is built from black women's lived experiences and attends to the different and sometimes contradictory or unexpected ways in which race, gender, social class, national origin, marital status, employment and other factors manifest themselves in black women's narratives. Intersectionality does not require a comprehensive explanation for every instance of these manifestations (Bowleg, 2008), but a demand for attention to the sometimes unanticipated intersections of mutually constitutive oppressions (Hamilton, 2019).

Black women intertwine intellectual thought and political activism

One of the most important features identified by Collins in her development of black feminist thought is the knowledge-building capacity of black women. Although it is rarely recognized in the academy and other traditional institutions of knowledge and learning (Brewer, 1993; Wane, 2002), black women's thinking, theorizing and organizing has played a crucial role in the survival of black communities. Black women have grounded their activism in concepts such as 'intersectionality' even when their activism is not identified in these terms. As Njoki Wane (2002) describes, black women have long expressed the 'fundamentals of Black feminist theory in their everyday lives and within their communities' (p. 30). The marrying of theory and practice that this principle expresses is also evident in black women's experiences of motherhood, informed by attention to the context in which they raise their children (Cooper, 2010). Black mothers draw on knowledge about parenting from a variety of sources, from mainstream or state-endorsed parenting suggestions to spiritual and culturally centred approaches to childrearing, and recognize the political implications of their parenting choices for both their children and their own subjectivities (Vincent et al, 2012).

The capturing of black women's everyday experiences is crucial for the development of critical analyses of their experiences and their position in broader structural hierarchies (Brewer, 1993). It is upon this experience that the social justice initiatives central to black feminist thought are formulated. Rather than abstract theorizing, the purpose of black feminist thought, and the analytical tools it develops, is the protection and improvement of black women's lives.

Black women recognize a distinct cultural heritage (or transnational blackness)

A critical interpretive black feminist framework attends to the transnationality of black women's lives as mothers and workers, as they are located as citizens and non-citizens within the UK and Canada, and as they experience interlocking oppression and exercise different forms of political activism to press these states for recognition and equity. Some black women grapple with the shifting meanings of identity as they cross borders, as they acclimatize to the demands of living in new countries, and as they come to terms with structural forms of gendered racism. These themes are evident in the black Canadian feminism and black British feminism that frame this book's analysis.

Both British and Canadian expressions of black feminism are integrally tied to and centre the transnational experience in their analyses and politics. Black Canadian feminism is developed from the experiences of a diverse group of black women who differ across 'class, sexuality, geography and national origin' (Wane et al, 2002, p. 14). The experience of migration, whether recent or historical, plays a significant role in the shaping of black women's experiences in Canada and thus informs their political organizing (Wane et al, 2002; Massaquoi, 2007; Wane, 2009; Norwood, 2013). Migration plays a similarly important role in black British feminism, with close reference to how colonial relations shape black people's migration from former colonies to the 'mother country' (Perry, 2015, p. 61; see also Fisher, 2012). In fact, the very foundation of black British feminism is its attention to the transnational nature of oppression and resistance, expressed, for example, in African, Caribbean and South Asian people's decisions to claim 'black' as a political identity (Samantrai, 2002; Brah and Phoenix, 2004; Fisher, 2012; Anim-Addo, 2014). Although the use of blackness as a political identity has since fallen out of favour (Fisher, 2012), it continues to inform how black British feminists organize today (Brah and Phoenix, 2004).

The themes at the centre of both British and Canadian black feminism are crucial to understanding AP as they reflect on the ways that black identities in these spaces are characterized by 'oscillation' (Massaquoi, 2004, p. 142) and fluidity (Reynolds, 2005). These struggles between an imagined home in the country of 'origin' and minority status in the Canadian and British nations reflect the need to consider black people's experiences contextually, attending to the 'dynamic nature of transnational flows' (Massaquoi, 2004, p. 140) and its effects on black people's sense of self. Such dynamism can inspire the creation of 'new modes of cultural identity', drawn from Caribbean or African cultural traditions and the 'particular social realities' (Reynolds, 2005, p. 48) of being black and British or Canadian. From such a perspective, cultural identity is 'fluid, transient, [and] mobile' (Reynolds, 2005, p. 51) and thus informs the experience of motherhood, drawing from British and Canadian ideas of good parenthood as well as African and Caribbean ideas, imagined or otherwise.

Collective memory plays a significant role in the development of black subjectivities, especially for black mothers. Collective memory rests on attending to transnational movement, which necessarily shapes black women's lives, regardless of the women's date of arrival in Canada or the UK. Shared experiences of migration, whether recent or historical, shape black mothers' identities and reflect a core principle of black feminist theory. This principle anchors an analysis of black women's experiences of AP by acknowledging both the transnational aspects of AP itself and the effects of globalization and migration on black mothers' lives.

This attention to migration, globalization and the transnational is crucial for understanding AP and the experiences of the women articulated in this book. As British and Canadian black feminist traditions show, black feminist praxis, albeit widely associated with the experiences of African-American women, is evident wherever black continental and diasporic women have encountered and resisted colonial, sexual and patriarchal violence (see, for example, Norwood, 2013, who provides a concise summary of black feminist activism in Africa, North America and the Caribbean). Moreover, although the term is deeply contested among and between black women for reasons related to race, social class, nationality, sexuality, disability and ethnicity, black feminism engenders the epistemological specificities, similarities and differences that emerge from the shared experience of colonial patriarchal domination that all black women have faced, and continue to face. In other words, at the centre of black feminism is an appreciation of the shared 'histories of oppression resulting from slavery, colonialism and racism' (Wane et al, 2002, p. 15) at the same time as there is an acknowledgement of a diversity of experience in black women's lives.

Drawing on these shared histories, black feminist theory contributes a conceptual framework that 'encapsulates the universality of intersecting oppressions as organized through diverse local realities' (Collins, 2000, p. 228). Therefore, black feminist theory constructs experience as both rooted and relational, recognizing its specificity and its link to a larger global context. This theory facilitates analysis of AP by acknowledging that black women's experiences with the philosophy are both entrenched within their specific Canadian and British contexts and shaped by global relations that, among other things, refashion the 'primitive' cultural activities of people in the South as the enlightened choices of privileged Northerners. This theory also enables an analysis of black women's mothering as it is framed by transnational dynamics of 'placement, displacement, and movement' (Massaquoi, 2004, p. 140).

The mothers

To answer the question of how black mothers engage with AP, I interviewed 19 women between June 2015 and May 2016. Ten women living in Britain were interviewed during a ten-week research trip to the UK in the summer of 2015. The remaining nine mothers were interviewed in Canada, between December 2015 and the summer of 2016. I chose Britain and Canada as research locations as part of an effort to capture the diversity of black women's experiences and attend to the expansion of black feminist theorizing beyond the US (Reynolds, 2002; Massaquoi, 2007). The two countries' similarities and differences also offer an interesting point of comparison with their similarly sized black populations and comparable histories of migration from the Caribbean and Africa. These experiences of migration are captured in the sample, which includes women born in the UK and Canada as well as those born in or tracing recent heritage from countries in Africa and the Caribbean.

The interviews were conducted in two phases: the first during a ten-week research trip to the UK in the summer of 2015, and the second during a longer period beginning in December 2015 and stretching into the following summer. Interviews were mostly conducted in participants' homes and workplaces and in cafés and restaurants, with two interviews taking place over Skype. The interviews lasted on average 90 minutes and were occasionally interrupted or elongated by children, spouses and other demands of family life. The recruitment process was difficult and began with a largely unsuccessful strategy of contacting nursery schools, community centres and churches to request access to their membership lists and networks (see Hamilton, 2019 for a longer reflection on the limits and opportunities of an intersectional methodology). Most organizations agreed to pass along my call for participants to their members but this strategy yielded only one interview. The remainder of the interviewees were recruited online and through existing networks. I posted a call for participants on social media sites and forums, asking those who self-identified as black women, had one child aged five years or under and had heard of AP to contact me.

Using awareness rather than practice of AP as a criterion attracted a wide range of views about AP. The 19 women interviewed fell into three broad categories: those who identified as attachment parents (or used another name to describe this kind of parenting), those who rejected the philosophy as 'extreme', and those who fell in the "middle", as one participant called her parenting. To introduce the sample, I have chosen three mothers, one from each of the aforementioned broad categories, whose narratives capture the wide range of experiences and dispositions of the wider sample. Table 3.1 offers more detail about the remaining 16.

Olive

I met Olive at a café close to where she lives in a large city in southwestern Ontario. During our email exchange before the interview, Olive told me that she would bring her two children, one aged three years and the other only a few weeks old, to the interview, inadvertently offering me a valuable opportunity to see her parenting in practice. She arrived at the café wearing the youngest of her two boys in a cloth sling, one of the more popular indicators of interest in AP and an interest that was soon borne out in the interview that followed. Olive received my contact information from another interviewee and sent me an email expressing an eager interest in participating in the project. On first meeting her, she appeared quiet and mild-mannered but as our discussion continued, the enthusiasm and belief in her particular approach to parenting became more apparent. When I first asked her if she would call herself an 'attachment parent', she seemed uncertain and continued to mull it over as we talked through the list of standard AP practice, assessing her approach to breastfeeding, babywearing and bedsharing. It was when I mentioned natural birth as a possible AP practice that her enthusiasm came alive:

'Yeah so as soon as I got pregnant with him, I was like, I really wanna do this naturally and I feel like women, our bodies are designed to do it naturally. So I started looking into it and I took a natural birth class and all that … it was not an option to have him in the hospital. Like if there was an emergency I understand, an emergency's an emergency but I would prefer to do everything as naturally as possible. I didn't even take Tylenol or Advil, nothing, while I was in labour … so it was hard but it was like "I can do this, it's what my body's meant to do" and I knew I could do it. It's like my grandmother did it and all of these women have done it so why can't I?'

Olive was 28 years old at the time of the interview and was enjoying spending time at home with her two boys until September, when her seasonal employment would begin again. She was unsure of how she would manage the return to work and told me that she had struggled to commit to working again at the end of parental leave with her first son. During this time away from work, Olive was not officially on parental leave and was not receiving any leave benefits because she had not worked the required 600 hours prior to the birth of her second son.

As her quote indicates, Olive's interest in and commitment to AP (or its like) was part of a broader effort to "do everything as naturally as possible". Olive was a vegan, shunned commercial cleaning products for having "all those chemicals" and wore her hair in dreadlocks. Although she framed the decision to wear dreadlocks as a signifier of "black culture" and "rebellion … [against] the standards of society", this perspective did not seem to directly inform her parenting style. Olive was among ten participants who either identified themselves as attachment parents (or some similar phrase) or described following AP principles, particularly the combination of babywearing, breastfeeding and bedsharing.

Olive was also one of five participants who named themselves as "working-class". This question, asked via a demographic form, inspired much discussion and debate with many participants, Olive included, asking me to explain what I meant by 'class'. Indeed, Olive's answer only came after I gave her the options of 'working-class' or 'middle-class'. While Olive's description of her financial circumstances, the kind of work she was doing prior to the birth of her second son and her ineligibility for parental leave benefits suggest a working-class position, my approach throughout this project has been to use self-declared class identity cautiously.

Claudia

Claudia was a 40-year-old US-born professional who had been living in the UK for over a decade at the time of the interview. Although she lived in a large city in southern England not far from my home base in Bristol, Claudia asked if we could hold the interview over Skype. Bar a few technological issues and interruptions by her adorable 20-month-old twin sons, the interview provided an interesting insight into Claudia's life, particularly as it was informed by her position as an immigrant from the US. This was evident from the very beginning of the interview, when she explained her plan to give birth to her third child, due later that year, in a third country, neither the UK nor the US:

> ''Cause we're [referring to her partner] both sort of avid travellers and we know that [country] has a really good standard of care, even though it's, you know, I could stay here and get it on the NHS for free. I guess because I'm American I'm used to the idea of paying for healthcare so that concept doesn't bother me.'

Although Claudia had little positive to say about AP (she described the philosophy as "a bit crazy"), she did recognize some of its appeal. Her assessment mirrors popular analyses of AP as a philosophy that takes accepted norms of good parenting and pushes them to 'freakish' extremes. Her description of her own approach to parenting followed this same pattern. For example, she prioritized breastfeeding but only for the first 12 months and practised bedsharing with her twin sons but only as a temporary solution to unexpected problems she experienced while moving house. Claudia was the only participant whose male partner played the role of caregiver while she described herself as the "provider", a division of labour she preferred given the twins' boisterous energy levels. At the time of the interview, it was actually Claudia's partner who was bedsharing with their children while she slept separately to ensure that she was "refreshed" for work.

Claudia's critique of AP was contextualized by her suspicion of government intrusion, a suspicion she attributed to her cultural identity as an American. For example, she described a greater pressure to breastfeed in the UK than what she experienced in the US, where she chose to spend her maternity leave. This pressure, she argued, was probably linked to the longer maternity leave available to mothers in the UK, which seemed to carry the expectation that women could and therefore *should* breastfeed. For Claudia, this government intrusion was also racialized and involved a sense of feeling 'monitored', particularly as a black mother:

> 'And I feel like … it just makes me feel like the UK is more of a socialist state than the US. I mean, I did not want a healthcare visitor, yet they came every week and I felt like I couldn't say no to it. And then at one point, I went to the doctor and the doctor said, "Oh, the healthcare visitor told me x, y, z" and I was just, like, so they're reporting back? Like, I just feel like … um … I just, it just makes me feel sus-, like I'm under a cloud of suspicion and I don't like that and I feel that … I, I feel like … they tend to be a bit more judgemental of black mothers and, this is only from my own personal experience so, so it could be the case that they aren't and I just had, you know, a bad healthcare visitor.'

Albeit of course shaped by her seemingly long-standing disdain for "socialist" approaches to government, Claudia's retelling of this experience also draws attention to the way seemingly neutral parenting support mechanisms can both reflect and perpetuate racialized norms of ideal parenting, especially in the way such mechanisms frame which populations are imagined as in need of intervention. This racial work that state bodies perform is a crucial theme in this book, particularly when concentrated on the three practices I identify as signifiers of AP: breastfeeding, babywearing and bedsharing.

Ida

I met Ida shortly before I returned to Canada when she invited me to her home in a small town in southern England. Ida was 41 at the time of the interview, and was home on maternity leave with her eight-month-old son, although she did not plan to return to her job. Ida described her circumstances as "slightly different" from those of other mothers because her husband's unique work situation meant that he was able to stay at home to share parenting more equally. Despite his presence, however, Ida still took on a greater share of the childrearing work. She explained that this division of labour was a result of an agreement she had made with her husband when they discussed having a second child (the couple also had a three-year-old daughter). Her husband agreed to have another child only if Ida agreed to take on more responsibility for the care of that child.

This compromise of sharing childcare labour is echoed in Ida's overall parenting style. Like the other women in this study who fell into this category, neither rejecting AP nor embracing it, Ida struggled to provide a name for her parenting style and instead used words like "combination" and "flexible" to describe her approach. In the interview, this meant distinguishing between an AP approach, which she defined as being "sensitive to [children's] needs … following them more than them following your needs" and which she viewed as a mainly positive value, and AP *practices* such as bedsharing and babywearing, which she found less valuable and not well suited to either her or her babies' needs. Describing how she worked out her son's sleeping arrangements, Ida explained:

> 'I got to the stage where actually he just, there was nothing I could do, so in the end I put him down and actually I found that he would often just cry himself off to sleep, it wouldn't take long. And then as we went through that journey, I found actually I could tell when he was crying and inconsolable, at which point I would pick him up and offer him breastmilk or pat him or whatever, or when he was just crying himself to sleep and that's just what he sort of seemed to do. Um … so it's been a bit of a journey with him. And then at another point, when he was about six months, we actively said, "Okay, now we're going to put him down awake and we'll go in at timed intervals and check on him until he goes to sleep." And he seemed to respond to that quite well, I think there are a few, there were some stressful times but on the whole, we've done that, um … but again we've been quite flexible so there have been other times where he's just waking in the night and [her husband] will go and pick him up and settle him and put him back down so it's been a bit of a mixed bag of different approaches.'

Ida's bringing together of the underlying values of AP and a more "routine-orientated" approach that she felt best suited the needs of her family was also evident in her commitment to breastfeed albeit not for too long. When we met, she was in the process of trying to "wean [her son] a little off breastfeeding" by offering him a cup or solid foods. However, she identified breastfeeding as the source of building a "strong bond" between mother and child and spoke at length about supporting women's right to breastfeed in public. Ida's "mixed bag" approach to breastfeeding aptly captures both the ubiquity of a 'breast is best' message, a message on which AP can build (after all, it was an image of a woman breastfeeding her child that visually represented the philosophy on the cover of *TIME* magazine), and draws the boundaries of AP's appeal, the point at which the philosophy becomes 'freakish'. While all participants in this study expressed some belief in the value of breastfeeding, many also pointed to 'extended' breastfeeding as an indicator of 'extreme' AP behaviour, revealing the philosophy's slippery status.

The remaining mothers

Table 3.1 provides information about all 19 mothers in the study. At either the beginning or the end of interviews, interviewees were asked to complete a demographic form that asked for information such as their age, highest educational qualification and occupation. Participants were also asked to describe their racial or ethnic identity and their class, questions that prompted much conversation and rapport building. Table 3.1 presents the information from these forms, with a few alterations intended to protect participants' identities. The mothers' class and racial or ethnic identifiers are presented verbatim and provide a glimpse of the diverse understandings and expressions of blackness as well as the complexities and currency of class in the sample.

Conclusion

The experiences of the black mothers at the heart of this study do not occur in a vacuum. That their parenting is even the subject of scrutiny is the product of myriad historical, cultural and political factors. One of the most significant of these factors is the sociopolitical context that informs notions of good motherhood and good citizenship. Contemporary mothers parent within the boundaries set by neoliberal rationality and its attendant risk consciousness, navigating a shrunken and disciplinary state that purports to be 'beyond' race while at the same time deploying it for the purposes of delineating good citizenship and, especially, good motherhood. When black mothers negotiate with popular parenting philosophies, they do so not just as an attempt to raise good citizens but to enable their children's survival against legacies of racism. Most significantly, they craft their parenting strategies

Table 3.1: Interviewees' demographic information

Interviewee	Age	Place of birth	Relationship status	Highest educational qualification achieved	Occupation	Self-ascribed race	Self-ascribed class
Angela	35	UK	Married	Undergraduate degree	Analyst	Black–Caribbean	Middle-class
Barbara	38	UK	Married	Postgraduate degree	Psychologist	Black Caribbean	Working-class background, middle-class education
Claudia	40	US	Living with partner	Postgraduate degree	IT manager	Black – other or African American	Middle-class
Demita	26	UK	Single	Undergraduate degree	Journalist	Black (Caribbean)	Middle-class
Eleanor	33	UK	Married	Post-16 qualification	Freelance life coach	African Caribbean British	Working-class
Florynce	29	UK	Married	Undergraduate degree	Teacher	Black British (Caribbean)	Working-class
Gloria	34	UK	Married	Undergraduate degree	Engineer	Black Caribbean	Middle-class
Harriet	34	UK	Married	Postgraduate degree	Blogger	Black Caribbean	Born working-class, now middle-class

(continued)

Table 3.1: Interviewees' demographic information (continued)

Interviewee	Age	Place of birth	Relationship status	Highest educational qualification achieved	Occupation	Self-ascribed race	Self-ascribed class
Ida	41	Africa	Married	Undergraduate degree	Manager	Mixed	Middle-class
Jayaben	44	Asia	Married	Postgraduate degree	Freelance editor	South Asian	Middle-class
Kimberlé	24	Canada	Single	Undergraduate degree (incomplete)	Student	Black	Working-class
Lorde	33	US	Married	Undergraduate degree	Doula	Black (Afro–Cuban)	Upper middle-class
Margaret	28	Caribbean	Married	Undergraduate degree	Consultant	Black	Middle-class
Notisha	34	Canada	Married	Undergraduate degree	Manager	Black – West Indian	Middle-class
Olive	28	Caribbean	Common law	Professional qualification	Stay-at-home mother	Afro-Caribbean	Working-class
Patricia	41	Canada	Common law	Professional qualification (incomplete)	Stay-at-home mother	Black	Working-class
Rebecca	38	Caribbean	Married	Postgraduate degree	Manager	Black	Middle-class
Stella	37	Canada	Single	Undergraduate degree	Freelance consultant	Black	Mid-high class
Tracey	31	Africa	Married	Undergraduate degree	Educator	Black/African	Middle-class

in different ways, reflective not only of their race but of a complex intersection of race, gender, class, immigration status and age. The examination of AP this book offers is rooted in black women's disparate, diverse experiences and in their responses to the state-sanctioned notions of what makes 'good' parenting.

PART II

AP and Parenting Advice in Britain and Canada

In a context where ever smaller childrearing decisions are framed as essential for optimal development, the booming parental expertise industry plays a vital role in guiding parents, informing state-produced parenting advice and delineating the boundaries of appropriate parenting practice. This is especially true for parenting in the infant and toddler years, where disciplines such as neuroscience, early childhood development and developmental psychology are deployed to identify the first years of a child's life as holding transformative (and finite) potential. Narratives of infant and parental determinism (Lee, 2014) suggest that the choices that parents make in these crucial early years are both immensely powerful and irrevocable. The decision to breastfeed or bottle feed, bedshare or sleep train, babywear or use a pram, cannot be made lightly.

How do parents navigate these treacherous waters? They turn to experts, like William and Martha Sears (2001), who offer seven tools or baby Bs to guide parental practice:

- birth bonding
- breastfeeding
- babywearing
- bedding close to baby
- belief in the language value of your baby's cry
- beware of baby trainers
- balance and boundaries

Although each of these seven tools plays a role in the construction of the kind of expertise AP espouses, there are three that are consistently identified by AP advocates, scholars (Liss and Erchull, 2012; Russell, 2015) and the mothers interviewed for this project: breastfeeding, babywearing and bedding close to baby (or bedsharing). These three tools or practices appear in different ways in state-produced parenting advice, though all are framed in ways that reflect neoliberal healthism, where good health is a key indication of good citizenship, and wider legacies of welfare reform. Within this fraught context, the Sears' provide the reassurance of scientific advice (both are medical professionals and refer to scientific studies throughout their parenting literature), personal experience (the Sears' have eight children) and the nebulous appeal of nature and instinct. As they explain in *The attachment parenting book*, their 'commonsense guide to understanding and nurturing your baby':

> Attachment parenting is what most parents would do anyway if they had the confidence and support they needed to follow their own *intuitions*. In a way, this book is our attempt to give back to the parents the *instinctual*, high-touch way of caring for their children that decades of detachment advice have robbed them of. (Sears and Sears, 2001, p. ix, emphasis added)

However, the path that the Sears' and AP philosophy offers to parents holds some dangers. On the one hand, AP's apparent theoretical congruence with attachment theory lends the philosophy legitimacy and capitalizes on the long-standing acceptance of John Bowlby's post-Second World War argument that infants require 'committed caregiving' from a primary caregiver to ensure normal mental development (Bretherton, 1992, p. 770). Despite critiques of the theory (Eyer, 1992) and the evidence on which it is based, appropriate maternal attachment and bonding remain the guiding principles of parenting advice in the early years (Allen and Duncan Smith, 2008; Field, 2010; Lowe et al, 2015). This influence is evident, for example, in the promotion of skin-to-skin contact after birth to aid bonding by health bodies in Britain and Canada, and indeed, across the world. The Sears', too, promote bonding through skin-to-skin contact, both explicitly, as one of their seven tools of AP, and underlying their other advice to ensure appropriate attachment.

But on the other hand, AP has also developed a reputation as 'weird' and 'extreme', for taking the standard practices of good parenting and extending them beyond their accepted norms (Freeman, 2016; Hamilton, 2016): breastfeeding but not just for the recommended and widely emphasized six months but beyond even the two years suggested by the WHO, not just keeping baby's crib or bassinet in your bedroom but bringing baby into your adult bed, and not just responding to baby's cries but wearing your baby in a sling 'all the time' (Sears and Sears, 2001, p. 65). Many of the women I interviewed for this project, even those who were most enthusiastic about the benefits of AP, described instances of AP "going too far" such as the oft-cited attachment parent who breastfeeds until her child is five or bedshares until her child is in primary school. These 'extreme' instances of AP, and the shaming and controversy that accompany them, demonstrate the limits of using the philosophy as a basis for good parenting.

It is AP's unique capacity to both express and guide good mothering and articulate its limits that is the subject of Part II of this book. The chapters in this section examine how AP appears in parenting advice in Britain and Canada, focusing on guidance issued by the UK's NHS and two public health bodies in Canada, PHAC and Health Canada. This focus on advice produced by health institutions reflects both the predominantly health-focused nature of early years parenting advice that prioritizes optimal physical and emotional health, and the role 'good health' plays in our contemporary context, as a marker of personal responsibility and appropriate lifestyle choices (Lee and Jackson, 2002; Cheek, 2008). Although a preoccupation with attachment, bonding and their significance for the parenting of infants and toddlers informs other forms of state power, this section of the book attends to those aspects that best capture advice for infant feeding, sleeping and carrying.

The chapters in this section draw on scholarship on neoliberal policy making to contextualize the development of feeding, sleeping and carrying advice in the two study sites. While neoliberalism cannot explain everything about the decision to promote specific parenting practices, it can help to explain the resurgence of these individualist, 'natural' recommendations for ideal parenting behaviour. In these chapters, my interest lies in the ideological assumptions that underlie decisions to promote one form of infant feeding, sleeping or carrying over any other. This goal is made possible by attending to black mothers' *experiences* of each of these practices and the *stories* they tell to account for these experiences. As with the *TIME* cover, the story begins with breastfeeding.

4

Best for Whom? Experiences
of Breastfeeding

'Breast is best' is the ubiquitous refrain that apparently captures state and public attitudes towards breastfeeding. However, as any media report of breastfeeding in public indicates, support for breastfeeding is far more fickle than such a slogan suggests. This contradiction between vociferous promotion and perpetual controversy does not prevent the close association between breastfeeding and good mothering, nor does it deter women from assessing their parenting against its parameters. With varying degrees of individual 'success', all of the women interviewed for this project expressed broad support for breastfeeding and described it as the normative practice of the good mother. This chapter examines this support for breastfeeding and the tensions it creates for women as they invoke the language of 'nature' to justify its superiority, account for breastfeeding 'failures' and risk breastfeeding for 'too long'.

That these are the themes that frame the women's experiences of breastfeeding is evidence of the diversity of socioeconomic circumstances that comprise this small sample (five described themselves as working-class and a further two reported "working-class backgrounds") and the complex conclusions about black motherhood that may be gleaned from their narratives. My intention here is to expand the predominant thinking around black women's breastfeeding experiences beyond claims that they reject breastfeeding for its risky proximity to nature (Blum, 1999) or that those women who embrace breastfeeding do so in acquiescence to white, middle-class norms (as suggested by Forna, 2000). The mothers I interviewed had different experiences with breastfeeding but each began from the premise that 'breast is best'. Their negotiation of this discourse was framed by their broader ideas about what constitutes good parenting and how such parenting is made possible by access to economic resources, and their disgust or reverence (depending on their attitudes towards AP) for breastfeeding beyond babyhood. This chapter considers these negotiations in greater detail.

As previous chapters have outlined, concern with breastfeeding has been a feature of state and public interest in the UK and Canada since at least 1900 (Carter, 1995; Baillargeon, 2009; Nathoo and Ostry, 2009). Independent of its association with AP, breastfeeding attracts a great deal of attention due to its many ascribed benefits and transformative capacities. Acknowledged by the World Health Organization (WHO) and the United Nations Children's Fund (UNICEF) as the 'crucial food for children's health and development' (UNICEF, 2017), efforts to promote breastfeeding have taken on greater significance in recent years.

In the UK, breastfeeding promotion has been marked by the development of a range of pilot studies and programmes to increase breastfeeding rates and the creation of legislation to facilitate working women's ability to breastfeed at work (Phipps, 2014). Similarly, the federal government in Canada has partnered with non-profit organizations such as La Leche League to promote breastfeeding, for example, through the Baby Friendly Initiative (Wall, 2001; Lee, 2018), which encourages hospitals, community clinics and birthing centres to adopt 'breastfeeding-friendly' policies and practices.

The promotion of breastfeeding is framed as essential for guaranteeing health protections 'lasting right into adulthood' (NHS, 2017). The NHS website[1] reports that breastfeeding reduces the rates of infections, diarrhoea, obesity and diabetes in babies and ovarian cancer, osteoporosis and cardiovascular disease in mothers, while the Public Health Agency of Canada's (PHAC) '10 great reasons to breastfeed' (PHAC, 2009) includes weight loss and delayed menstruation among breastfeeding's benefits for mothers. AP's primary experts, William and Martha Sears, repeat much of this advice, identifying ten health benefits of breastfeeding for mother and baby. For both the Sears' and these health agencies, breastfeeding plays a crucial role in strengthening the 'special emotional bond' (PHAC, 2014) between mother and child and all three sources recommend that mothers initiate breastfeeding within an hour of giving birth to ensure the beginning of a successful breastfeeding relationship. The Sears' explicitly link breastfeeding to the work of securing attachment, describing the hormones associated with breastfeeding as 'attachment hormones' (2001, p. 53) and emphasize the practice as both biologically and 'naturally' superior.

"Nature's milk"

This claim that breastfeeding is 'natural' has a long and enduring history, exemplified, for example, in the activist efforts of breastfeeding promotion organizations such as La Leche League. Since its inception in the 1950s, League founders wished to reclaim women's maternal authority and expertise and promote breastfeeding, not only because of the benefits it afforded to babies but as part of a broader view of what constitutes good mothering (Faircloth, 2013). While the League's initial framing of breastfeeding as natural responded to the scientization of mothering discussed in Chapter 2, in the contemporary era, this frame has been revised and expanded to now include scientific expertise: breastfeeding is natural *because* science has established that it is superior. Breastfeeding is 'perfectly designed for your baby' (NHS, 2017) and 'contains the perfect amount of protein, carbohydrate, fat, vitamins and minerals' (PHAC, 2009).

Though they were not all able to successfully breastfeed their children, all of the mothers I interviewed agreed that breastfeeding was the optimal infant-feeding method and described a wide range of benefits that the practice conveys:

> 'I think it was my mother instinct, it's so weird but I didn't trust anything. I felt everything looked nasty and I didn't trust anything and I wanted to give him what was the best, the best of the best and that was my milk....' (Kimberlé, 24, one son aged three years, interviewed in Canada)

> '… first of all it's our bond. And it's the way for her to live. I didn't want to give her formula if I had nature's milk for her. Right? I understood that … well, first of all breastfeeding is just … who doesn't wanna hold a baby?' (Stella, 37, one daughter aged four years, interviewed in Canada)

> '… breastfeeding is best for your baby. So, long-term effects of that on people who are adults. And mums, it's meant to lessen your chance of breast cancer and things like that. You're talking about raising happy, healthy, confident children. That's gonna have a good effect.' (Harriet, 34, one son aged three years and one daughter aged one month, interviewed in the UK)

As Harriet, Kimberlé and Stella's reflections on breastfeeding suggest, there is slippage between claims that 'breast is best' and 'breastfeeding is natural'. Kimberlé's description aptly captures the kind of good motherhood that La Leche League strives to promote, relying on her "mother instinct" to determine the "best" method for feeding her baby. Harriet's description goes further, revealing the weight of expectation on mothers' shoulders as the decision to breastfeed or not is invested with lifelong and society-wide consequences. Given the gravity of these consequences, the choice between bottle and breast is not a choice between two equal options but a 'moralized and constrained choice' (Knaak, 2005, p. 198). After all, mothers' commitment to the project of raising "happy, healthy, confident children" is taken as a given (Baker, 2010). As Stella asked, "Who doesn't wanna hold a baby?" That breastfeeding can be equated with an act so innate to infant caregiving as holding a baby suggests that breast is not only 'best' but the *only* appropriate 'choice' for a good mother.

Contradictions abound in this depiction of breastfeeding as 'naturally' superior. Although the practice appears to be as 'natural' and innate as holding a baby, reports of low breastfeeding rates and the catalogue of experts now required to instruct mothers on breastfeeding suggest otherwise. Mothers' (and broader society's) taken-for-granted investment in the production of "happy, healthy, confident children" is license to intervene in and constrain women's infant-feeding choices. That breastfeeding is both natural but requires instruction neatly aligns the goals of a medicalized promotion of breastfeeding articulated by public health bodies and the maternalist celebration of women's innate caring and breastfeeding capacity as espoused by the Sears'. Both rest on a model of motherhood that requires mothers' 'reliance on expert advice' (Lee, 2018, p. 36). While the Sears' claim that their goal is for mothers to believe that they are experts of their own experience, such experiential expertise is realized through the authority of the Sears' own expertise. Indeed, the Sears' offer numerous books and an expansive website of breastfeeding and parenting advice *because* mothers' experiential expertise is insufficient.

The importance of adhering to the expertise of authorities such as the Sears' is well captured in Harriet's goal of "happy, healthy, confident children" and the wider effects of such a goal. Breastfeeding has attracted increasing attention because the health benefits it promises are now explicitly linked to intelligence quotient, academic performance in school and even future earning potential (Boseley, 2015). The desired "good effect" Harriet describes is widely shared across societies but must also be understood through a race-specific lens in the wider context of racialized health inequalities that inspire movements such as Black Women Do Breastfeed. The opportunity parenting seemingly offers to address inequalities similarly spurred many of the AP enthusiasts I interviewed to promote the philosophy in black communities. For example, Olive, a working-class attachment parent, spoke explicitly about the potential consequences of her commitment to breastfeeding for future (black) generations:

> 'Maybe my son will think all this is normal, like, "My wife needs to breastfeed my kids"'cause that's what he saw. So I think maybe, maybe future generations, even black kids will start seeing that as the norm and even just little things like breastfeeding, even if it's not all attachment parenting, just the breastfeeding. Because that's becoming more of an issue where people are learning about it....' (Olive, 28, two sons aged three years and two months respectively, interviewed in Canada)

If individual parenting decisions such as breastfeeding have the potential public health authorities and experts say they do, the infant feeding decisions of black mothers are that much more meaningful, packed not only with immune-boosting but also disadvantage-busting possibilities. Supporters of AP such as Olive imbued breastfeeding with transformative potential that stretches beyond its health-protective mechanisms to encompass community transformation. Breastfeeding and AP's naturalness was not a threat to be avoided, as articulated by the working-class African-American women Blum spoke to, but was instead a characteristic to be embraced, a call to community.

Accounting for breastfeeding difficulties

"Nature's milk" did not capture the experiences of all the mothers, however. Contesting the claim that breastfeeding is 'natural' and innate, many of the women I interviewed reported difficulties with breastfeeding. Whether resulting in the desired successful breastfeeding relationship or ending in 'failure', the women's difficulties paint a more complex picture of breastfeeding experience than the idealized vision suggested by the 'breast is best' discourse. These experiences include negotiating with family members who disapprove of breastfeeding in public (as described by Eleanor and Ida), the challenges of maintaining a breastfeeding relationship on returning to full-time paid work outside of the home (despite the guarantees of the Ontario Human Rights Code, as recounted by Margaret and Rebecca) and disregarding the advice of the very state representatives responsible for promoting breastfeeding. It is these difficulties especially that reveal the contradiction between a state ostensibly committed to breastfeeding and the enactment of policies and practices that undermine it. Breastfeeding is natural and mothers' individual responsibility, but, for some of the women I spoke to, would not be possible without an extensive support structure. Tracey offered an illustrative example:

> 'In order to get breastfeeding established, for two months, I didn't do *anything* but try to do that while my husband did everything else. I didn't know how our bills got paid, I didn't do [my daughter's] birth certificate, I didn't do anything [chuckles] my husband did that all. I can see how somebody would give up breastfeeding if they weren't getting that support. Like even when it came to me eating, he would get me to eat. More aside from the fact that you're like starving when you're breastfeeding but he made sure that there was food for me to eat, right?' (Tracey, 31, one daughter aged five months, interviewed in Canada)

Tracey explained that she was able to dedicate this time to establishing breastfeeding because her partner was just as committed to their attachment-influenced parenting philosophy as she was. Both parents were each responsible even in their efforts to facilitate an act that required Tracey to carry a much greater burden of the parenting labour. In Tracey's telling of her breastfeeding story, the stark unevenness of their division of labour (her husband did it "all") is evidence not of the gendered inequalities that the 'breast is best' discourse produces but of the enduring power of that discourse, of breastfeeding's role as arbiter of not just good mothering (in succeeding at it) but of good fathering (in enabling it). Crucially, in naming and detailing the necessity of support in the establishment of a successful breastfeeding relationship, Tracey complicated the individualism of 'breast is best' by drawing attention beyond the mother–child dyad (Kukla, 2006).

For other participants, attempts to maintain good motherhood had to be improvised to account for breastfeeding 'failure'. Claudia, for example, reported that she "really wanted" to be able to breastfeed but "just couldn't", citing her twins and an inability to produce enough milk to feed them as the reason she was unable to breastfeed. Angela used similar language, expressing her keenness to breastfeed but finding that "it just didn't work out in the end". As all of the women's narratives revealed, the discourse of 'breast is best' informs mothers' interactions with medical professionals, spouses, family members, friends and sometimes even strangers, which brings the 'failures' of mothers such as Claudia and Angela into sharp relief.

Both these women described the pressure of needing to get breastfeeding right and the sense of failure that accompanied their realization that they would not be able to breastfeed. As Angela explained:

> 'I had a really difficult time and that was 'cause breastfeeding wasn't working at all and I was getting mastitis and all sorts, and I just couldn't sleep and I knew that she wasn't getting enough milk so I knew that she was crying, she was always … and I just got to the point where I was just like, in tears and I'm just like "I can't do this anymore" and I'm just having a breakdown and stuff and I saw the doctor and she said, "You know, you just need to, I'm not saying take a break but just be a bit … not so hard on yourself" and that's when I decided, fine, I'm gonna just give formula a go and see what she's like and she was just … changed overnight [laughs]. 'Cause she'd been fed and she was happy so I was like, okay, we're just gonna, we'll stick with it if, you know, if … next time, if I have a child hopefully breastfeeding might work that time if it doesn't, it doesn't matter, it's not done her any major harm I don't think.' (Angela, 35, one daughter aged two years, interviewed in the UK)

Angela's account starkly captures the emotional effects of pressures to breastfeed. Her experience of 'failure' is evidence of the trap mothers find themselves in as they attempt to balance the demands of breastfeeding and good mothering, and the physical and material limitations of childrearing. The notion of suffering through pain and difficulties, especially to achieve a successful breastfeeding relationship, is a common feature of the 'breast is best' discourse (Phipps, 2014). The heightened emotions that punctuate Angela's narrative suggest her efforts to negotiate and assert her own expertise with regard to infant feeding when the dominant model of good mothering renders formula milk socially and ideologically unacceptable.

Given this pressure and the high stakes, embodied both in breastfeeding's role as a guarantor of children's future health and wellbeing *and* as a signifier of good mothering, it is unsurprising that some formula-feeding mothers go to great efforts to defend their infant-feeding choices and re-present themselves as good mothers (Murphy, 2003; Lee, 2008). Angela's narrative can be read as an attempt at such a narrative recuperation, countering the association between a failure to breastfeed and poor mothering. First, she invoked the expertise and authority of a doctor to support her decision to stop breastfeeding. Careful to avoid portraying the doctor as advising her to stop breastfeeding altogether ("I'm not saying take a break") and thus assuring the doctor's investment in the mantra of 'breast is best' and the quality of her expertise, Angela described the dramatic effect on her daughter's wellbeing: "… she was … changed overnight … she was happy." Indeed, in Angela's narrative, her daughter was *not* happy before, when being breastfed. If the aim of breastfeeding and good mothering is the production of "happy, healthy" children, as Harriet argued, Angela affirmed herself as a good mother, despite her 'failure' to breastfeed, through her daughter's achievement of this desired happiness and health. Towards the end of her narrative defence of formula use, Angela offered one final concession to the superiority of breastfeeding and suggested that she might try breastfeeding again if she chooses to have a second child, but ultimately concluded that "it doesn't matter" and asserted that her daughter had not suffered any "major harm" from the lack of breastfeeding. Angela concluded with her status as a good mother cautiously secured.

Through a combination of her own experiential expertise (Murphy, 2003) and that of a medical professional, Angela attempted to disrupt the narrative of failure that accompanies not breastfeeding. Angela's narrative recuperation of her 'good' mother identity, mediating the 'risk' that formula-feeding mothers navigate as they challenge the 'cultural problematisation of formula feeding' (Lee, 2008, p. 476), cannot be separated from the 'cultural problematization' of black motherhood (Roberts, 1995). Angela's claim on a good mothering identity was not straightforwardly achieved by relying only on experiential expertise but was bolstered through invoking a medical expert's cautiously recited advice to "take a break". This identity was further assured by Angela's commitments to working and taking responsibility for her child. As our conversation turned to the Conservative party's 2015 electoral victory, which took place shortly before our interview, Angela told me that she did not mind the much-debated austerity measures and benefit cuts promoted by the Conservatives "because at the end of the day it's not [the government's] responsibility to bring up my child, it's mine and my husband's". Firmly locating herself against racialized stereotypes about welfare dependency, Angela shored up her good mothering, despite her 'failings' in the arena of infant feeding.

Florynce, a self-described working-class mother interviewed in Britain, offered another take on breastfeeding 'failure'. When we met, Florynce was in the middle of her maternity leave with her second child. She was enjoying breastfeeding (as she had with her first child, who was six years old at the time of the interview) and spending time with her baby. Though the UK secures parents' jobs for 12 months while they take parental leave, the low level of funding provided to cover this time has often meant that parents feel compelled to return to work long before this period (Hawkins et al, 2007), and this was true for Florynce. Although she was employed in a reasonably well-paid profession and married to a partner who contributed financially, Florynce could not afford to stay at home for the full 12 months. Her need to return to work (and the demanding nature of that work) shaped her parenting choices, specifically her decision to wean her daughter:

> '[If I could] I'd probably breastfeed for a year and a half. Probably up to maybe two ... and there's no reason why I still couldn't do that, I just think it'd be difficult. You know, going back to work ... they do have to allow you time to express if you want to do that. But actually, then that compromises the time I get home because I already work through my lunches and my breaks.... So if I want to get home at a reasonable time ... I'll generally work through everything and I can't be using those times to express milk. I know some people say, "Oh, but it's for the benefit of the child, it's good" and it *is* good but at that time she will be on solids, you know, she is getting her food from other places. And, you know, I'm going to make sure that she has a very good diet, um, I've already met a childminder, you know, spoken about the types of things she cooks and if I want her to have anything different then I must provide it but the menu looks healthy enough.' (Florynce, 29, one son aged six years and one daughter aged six months, interviewed in the UK)

Florynce's detailed and careful accounting of her decision to end breastfeeding 'early' is a marker of the scrutiny subject to every parenting decision, especially those associated with breastfeeding, that key signifier of good mothering (Blum, 1999; Kukla, 2008). Florynce could not simply choose to stop breastfeeding, not when she and the world at large have accepted its indisputable superiority. Instead, she explained, in painstaking detail, all the ways that her decision to deviate from the demands of 'breast is best' still served her child. Like Angela, this was primarily achieved through the prioritization of health as a justification for the decision not to breastfeed.

Florynce then deployed another characteristic of good mothering, the responsibility to carry out research (Murphy, 2003), and explained that she had already spoken to a childminder and assessed the quality of the services provided. As the Sears' explain, one of the strategies for balancing the practice of AP and working outside the home is the employment of an 'AP-friendly sub[stitute]' (2001, p. 37). Florynce demonstrated her commitment to good mothering by ensuring that her child will continue to achieve good health, particularly nutritionally, albeit not through the exalted act of breastfeeding. Further, it was her dedication to her family and her desire to get home from work at a reasonable hour to spend time with them that made continuing breastfeeding difficult. In this case, it was not the absence of a legal requirement to support breastfeeding but the taxing demands of Florynce's profession itself that prevented successful breastfeeding. Florynce's dilemma captures the contradictions as well as the raced and classed implications of attempting to perform good mothering. In weighing the benefits of staying at home to breastfeed and her financial need to work, including the ability to provide her household with what she called "luxuries" such as holidays, Florynce concluded that she would prefer to work. This is despite her belief that she would be a "better mother" if she did not work. However, earlier in the interview, Florynce praised the childrearing strategies of parents who are "interactive with [their children], take them to museums, take them away, take them on holiday, talk to them a lot". For Florynce, good parenting requires time and the financial resources to provide children with stimulating activities. Her decision to work compromises the former but ensures the latter, thus making Florynce's hold on 'good' motherhood precarious, a common refrain for black mothers categorically excluded from fulfilment of good citizenship through either economic productivity or dedicated mothering.

'Breast is best', but not for too long

The length of time spent breastfeeding represents one point at which AP departs from public health policy and parenting advice, demonstrating the limitations of the alignment between AP and state-produced parenting expertise (Hamilton, 2016). While both the NHS and the Public Health Agency of Canada repeat the WHO's recommendation that children can be breastfed for 'up to two years or longer', much of the advice concentrates on the work required to establish breastfeeding and the importance of exclusive breastfeeding for the first six months of a baby's life.

During our interview, Rebecca noted this disproportionate focus on the initial months and argued that breastfeeding is "acceptable when you're on mat leave but it's almost like when you go back to work then there doesn't really seem to be a place for it". Given that both Canada and the UK offer mothers up to 12 months of maternity leave and research has suggested a positive correlation between the availability of paid parental leave and increased breastfeeding rates (Ruhm, 2000), participants understandably often linked breastfeeding and maternity leave, with Claudia, for example, including Britain's "lengthy" maternity leave among the sources of pressure to breastfeed. This link suggests that there is concentrated and explicit public support for breastfeeding in the first 12 months of an infant's life but that this support eventually tapers and disappears as babies become toddlers. Breastfeeding beyond these acceptable 12 months is an invitation for suspicion and negative attention (Faircloth, 2013). News reports that frame AP as 'extreme' often equate the philosophy with extended breastfeeding, which is constructed as especially problematic (as my discussion of the 2012 *TIME* cover story in Chapter 1 reveals). This conflation of 'long-term' breastfeeding (Sears and Sears, 2001, p. 62) and 'extreme' AP was shared by at least two participants who voiced an aversion to AP and to the practice of breastfeeding beyond the 'appropriate' period the philosophy required. Gloria, a middle-class mother who breastfed her daughter for seven months, offered the following response when I asked her whether she believed that AP was popular:

> 'I think it's getting more popular ... when I was first quite a new mum I went to quite a few groups where, um, somehow I just felt I didn't fit, you know, there was a breastfeeding group where they all seemed to be into, you know, eating nuts and breastfeeding their babies until they're seven and that, you know, and like, it works for some people, it wasn't gonna work for us.' (Gloria, 34, one daughter aged eight months, interviewed in the UK)

Gloria's sense that breastfeeding "until they're seven" was not going to work for her was part of a pragmatic approach to breastfeeding that, while recognizing its benefits, did not require the Herculean efforts described by Tracey to continue or by Angela to justify stopping. Gloria's daughter stopped breastfeeding when they were separated for a few days while she was on holiday, a story Gloria recounted nonchalantly, with none of the emotionally charged language of failure or disappointment. Gloria's pragmatism about breastfeeding seemed to rest on a wider confidence that she was doing what was "good for her child", a doing that could not be separated from her own class position. Recalling a story she read on the effects of breastfeeding in different contexts, she stated:

> '[I was] reading this article about it. In England, they said that the best form of feeding your baby is breastfeeding whereas places in Asia, the best form of feeding your child was formula. Actually, when they broke it down and looked at the classes of people, they were both middle-class so actually the best … way of looking after your child is apparently to be middle-class. 'Cause if you looked at wherever it was whatever the cla-, that class in that country was that was the best. So whether you were in India and you're middle-class and it's formula-fed or in England and you're middle-class and it's breastfeeding, then that's the best. So actually it's best to be middle-class [laughs].'

Echoing the critique of scholars such as Joan Wolf (2011) who argue that claims about the superiority of breastfeeding fail to take into account variables such as class, Gloria incisively cut through the noise of 'breast is best' to position her own middle-class parenting as good, regardless of her breastfeeding 'successes' or 'failures'. Indeed, it was those mothers "eating nuts and breastfeeding their babies until they're seven" who were engaging in behaviour that might risk their good motherhood, a point made more overtly by Claudia:

> 'I have a friend whose sister-in-law is very much into attachment parenting and the child is eight and still breastfeeding and that really sort of freaks me out, like, that doesn't, that seems a bit wrong to me and I don't wanna be too judgemental here but um, it just seems like after the point where they have teeth you should start to wean them….' (Claudia, 40, twin boys aged 20 months and expecting a third child, interviewed in the UK)

Particularly for Claudia, the collapsing of extended breastfeeding and 'freakish' AP was racialized. At the beginning of our interview, I asked Claudia about her first impressions of AP and she responded that it was "more like a thing that white people do". Angela, too, suggested that AP was probably more popular among white parents. I suggest that this association between white parents and 'extreme' AP practice complicates and, perhaps, facilitates claims on good motherhood. If AP is understood as freakish rather than an appropriate expression of good mothering, Claudia and Gloria's distancing from its practices enables their own claim on good motherhood, especially when practices are stripped of their significance in favour of the benefits of class, as Gloria suggests.

For two of the women I interviewed, however, it was extended breastfeeding that offered a path to good motherhood:

> 'But I think the majority of people think by the age of one it's like enough breastfeeding. And when they would ask me when I'm gonna stop breastfeeding I'd be like, "I don't know, whenever he wants to stop" and they're like, "Oh my god! That's crazy! What if he's breastfeeding until the age of five?!" I feel like that's not normal, that's not gonna happen. Maybe there's one person in the world [who does that], you know? It's extreme and it's different.' (Olive, 28, two sons aged three years and two months respectively, interviewed in Canada)

While, like Gloria and Claudia, Olive distanced herself from the activities of 'extreme' mothers, she did so in an attempt to normalize extended breastfeeding. Her AP-informed expertise required her to adopt a child-centred approach that assigns the decision to stop breastfeeding to her son but involves negotiating a social context that promotes breastfeeding under particular circumstances. Her claim on good motherhood was precarious, as is AP's position as an appropriate parenting philosophy, as Rebecca described:

> 'And I think what people's minds go to is like, the minute you say attachment parenting they think, "Oh, my gosh, you're gonna be breastfeeding your child at five." Like that's what everybody associates it with, that negative image, I guess.' (Rebecca, 38, one daughter aged 13 months, interviewed in Canada)

The image associated with AP and with its affiliated practices influence mothers' ability to use an AP-informed expertise to claim good motherhood. If it is true that AP only evokes 'negative' images of extended breastfeeding, those mothers who frame themselves as attachment parents risk drawing censure, while those who reject AP as 'strange' can build their claim to good motherhood on this rejection. While extended breastfeeding presents the opportunity to take the accepted norms of good mothering and push them that much further (Freeman, 2016) and troubles the simple assumptions that neoliberal models of mothering make about women's pathway to good citizenship (Hamilton, 2016), it is only one indicator of AP. The other practices with which AP is associated, particularly bedsharing and babywearing, offer new ways for the parenting philosophy to cast off the 'freakishness' of extended breastfeeding and rebrand itself as the ideal approach to parenting.

Conclusion

Breastfeeding occupies a unique role in contemporary mothering ideology. It is a site of disgust and controversy (Tomori, 2014; Lee, 2018), and yet loudly and widely promoted, linked to good health, nature and economic savings. However, these promotion efforts apparently have little effect. After years of advocacy, both Britain and Canada remain concerned with their 'low' initiation, duration and exclusivity rates (Weeks, 2010; Gallagher, 2016). And yet promotion efforts remain largely the same. For example, new interventions have focused on financial incentives as a means of attracting low-income subjects with low breastfeeding rates, rather than devising structural responses to the association between low income and lower levels of breastfeeding (Hamilton, 2016). I suggest that such efforts concentrate on convincing individual women to breastfeed (but not for too long!) because the net result will be not just increased breastfeeding rates (and the alleged society-wide economic benefits) but the cultivation of particular values among mothers. These efforts promote a vision of mothering that requires intensive efforts, resources and energy to give children the start they 'deserve'. They also idealize a self-responsibilized citizenry, for whom the appropriate amount of breastfeeding is merely one among many consumer choices they are expected to make with no attention paid to the structural constraints that might make another choice more appealing or appropriate.

AP capitalizes on this self-disciplining promotion of breastfeeding to frame itself as a normative parenting style. Like 'breast is best', AP emphasizes individual responsibility, both to produce an 'empathic, well-disciplined, bright and successful' child (Sears and Sears, 2001, p. ix) and in the performance of the minutiae of day-to-day parenting decisions such a production requires. However, in its emphasis on 'long-term breastfeeding', AP risks ridicule and accusations of going 'too far' and expecting too much of mothers. Intensive mothering requires a delicate balancing act of giving oneself unceasingly to the 'sacred child' *and* maintaining economic productivity. This balance is played out in the frenzied promotion of breastfeeding in the first months of a child's life that evolves into rhetorical pledges to mothers' right to pump at work (Boyer, 2014). AP upsets this balance by insisting on the long-term benefits of continued breastfeeding, which includes 'greater ... intellectual advantage' (Sears and Sears, 2001, p. 63), that arguably requires mothers' greater absence from the paid workplace. In this way, AP limits mothers' deployment of the philosophy for the purposes of claiming good motherhood, particularly for black mothers, whose precarious hold on good motherhood status is entwined with and undermined by black women's generic 'naturalness' as well as a specific 'natural' proclivity for work.

However, as some of the women's narratives affirm, more than just closing down opportunities to claim good motherhood, the trifecta of breastfeeding, AP and nature also provides openings. Stella's praise for "nature's milk" leans in to stereotypes of black women's naturalness to undercut another controlling image of black womanhood: pathologically poor mothering. As Demita argues, black women "have been doing it for years ... it's natural for many of us". The innate rightness of breastfeeding is in this way constructed for the purposes of revealing and promoting black motherhood.

For other mothers in the study, breastfeeding was fraught with complication and challenge. Tracey's difficulties led her to conclude that breastfeeding requires a level of support thus far absent from dominant narratives of 'breast is best'. Florynce's economic constraints compelled her to reset her framing of breastfeeding and its role in good mothering, embodying the lack of support identified by Tracey. For Angela, acceptance that 'breast is best' required an explanation of her 'failure' but did not preclude good mothering. The difficulties women faced with breastfeeding brings into view both the success of the 'breast is best' discourse and the creativity inspired by negotiating such a ubiquitous discourse.

The diverse breastfeeding experiences relayed by women in this study move beyond the dominant stories of black mothers breastfeeding as either rejecting the animality and loss of autonomy breastfeeding allegedly requires (Blum, 1999) or facing neglect at the hands of an indifferent healthcare system more concerned with protecting the health and opportunities of those white, middle-class women most likely to meet public health breastfeeding targets (Hausman, 2003). The women I interviewed believed (with different levels of intensity) in the transformative power of breastfeeding and their deployment of this power was contextualized by differing circumstances, as described by Gloria's protective middle-class position, regardless of infant-feeding choice and Florynce, whose breastfeeding journey was curtailed by constrained finances. For those women who agreed with its principles, AP offered an additional protective mechanism to facilitate breastfeeding, even when facing difficulties, but this carried risks, given the scrutiny attracted by 'extended' breastfeeding and wider suspicion of racialized women's bodies. Still, AP offered some of the women I interviewed a clear and unambiguous tool for mothering their children 'well', allowing them to give their children the 'best start' so often championed in breastfeeding advocacy and offering them the time and attention so often denied black children whose mothers are expected to work or are dismissed as feckless.

In the range of experiences reported by the women in this study, the contradictory positions occupied by both breastfeeding and AP in the contemporary parenting landscape is evident. Depending on the mother, breastfeeding and AP might represent a danger to their claim on good motherhood or a path towards it. Neither could class definitively determine the route to good mothering: the protections afforded by middle-classness either enabled a casual approach to breastfeeding (as with Gloria) or ensured the support necessary to commit to breastfeeding steadfastly (as with Tracey). The stories the mothers tell about breastfeeding suggest a complex relationship between race and class, nature and good mothering, that AP provides but one strategy for understanding.

5

Mother Knows Best? Bedsharing against Expert Advice

Sleep is a universal and widely debated topic for parents and parenting experts. The where, when and how of infant sleep motivates public awareness campaigns, forum discussions, scholarly research and parenting literature, each offering different solutions to the problem of managing babies' sleep. Sleep is the subject of this level of debate and interest not only because babies are universally known for sleeping erratically but also because of the danger associated with sleep, specifically Sudden Infant Death Syndrome (SIDS). Also known as cot death or, more recently, Sudden Unexpected Death in Infancy, SIDS is the unexplained or undetermined death of a child within its first year of life. While the cause of SIDS is unknown, research has identified a number of risk factors such as smoking, and preventative measures such as a supine sleep position. The latter spurred perhaps the most famous anti-SIDS campaigns in the mid-1990s: Back to Sleep. The campaign advised parents to put babies to sleep on their backs and successfully lowered SIDS incidence rates in the UK, Canada and other countries. Although rates have fallen dramatically since this campaign, SIDS remains a cause for concern in both countries, remaining one of the leading causes of death in children under two, and has inspired ongoing Safe Sleep campaigns that advise parents of the merits of breastfeeding and the dangers of smoking, alcohol and drug use while caring for an infant.

In this chapter, I examine AP's solution to the problem of sleep: bedsharing,[1] defined as a baby and its caregiver sharing an adult bed. The status of bedsharing is controversial in the world of public health and, indeed, among mothers, whether they reject or embrace AP practice. The sleeping habits reported by the mothers I interviewed echoed the findings of a 2019 study in the UK that reported that over three quarters of parents had bedshared despite public health warnings against the practice. Motivations for disregarding public health advice varied, but in this chapter, I highlight how these narrative defences of bedsharing reveal the currency of 'nature', enduring gendered divisions of labour in infant care and the complexities of competing sets of parental expertise in contemporary parenting culture. In these myriad ways, AP is revealed as an expression of intensive mothering ideology uniquely suited to the neoliberal context. It requires *mothers*, in particular, to take responsibility for not only choices about where and how their babies should sleep but also the consequences of those choices, whether bedsharing results in an overly dependent adult or an impressively self-reliant one. Such choices are, of course, not made autonomously, devoid of an individualized or racialized context, and it is this context to which I draw attention throughout this chapter. One institution that provides significant contextual information for parents' choices is the state.

What say the state? The dangers of bedsharing

Overwhelmingly, Safe Sleep guides discourage bedsharing, putting state-produced parenting advice at direct odds with promoters of AP such as William and Martha Sears, who view 'bedding close to baby' as an extension of the AP an infant requires when they are not sleeping. The Sears' acknowledge the 'controversy' associated with their advice at the very beginning of their chapter on AP-style sleeping:

> Not a week goes by that I don't get a call from a writer wanting to interview me for an article on 'the controversy about sleeping with your baby.' I laugh and think to myself, what is so newsworthy about parents sleeping with their babies? Parents have slept with their babies for thousands of years, and even today the practice is not unusual. Most parents do sleep with their babies, at least some of the time – they just don't tell their doctors or their relatives about it. Why is this practice kept so hush-hush? The reasons go back to parents' and advisers' focus on making children independent, while failing to understand how children really become independent. Of all the Baby B's [sic], bedding close to baby seems to be the most controversial. (Sears and Sears, 2001, p. 89)

The Sears' opening gambit in favour of bedsharing is remarkable in two ways. First, the absence of any reference to SIDS is sharply contrasted with the SIDS-focused tone that characterizes any reference to bedsharing in the advice issued by the NHS, Health Canada, PHAC and their partners. Health Canada and PHAC's 'Safe sleep for your baby' brochure explicitly warns against bedsharing:

> Bed sharing or co-sleeping, is when a baby shares the same sleep surface such as an adult bed, sofa or armchair, with an adult or another child. Sharing the same sleep surface increases a baby's risk of SIDS and suffocation. This risk is even higher for babies less than 4 months old. (PHAC, 2010/2014)

In the UK, the National Institute for Health and Care Excellence, the institutional body responsible for guiding healthcare workers, has issued postnatal care guidance whose only mention of 'co-sleeping' pairs it with SIDS, and advises workers to inform parents about the 'association' between the two (NICE, 2006/2015). Health organizations in both countries instead recommend room sharing, defined as 'placing your baby to sleep in a crib, cradle or bassinet next to your bed, in your room' (PHAC, 2010/2014) for the first six months. While these organizations promote room sharing because of its link to a reduced risk of SIDS, a 2011 statement directed at Canadian healthcare practitioners also notes that room sharing 'facilitates breastfeeding and frequent contact with infants at night' (PHAC, 2011, p. 2). This expressed link between room sharing and breastfeeding points to public health bodies' overarching investment in the promotion of attachment and bonding and, indeed, of breastfeeding in general. This overlap between breastfeeding, sleeping practices and the generic goal of 'good' bonding is a significant theme in the interviews, highlighting the messy interconnectedness of modern parenting advice, especially as parents, and particularly mothers, are framed as responsible for risk avoidance (Wolf, 2011).

The second noteworthy aspect of the Sears' introduction to the benefits of bedsharing (Sears and Sears, 2001) is the way that it so deftly captures the contradictions engendered by AP's rise to infamy. AP is meant to represent 'natural' and 'instinctual' parenting behaviour and yet it is the subject of much controversy and critique. The philosophy is ridiculed for producing clingy, dependent children but claims it offers the best path to independent, well-disciplined adults. It suggests individual parents are experts of their own childrearing experience but still asserts its own superior expertise, backed by (often questionable) science, nature and the Sears' own experience. The Sears' claim that 'there is no right or wrong place for baby to sleep' (Sears and Sears, 2001, p. 91) but proceed to spend the rest of the chapter describing why bedsharing in particular, not merely 'bedding close to baby', is superior, ending with an audacious claim (boldly stated but under-researched) that bedsharing *reduces* SIDS.

Justifying bedsharing

Still, the Sears' introduction to bedsharing does offer some foreshadowing of how many parents, including the women interviewed for this project, negotiate bedsharing in a context that frames it as risky. For many of the mothers I spoke to, participating in a project about AP was an invitation to openly proclaim their bedsharing habits even when they had previously kept them from family, friends and the healthcare professionals they interacted with. As the Sears' suggest, despite warnings against the practice, the majority of the participants (13 out of 19 mothers) reported at least one instance of bedsharing, suggesting the possibility of claiming good motherhood even against (and perhaps, *especially* against) policy guidelines:

> 'Co-sleeping felt natural. But my youngest brother-in-law is a doctor here and he's very vocal about ... he doesn't think co-sleeping's a good idea so I just kept that to myself. As did [her husband].' (Jayaben, 44, two daughters aged six and three years respectively, interviewed in the UK)

> 'You know what? Some people have said to me, "Co-sleeping, I can't believe you do that. There's a cot for a reason, [otherwise] it's just an expensive toy." But the way I see it, she's not gonna be in my bed forever is she? I mean, it will come to an end. If she's still in my bed at 18 we'll have a problem. We'll call the doctors in. But I think she'll be fine. I mean, I co-slept with my son until he was two. He had a bed, he had a room, just, you know, he just wanted the comfort. But you know they change so much, I don't see there's no reason to push them out too early.' (Florynce, 29, one son aged six years and one daughter aged six months, interviewed in the UK)

As Jayaben and Florynce suggested, choosing AP practice, particularly its more controversial 'tools' such as extended breastfeeding or bedsharing, carries risks of public censure, particularly from medical authority. Although both William and Martha Sears are themselves medical professionals and medical studies are often cited in their books, the discourse around AP suggests that the practice is at odds with mainstream medicine. Attachment parents, therefore, have to manage particularly medical assessments of their choices. Both Jayaben and her husband chose to keep information about their bedsharing from their disapproving doctor relative. Florynce, on the other hand, chose to respond directly to criticism by jokingly invoking medical authority and the oft-used trope of the overly attached older child. Her defence also suggested that not only is bedsharing not dangerous (yet) but that it might be superior. By explaining that she does not want to "push" her children out of her bed "too early", she redirected the scrutiny to those who use cots "too early" for their babies, undermining the widely accepted attachment and bonding that all parents ought to be aiming for. Here, AP's precarious position in parenting culture provides an avenue for defending the practice.

Pairing bedsharing with another accepted (albeit still controversial) practice was another method of defence:

> 'The co-sleeping, which I loved, for me, personally, it was twofold. It was helping her sleep better, knowing that I was there for her ... it made it easier to nurse in the middle of the night ... and it was peace of mind for me, you know, it was peace of mind for me.' (Stella, 37, one daughter aged four years, interviewed in Canada)

> 'Co-sleeping helps be able to breastfeed during the night, it makes it a lot easier ... I'm getting enough sleep, I think ... he just feeds and he goes right back to sleep, it's not like we're up and doing stuff you know?' (Olive, 28, two sons aged three years and two months respectively, interviewed in Canada)

The overlap between breastfeeding and bedsharing, mentioned here by Olive and Stella but also by other AP-inclined interviewees, demonstrates AP as a 'package' of parenting practices (Berry, 2010, p. 1) and opens the door for a defence of bedsharing. The pursuit of a successful breastfeeding relationship, which is explicitly and vociferously promoted in public policy, as detailed in the preceding chapter, engenders bedsharing, despite policy warnings to avoid the practice. This contradictory coalescence between the two acts is further evidence of AP's ambiguous position. AP involves an extension of what public health bodies already advise, promoting breastfeeding and 'bedding close to baby' only for longer periods (Freeman, 2016), and yet it is often the subject of ridicule, particularly as it embodies an excess of 'maternal attentiveness' (Stephens, 2011, p. 108). Mothers are forced to navigate cautiously between accusations of 'caring too much' and claims of maternal neglect, both of which have racial dimensions and are understood to have lifelong impacts on children's capacity to develop appropriately.

The mothers in this study employed different sources of expertise to guide this navigation, relying on the widespread acceptance of one practice (breastfeeding) to justify their decision to perform a less acceptable one, as Olive demonstrated, or tapping into a broader and increasingly popular narrative of 'nature' to explain their practices, as Tracey did:

> 'Having her in a bassinet next to me felt so unnatural and I know it was probably just like the postpartum craziness but it literally made me upset [chuckles] to see her ... so far from me so I woke her up and put her in my bed and then we never looked back after that.' (Tracey, 31, one daughter aged five months, interviewed in Canada)

Tracey's decision (as well as that of Jayaben and other participants) to employ the language of the 'natural' to explain not only her preference for bedsharing but her wider approach to parenting deserves close attention as it carries particular risks for racialized and especially black mothers. The claim that black women are closer to nature has a long history and has been used to justify a number of exploitative practices, particularly those related to reproduction. The same narratives of 'obstetrical hardiness' that facilitated gynaecological experiments on enslaved women have informed neglectful treatment more recently, such as the denial of adequate pain relief or the failure to provide support services during birth (Phoenix, 1990; Bridges, 2011, p. 117; Morris and Schulman, 2014).

The belief in black women's 'natural' capacities that underlines this kind of negligence by disinterest is further bolstered by the stereotype of the 'strong black woman', which in turn facilitates the withdrawal of services. The 'nature' that is invoked in these kinds of narrative can cohere neatly with neoliberal purposes. If mothers are naturally adept at caring for their babies, there is little need for the provision of services to support infant care. And yet, the proliferation of advice in the form of leaflets, videos, posters and the booming parenting literature industry suggests that nature is an insufficient source of parenting expertise. While the Sears' reference ancestral parenting practices, they also rely on 'science' to justify their claims about optimal parenting styles. Similarly, in the mothers' narratives, the coalition of science and nature, with each discourse foregrounded at different moments, was an effective defence for women's use of unsanctioned parenting practices in their ongoing and complex efforts to claim good motherhood.

However, the claim of 'nature' cannot be understood only in terms of the work it performs for the advancement of neoliberal ideology. Turning to the way that mothers frame their reliance on 'nature' draws attention to how 'nature' can be utilized to resist oppressive narratives about black parenthood, even if doing so requires rejecting policy recommendations. To draw from Tracey's narrative again, she described her practice of bedsharing and natural parenting more generally as a reflection of her family background as the child of East African immigrants. Her assertion of expertise was against a purportedly culturally neutral form of 'good' parenting that has variably appropriated parenting practices, enabling Tracey to claim good parenting:

> 'There's a book, *Happiest kid on the block*, and it talks about babywearing and things like that and, um … it associates it, and like it bugs me 'cause it says "in Africa" it doesn't pick a country but, um, that kids don't cry, like African kids rarely cry, in Africa, and that's because they're worn all the time and that is a big, well, if you think about it, that is probably the biggest part of attachment parenting because that's the thing that you're doing all day long, wearing your child, and I know it's because we don't, they don't have these fancy gadgets that we have but now … it's making full circle that you don't need all these fancy gadgets to be a, to have a baby that doesn't cry and if that's like the good parent then African babies have the best parents if that is the equation that you're trying to make, right?'

While Tracey's focus was on babywearing in this quote, her broader claim about the origin of AP sought to extract the philosophy from the white experts, such as the Sears' and the author of the book Tracey references, with whom it is currently associated and return it to its 'source', allowing black mothers, particularly African mothers, to name themselves as good mothers. But this championing of an African-derived AP carries risks if, as Tracey suggested, it is built on a Eurocentric, monolithic construction of Africa in which all babies are worn and happy. Although she acknowledged the danger of such a construction, she exchanged acceptance of this homogenizing stereotype for the image of good African mothering it generated. This tension between Tracey's support for and criticism of AP appeared at other moments in her interview but was largely subsumed in the larger and arguably more important project of invoking her own immigrant African background for the purposes of claiming natural and therefore good parenting.

Bedsharing as intensive mothering

The women's descriptions of their experiences of bedsharing reflects not only racialized ideas about nature but also the gendered demands of good parenting. As I suggested earlier, the participants justified their use of bedsharing by drawing attention to its facilitation of other assuredly good parenting practices. Their defence for bedsharing against public health advice is only legitimate if the optimal development of their children is their primary goal. In the cases where a mother did mention her own ability to get more sleep while bedsharing, for example, it was only positively framed in so far as it enabled her to perform other good mothering practices. These additional pressures that mothers experienced, to subordinate their needs to that of their child by, for example, compromising their own ability to sleep well, was also expressed in the way many participants described their partners' involvement in the sleeping arrangements. For example, Kimberlé and Stella, both mothers to older children, recalled that they found bedsharing nerve wracking (Stella) or impossible (Kimberlé) because they feared that their partners would "crush" the baby. Although both women referred to the (larger than average) size and height of their partners as an explanation for this fear, the subtext of our conversations suggested that, as mothers, they could monitor their positions even while asleep and were thus more capable of successful bedsharing:

> 'I co-slept. That was cool, that was cool for a bit until it was like, her dad is really tall, he's about six foot five, big guy, and I'm about five eleven, right? And we have a queen-size bed, which is fine but he's a big guy and she would sleep between the two of us and he'd roll and I'm like, "You're gonna kill her! Smother her [chuckles].... Get out of the bed!" Right, you know, but I just ... she slept better when she was with us, I think more so me than him because she

would just kinda roll underneath him, it wasn't his fault, he was a heavy guy, in a bed you know somebody who's light's gonna … roll [chuckles] all the time, "You're gonna kill her, get out of the bed!"' (Stella, 37, one daughter aged four years, interviewed in Canada)

Following the end of her relationship with her daughter's father, Stella continued bedsharing, and even described a touching occasion when she spent the night holding her infant daughter's outstretched hand. The implication in Stella's story is that bedsharing is gendered, a practice that mothers are especially suited to even as it might require compromising their own sleep or spending time away from their partners and thus, enables a claim to good motherhood. Such a claim was more emphatically stated by Eleanor, who first explained that men are less likely to be "in tune with their emotions" and then described her take on bedsharing:

'… it felt weird having a cot, my baby being so far away from me and that fear of cot death. I know the implications that are suggested with having your child sleep in with you but I also feel like, not all cases, but in many cases where, depending on how you are as a person determines what kind of parent you're gonna be. So if you're kind of like a slightly in tune kind of person, if you're a more self-reflective kind of person, I dunno if it's as cut-and-dry and black and white as that but … I dunno, there's just something about your connection with your child so things like co-sleeping with my babies, I didn't, you don't go into a full, deep sleep, you're always kind of like half asleep and you're kind of aware that your child is there.' (Eleanor, 33, two daughters aged 12 and six years respectively, and one son aged four years, interviewed in the UK)

First, like the Sears', Eleanor both acknowledged the fears associated with bedsharing and rejected them, suggesting instead that bedsharing offers protection against SIDS, invoking its now less common name, "cot death", to make her argument. And second, again following the same logic employed by the Sears', Eleanor argued that bedsharing suits a particular "kind of person", a woman, a mother, a *good* mother, whose sleep patterns are altered by motherhood making her capable of responding to any dangers potentially posed by bedsharing. Eleanor's husband, while clearly supportive of attachment-style parenting, was not imagined as capable of the kind of "in tune" responsive parenting that bedsharing and AP more generally required.

For some women, the solution to the potential threat faced by inattentive fathers was to have their partners sleep separately. Tracey, Rebecca and Margaret reported that their husbands either currently or previously slept in a different room while they bedshared with their young children, a situation that Rebecca's husband hoped would soon change. Rebecca's explanation of her husband's reluctance was couched in a wider discussion about the limits of AP:

> 'So it's almost like you go too far, maybe it's my kind of, my thing in that I've gone too far in that direction where I've made everything sort of baby-centric as opposed to taking into account ... you know the whole family in terms of having a balance. 'Cause I'm sure for him, it's no fun ... your wife's not there anymore basically ... she's off in the other room and you've kind of been relegated to the guest room or whatever in favour of baby so that can't be easy, right?' (Rebecca, 38, one daughter aged 13 months, interviewed in Canada)

In this quote, Rebecca claimed full responsibility for the "baby-centric" approach her and her husband had taken to childrearing. While this is, of course, a natural consequence of conducting an interview about parenting with only one of the parties involved, in this claim, Rebecca's explanation reflects a model of good mothering that requires her, as the mother, to peruse the available expertise and make the decisions, and that holds her responsible for the results. In such a scenario, Rebecca was not only physically responsible for all of what she called the "night-time work" but also took on much of the 'cognitive labour', reflecting wider gendered divisions of labour in the household where women feel particularly responsible for the outcomes of particular parenting decisions (Daminger, 2019). As the quote suggested, Rebecca's husband was "relegated" in this process because he does not bear the burden of responsibility that Rebecca does with regard to the wellbeing of their child. Her claim that bedsharing is the superior option for her child was made not just against public health bodies that suggest that such a practice is dangerous, but against her husband who, despite sharing their daughter's care "fifty-fifty", was unable to match Rebecca's maternal expertise.

Sleep also emerged as a site at which to negotiate gendered dynamics and responsibilities of ideal parenthood in my interview with Barbara.

Having only just returned to work (which ironically sometimes involved working through sleep problems with other parents) in the weeks preceding our meeting, Barbara described her parenting style as "gentle" or "peaceful", preferring these descriptions over 'attachment parenting' but acknowledging the overlap between them. While outlining the various "paraphernalia" associated with AP, Barbara provided a long and detailed account of the sleeping arrangements with her 12-month-old daughter:

> 'The co-sleeping. Um, yeah, I hadn't planned on that one [laughs] and actually, well, it depends how you define it. We did get a little cot that attaches to the bed when she was newborn so she was next to me with, it has a kind of little doorway, one of the sides drops down so she was always close … we hired that for six months and also by six months she was getting kind of big for it so then when she was six months we tried to transfer her to a normal size cot still in our bedroom but not right next to our bed … 'cause it was bit of a squeeze to fit it in next to. [But] she just literally wasn't having it, like every night we put her in it she just screamed as if we were putting her in prison, she just hated it. And [in the previous cot] she had got to the stage of pretty much like literally sleeping through so going to bed about 7, half 7 and then waking up maybe at 6 and going to bed awake but tired … and she would kind of just drift off happily and was like the most like easy baby in that respect and I thought, "Oh, sleep's a doddle! This is great!" And then yeah, we changed cot and that was it.' (Barbara, 38, one daughter aged 12 months, interviewed in the UK)

Barbara's unplanned and unique version of "co-sleeping" was a common theme in other interviews, particularly among those mothers who were less enthusiastic about, or in some cases, outright suspicious of AP. Participants described bedsharing occasionally when their babies were sick (Gloria) or only in the morning, before officially waking up for the day (Rebecca and Notisha). This latter practice enabled parents who otherwise slept separately to bedshare in the first place to enjoy what the Sears' and other AP enthusiasts call 'family bed' (Sears and Sears, 2001, p. 90), if only briefly. As discussed earlier, others mentioned that bedsharing facilitated breastfeeding or allowed them to get more sleep and thus be better able to perform the duties of good mothering.

But as with Rebecca, I want to suggest here that bedsharing can also aid in the wider shift to assign responsibilities to mothers even when they have to return to work, as in Barbara's case. Her choice of sleeping arrangements, which involved a "sidecar" setup with her daughter's cot attached to the adult bed with no barrier between the two, was chosen precisely because it compensated for the excessive (according to Barbara) time her daughter spent in childcare while also reasserting her own maternal expertise:

> '... and maybe that's probably another reason why with the sleep, I'm not fussed about tryna push her to "You will be in your cot by yourself!" kind of thing. 'Cause it's like "Hey, you've had nine hours of being independent and managing with other people" and all the rest of it. And as I say, she does fall asleep and I can leave her in the evening and then, you know, when she wakes up in the night I'm usually there. If she still needs to wake up in the night and wants to be close and stuff I'm okay with that, I don't think that's sort of pathological or needy or clingy [laughs].'

Barbara's attachment-inspired sleeping arrangement served as a 'buffer zone' (Christopher, 2015), counteracting the implicit 'damage' her daughter was enduring because she spent four full-time days a week in paid childcare. Like many mothers, Barbara's return to work was financially motivated rather than borne of a deep-seated commitment to her career but AP practice offered her the opportunity to offset the way this financial obligation had encroached on her preferred mothering style. Even better, this style of mothering did not impede her child's ability to develop the independence and mental wellness expected of good citizens but instead facilitated it, repairing what Barbara viewed as the harm of forcing independence on to children too early through decisions such as enrolling them in full-time childcare.

Barbara's retelling of how her daughter came to sleep in a cot attached to the adult bed also explicitly offered a glimpse into the division of labour in her household. Early in the interview, she explained that while her husband was "very active and involved ... he also kind of feels like mum's in charge" and this became apparent as she described her husband's single and unrepeated experiment with a moderate form of sleep training ("my husband thought he would try the 'picking up and putting down' approach") and its consequent and seemingly unsurprising failure ("[our daughter's] reaction was so strong that he was like, 'I can't do this.'"). Having eliminated sleep training in favour of gentler (almost) bedsharing, Barbara's command of the parenting in her household was assured. And further, the threat posed by her return to work was mediated by AP and her assertion of an especially *maternal* expertise that subordinated her husband's expertise.

Whose expertise?

Even in their carefully delineated and AP-inspired maternal expertise, there remains the fundamental contradiction of a parenting philosophy that suggests mothers are both naturally and instinctively capable but still require external guidance. Maternal expertise is only valid in so far as it conforms to the standards determined by hegemonic discourses about good parenthood, including its gendered and 'scientifically natural' dimensions. Its limits can be tested and perhaps even expanded (seen here in the fact that so many women reported bedsharing, even as most sources of parenting advice recommended against it) but it remains bounded by an external, and sometimes superior, expertise. This is evident in Olive's description of her bedsharing arrangements, which involved balancing the needs of her oldest son, a toddler, with those of her two-month-old baby:

> 'It's only been two months since [her younger son is] here, before that we co-slept ... and I felt so bad to push [her older son] into his own bed because they say it's not safe for toddler and baby to sleep together but if it was up to me, I would've kept him in the bed.' (Olive, 28, two sons aged three years and two months respectively, interviewed in Canada)

Olive's explanation demonstrates the complex and contradictory nature of the kind of maternal expertise that intensive mothering ideology engenders: she was able to choose bedsharing, despite public health warnings about its risks, but this choice did not extend to practising family bed. Her language is revealing; "if it was up to me" suggests an acquiescence to dominant ideas about appropriate sleeping arrangements and yet much of Olive's interview was taken up with her objections to "normal" parenting. It reveals the limits of a mothering ideology that makes mothers too responsible and yet incapable of that responsibility (Apple, 1995). It also highlights the knot that mothers find themselves in as they attempt, and are encouraged, to assert their own experiential or cultural expertise against the standards and boundaries set out by dominant ideologies about ideal parenthood.

These boundaries curtail choice and entrench responsibility for both mothers like Olive, who ignore advice about bedsharing, and Patricia, who reject the compulsions to room share altogether. Patricia was unsure about whether to call herself an attachment parent, a reluctance that revealed itself in her attitude towards even room sharing:

> 'We were never really a big fan of [room sharing] …it was just 'cause I had a bad, not a bad experience but I know what my sister went through with her co-sleeping and I was just like, "No, we're not having this, right."' (Patricia, 41, two daughters aged six and three years respectively, interviewed in Canada)

Patricia was concerned, in particular, about the long-term effects of room sharing and reported that her nieces, aged eight and older, still required assistance at bedtime in order to fall asleep. As named by Florynce, this represents a popular criticism levelled at AP, that it produces coddled children unable to manage autonomy and who will fail, as Stella contended, to learn to be "independent" (Jenner, 2014). These critiques endanger AP's status as an appropriate parenting ideology and suggest, once again, the contradictory position the philosophy occupies as both conforming to a neoliberal model of good parenting and inevitably representing its limitations. At its core, parenting is an undeniable representation of human dependency; an infant is unable to care for itself and thus must rely on another to provide this care. AP emphasizes this dependence, extending duties of infant care beyond the boundaries determined by public health bodies. Such dependence is an affront to the narratives of self-reliance and self-sufficiency that punctuate neoliberal discourse and form the basis of good citizenship, and thus requires strategies of governance that aim to cultivate these qualities. AP survives as a 'good' parenting philosophy insofar as it represents itself as a tool capable of *developing* self-sufficiency in dependent infants and children, as Barbara contended. AP repairs its reputation by highlighting the greater levels of independence attachment practices can generate. Similarly, Patricia atoned for her rejection of room sharing by emphasizing the bonding and security her particular articulation of AP can attain:

> 'I think for me, feeling secure, you're still attached in a sense, right? Where I'm not just shutting you out. Like when we did sleep training I took a whole, I read a whole, like all the different types of methods that I could read up

on and I meshed it together to work for us so I didn't just stick with Ferberizing[2] or cry-it-, well I think Ferberizing and cry-it-out are just the same but I just did it so that it worked for us. And, um … yeah, like I mean for me I was … proud to know that at six months my daughter was able to … understand that … she could fall asleep, she could put herself to sleep.'

Patricia's expertise is assured, despite her use of sleep training, through the evidence of her child's development. Any doubts about this expertise are put to rest by Patricia's namechecking of other parenting experts. She did not reach the decision to sleep train without carrying out the research and assessment required of all 'entrepreneurial citizens' (Murphy, 2003). Patricia was "proud" of her daughter's ability to "put herself to sleep", suggesting a claim on good mothering made against AP practice. Patricia's narrative demonstrates the pressures mothers experience, regardless of the actual choices they make about parenting. Whether bedsharing, room sharing or sleep training, mothers' capacities to not only choose appropriately but justify that choice with suitable references to the accepted but sometimes contradictory industry of professional expertise and the particular kind of expertise crafted by state-produced parenting advice is the basis on which their parenting is measured.

Conclusion

In March 2019, supporters of AP in the UK celebrated a subtle but important shift in mainstream advice about infant sleeping arrangements. March held Safer Sleep Week, an annual campaign to promote safe baby sleep practices, and in 2019, the focus of the campaign was co-sleeping (or bedsharing, as I have referred to it). Responding to research that found that 76 per cent parents had shared a bed with their babies and over 40 per cent had done so 'in dangerous circumstances', the 2019 campaign focused on advising parents about how to bedshare safely and involved working with Public Health England and UNICEF UK Baby Friendly to produce resources for both parents and the healthcare workers with whom they interacted (Lullaby Trust, 2019). For many attachment parents, the campaign's acknowledgement that parents shared their beds with their babies was cause for celebration, marking a clear break from previous NHS advice that merely stated 'never bed-share' and perhaps signalling the philosophy's increasing recognition. However, this new acceptance of bedsharing remains intrinsically risk focused. For example, guidance for NHS workers continues to link bedsharing and SIDS, and the Lullaby Trust, the organization responsible for the bedsharing-focused Safer Sleep Week of 2019, is a SIDS awareness-raising charity, dedicated to halving SIDS rates by 2020. The decision to advise parents about safer bedsharing practices is motivated, not by a belief in the closer bond achieved through bedsharing but in response to a recent increase in SIDS rates, rates that had consistently and dramatically fallen since Lullaby Trust's involvement in the Back to Sleep campaign in the 1990s.

Some of the mothers I interviewed attempted to undermine this risk-centred view of bedsharing constructed by public health bodies by calling attention to the myriad ways that bedsharing enabled other, more palatable, good mothering practices, including breastfeeding, the development of an appropriate and secure bond, and the promise of future independence. They claimed that bedsharing was "natural", in a particularly gendered way, evoking the ideological tenets of intensive mothering to rewrite their apparently risky decision to bedshare. However, there is only so far that this recuperative work can go. Bedsharing's association both with AP and a higher risk of infant death is a vivid illustration of AP's precarity as a contemporary parenting philosophy. As I have argued elsewhere (Hamilton, 2016), AP captures and expresses the child-centric, time-consuming, resource-heavy demands of intensive mothering ideology while also delineating (and exceeding) its limits. AP appoints individual parents the 'experts' of their own babies (Sears and Sears, 2001) but only insofar as they follow the advice and guidance of figures such as the Sears'. This tension between women's natural capacity for mothering and their apparently obvious need for instruction is tested by these particular women's construction of AP as not just the received wisdom of white experts such as the Sears' but as African, cultural, familial and *black*, when received wisdom about black mothers constructs them as failures and AP presents itself as the possession of white, middle-class experts. Black women's reclaiming of this philosophy may suggest new possibilities for carving a route through these contradictory visions of mothering (and particularly *black* mothering), a possibility that may best be represented in attitudes towards babywearing, as discussed in the next chapter.

6

Babywearing: Fads, Dangers and Cultural Appropriation

Between the techniques of (extended) breastfeeding, bedsharing and babywearing most commonly associated with AP, the latter is perhaps the most mainstream and uncontroversial. As the preceding chapters reveal, while the message that 'breast is best' suggests unequivocal support for breastfeeding, the reality is more complicated and involves mothers negotiating competing notions of expertise to claim the good motherhood that the 'breast is best' discourse promises. Bedsharing is more explicitly controversial, although there are now recent shifts towards advising the apparently significant proportion of parents who bedshare against advice to do so safely. Reflecting a parenting culture that assigns meaning to the most minute of parenting choices and tasks, both breastfeeding and bedsharing require mothers to articulate an explanation of their choices, whether addressing their 'failures' to feed appropriately or the dangers associated with sharing a bed with their babies. The mothers I interviewed for this study offered many justifications for these parenting decisions but most striking among them was the use of 'nature'. 'Nature', especially when paired with experiential or maternal expertise, could be deployed to celebrate the benefits of extended breastfeeding or the 'instinctive' desire to sleep close to one's baby. However, recourse to the natural carries risks, both racialized and uniquely suited to the neoliberal moment, where women's 'natural' proclivities for childrearing can be cited as justification for the withdrawal of supportive structures and resources. This tension between what 'nature' discourses can open up and what they close down is mirrored in the wider work accomplished by intensive mothering ideology as it identifies mothers as uniquely suited to infant care while at the same time subordinating maternal 'instinct' to the authority of parenting experts. These same tensions are at work in state-produced advice and the women's narratives about babywearing.

When compared with the debates around breastfeeding and bedsharing, babywearing appears relatively innocuous. Although there have been some concerns about safety, state bodies in both Britain and Canada have addressed these concerns matter-of-factly while still suggesting the practice as one option among many for carrying an infant. Babywearing is an inoffensively visible marker of the values of bonding and attachment so ubiquitous and unquestioningly accepted in contemporary parenting cultures. And it is this ubiquity and acceptance that AP trades on as it attempts to journey from fringe parenting style to popular, and ultimately, normative approach to raising children. This chapter will examine whether AP has been successful in making that transition, describing babywearing's appearance in state-produced parenting advice and the 19 black mothers' experiences with and ideas about the practice. Both public health bodies and the mothers largely viewed babywearing in positive terms. However, the women's narratives also draw attention to its dangers, both in terms of physical safety and cultural relevance. These tensions highlight the complex position occupied by babywearing (and by implication, AP) as both recently popular parenting trend, reflecting dominant ideas about what constitutes good parenting, *and* tool for critiquing the individualist, self-reliance contemporary parenting culture demands. As argued in the preceding chapter, the centrality of attachment and bonding as taken-for-granted features of good parenting both enables AP's emergence (AP ensures bonding) and reveals its primary weakness (AP produces coddled children). In such a milieu, both supporters and detractors of AP reinterpret advice about feeding and sleeping so that *their* choices are sanctioned, an action made possible only by a parenting culture that celebrates experiential expertise at the same time as diminishing it. Babywearing provides a unique avenue for this reinterpretation, drawing on 'nature' once again.

Babywearing? "What's that?"

Babywearing describes the act of 'carrying an infant on the body using a sling or cloth carrier' that has grown in popularity over the last 30 years (Russell, 2015, p. 1131). Although the practice is associated with AP, and is arguably its most visible and public display of this style of parenting, babywearing has spread beyond AP communities as a popular alternative (or addition) to prams, strollers and pushchairs. There are many different types of baby carrier that broadly fall into two categories: first, the more 'engineered', buckle-and-go carriers such as the BabyBjorn, and second, carriers that require substantially more knowledge, preparation and education, such as the pouch, ring sling or the wrap (Russell, 2015) (see the ring sling pictured in Figure 6.1).

I dwell on the distinction between these two kinds of carrier because it is in this difference that babywearing's (and AP's) multifaceted potential is brought into view. The difference between these slings lies not only in the preparation required to use one but also in what kind of parenting they signify. Use of a more engineered, soft-structured carrier is often in addition to and not a replacement for a pram or a stroller and is therefore a mainstream parenting choice. Babywearing, on the other hand, is a clearly demarcated practice closely associated with AP and seen as enabling other AP tools. Such a distinction appeared in the interviews between those who rejected AP, such as Kimberlé, and those who called themselves attachment parents (or an equivalent name):

PH: 'Okay. So what about things like babywearing. Did you do any of that?'
Kimberlé: 'What's that?'
PH: 'So the slings …'
Kimberlé: 'Oh, yes. Oh, the, yeah, um, uh … the Snugli yeah, I call it the Snugli. He [her son] was such a chunky man. It was the dad that did the Snugli a lot 'cause I couldn't do it. He was [indicates large size], seriously, he killed my back but yes, yes, huge Snugli. Um … Snuglis are huge here, like even they do the, I wanted the wrap, like, you know, the African wrap? That's what I wanted so I could have him [gestures towards chest] but he was so big and chunky….' (Kimberlé, 24, one son aged three years, interviewed in Canada)

Kimberlé's lack of familiarity with the term 'babywearing' was unsurprising given her indifference (and arguable disdain for) to AP. Although my clarification was more familiar to her, in her answer, she distinguished between a Snugli, a brand-name, soft-structured carrier, and an "African wrap", suggesting a distinction in carriers and their associated meanings and value. The Snugli, developed in the 1960s, is one of the earliest baby carriers produced in the US and while it is recognized as playing a crucial role in the shift in American infant-carrying practices (Warren, 2001; Szalinski, 2019), its design is considered outdated (Russell, 2015), especially when compared

Figure 6.1: Visible & Kissable campaign poster

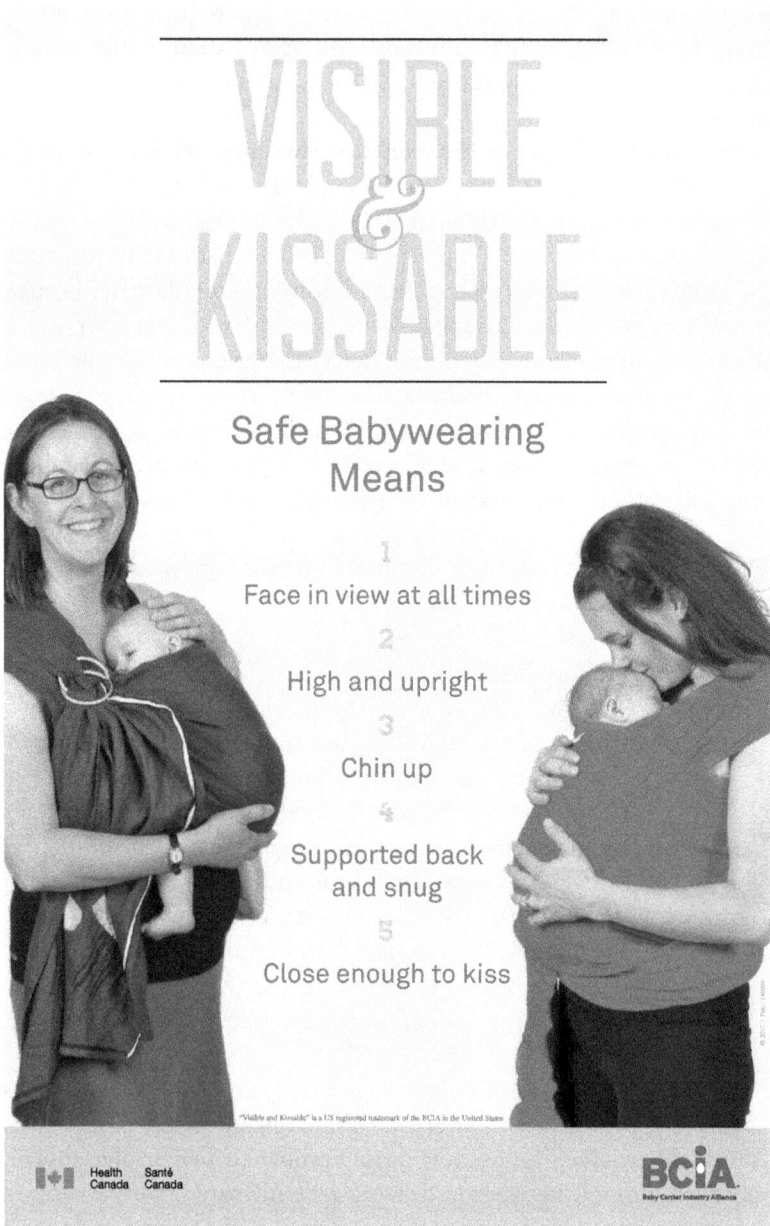

VISIBLE
&
KISSABLE

Safe Babywearing
Means

1
Face in view at all times

2
High and upright

3
Chin up

4
Supported back
and snug

5
Close enough to kiss

"Visible and Kissable" is a US registered trademark of the BCIA in the United States

Health   Santé
Canada Canada

BCiA.
Baby Center Industry Alliance

Source: © All rights reserved. Visible & Kissable. *Health Canada, 2013*. Adapted and reproduced with permission from the Minister of Health, 2019.

with the less structured but significantly more difficult-to-master wraps named by Kimberlé and sported by AP enthusiasts. Both Harriet and Olive, two supporters of AP, arrived at their respective interviews wearing their babies in softer slings comprising loose fabric, visibly displaying their commitment to and expertise in AP. Harriet's description of her introduction to baby carriers offered a pertinent example of this difference:

> '[B]ut I only knew about the big kind of harnesses and I thought, "Oh, that would be good." And then in my first pregnancy I learned about kind of soft slings and how important it was to kind of carry him around and keep him close….' (Harriet, 34, one son aged three years and one daughter aged one month, interviewed in the UK)

Harriet linked "soft slings" to the closeness, attachment and bonding so widely promoted in contemporary parenting culture and extended by AP. While the harness-type carriers might be more well known, it is the sling-type carriers that appear to specifically aid in the development of a close mother–child bond. Eleanor echoed such a description, calling the harness carriers a "fad", indicating "mainstream" parenting behaviour:

> '[It's] a fad to use a sling but it's more so the mainstream, commercial, like BabyBjorn kind of slings that you click in place and those kind of things and you only breastfed your children for three months … that's all you need and then it's formula fed after that.' (Eleanor, 33, two daughters aged 12 and six years respectively, and one son aged four years, interviewed in the UK)

For Eleanor, use of soft-structured carriers such as the BabyBjorn was wed to other parenting choices such as abbreviated breastfeeding and an acquiescence to the vagaries of parenting trends. Her description aptly conveys the difference between baby carriers and their attendant signification. Such a distinction is played out in the contrast between the "mainstream" advice offered by Health Canada and the NHS and the recommendations of the Sears'. For the two health bodies, information about slings and carriers is offered alongside guidance about playpens, high chairs, carrycots and strollers, while the practice of babywearing does not appear at all. The Sears', on the other hand, are explicit about the particular benefits of a 'sling-type carrier' (Sears and Sears, 2001, p. 66). Their chapter on the subject is illustrated with a drawing of the more difficult-to-master ring sling and describes prams and strollers as a tool by which to facilitate separation between mother and child (Sears and Sears, 2001, Chapter 6). Echoing Eleanor, the Sears' link choice of babywearing paraphernalia to other parenting choices and wider parenting philosophy, outlining the myriad benefits of babywearing including enhanced 'speech development' (2001, p. 71), easier breastfeeding and calmer babies. The difference between genuine babywearing and 'faddish' use of brand name carriers is also played out in the arena of safety.

Safer babywearing and its consequences

Missing from the Sears' 16-page treatise on the benefits of babywearing is any reference at all to safety (Sears and Sears, 2001, Chapter 6). Public health bodies, on the other hand, have recently focused on the dangers associated with baby carriers. Health Canada (2014) states that while wearing a baby might have 'practical' benefits, 'using these products incorrectly can lead to injury or suffocation'. While the public health response to babywearing has been much less fraught than breastfeeding or bedsharing, media reports of infants who have suffocated while being worn in this manner (Howard, 2014) have sparked more safety-orientated advice. In both countries, sling manufacturers have issued advice about 'safe babywearing': the consortium of UK sling manufacturers and retailers has developed the TICKS rule which states that safe babywearing is achieved with a **T**ight sling, with the baby **I**n view at all times, **C**lose enough to kiss, making sure that the baby **K**eeps their chin off of their chest and **S**upports the wearer's back (UK Sling Consortium, nd). In May 2013, the Baby Carrier Industry Alliance worked with Health Canada to launch the 'Visible & Kissable' campaign (see Figure 6.1).

It is these safety concerns, especially as they are associated with sling-type carriers rather than their engineered, commercial counterparts, that begin to endanger babywearing as one of the few innocuous AP practices, thus hindering the practice's ability to quietly promote the philosophy. But as suggested elsewhere in this book, AP appears to revel in this unique position between acceptance in mainstream parenting culture (insofar as it adopts and expresses intensive mothering, for example) and distinguishing itself from this very same context. The tension between a desire to promote AP as the normal (and indeed, natural) way to approach parenting and the possible dangers of that normalization was aptly captured by Eleanor.

Although reluctant to call it a business (she repeatedly corrected herself, calling it a "hobby" instead), Eleanor worked as what she called a "parenting lifestyle consultant": "I just make things that I like, I'm a creative person and I just put it out there and a lot of them are for babies and a lot of them aren't for babies, it's whatever I feel like making at the time." At one point, some of these items for babies were sling-style baby carriers but this aspect of her business had since been compromised by safety concerns:

'… I had people in America interested in what I was doing. I got asked quite a few times to go out there and talk about it and share the information that I had but … it didn't work out because … within the babywearing industry there's certain legislation that don't allow me to do certain things without doing certain things. It's becoming more and more restrictive so all the mums that were homework makers that set up their own businesses making slings and things, they've had been put out of business because of the new legislation.… There was this particular sling that was put on the market that looks more like a bag than a sling and I think there was a death as a result of that and, um, there has been scares with, and it's … it's not okay, it's very tragic but when people are not educated properly and that's one of the reasons why I wanted to speak up, become a babywearing consultant so I let people know about these things. It lets people know.… And certain slings have gone out of business as a result of those things happening. Um, so, yeah, now the whole babywearing community, industry, is reshifting and changing and a lot of legislation are coming in place where there's certain things that need to be put in place that cost a lot of money to do and it makes it more, like, um, you need to have your product tested, it can cost about a couple hundred pounds to do that.… And of course, if you're a company that's been doing your sling business for ten or 15 years then you've made enough money to be able to handle those new changes. Whereas somebody who's just starting out or just making things from home, they're not going to be able to afford to do that. And a lot of women have been, have had to shut down their businesses although they have no issues, they've had no problems or no complaints with their products.' (Eleanor, 33, two daughters aged 12 and six years respectively, and one son aged four years, interviewed in the UK)

The professionalization of babywearing is clearly a marker of the practice's growing popularity. As more parents use slings and the variety of slings available and sling producers proliferate, so the potential for errors and the need for industry-protecting intervention increases. That the babywearing "community" can now be described as an "industry" is evidence of the shift from a perhaps romanticized image of "mum homework makers", exchanging slings made on 'kitchen tables' (Baby Carrier Industry Alliance, 2019) to commercial enterprise. This is not to discount the opportunity for financial security that participation in the babywearing industry might afford women otherwise excluded or removed from the paid workforce, especially black working-class mothers such as Eleanor. Eleanor's responsibilities as an attachment parent had continued and perhaps even intensified as her children exited babyhood. She was homeschooling her three children and described her day-to-day routine as "driving [the children] all over the place" as they participated in sports, music lessons and other educational activities. Eleanor's decision to homeschool was in direct response to the racism that her oldest daughter suffered in a mainstream school and the belittling and dismissal of black children that she argued characterized British society. To make such an arrangement possible, Eleanor did not work outside the home and the family relied only on her husband's earnings, requiring them to "live frugally to be able to make things work". Thus, making and selling slings allowed her both a creative and financial outlet that cannot be easily dismissed. Eleanor's sling making also meant she remained engaged with parenting-related issues about which she was clearly passionate.

However, as she described in the quote, the "reshifting" of the babywearing community/industry had dire consequences for her own small business and that of others. Although she conceded that it was necessary, the introduction of safety-related legislation has benefited only those sling makers who were already commercially successful, and as her dismissal of the "fad" of BabyBjorns suggests, it seemed Eleanor was suspicious of commercial success. This may explain her reluctance to call her activities a "business", both in that the 'business' parts of it have been immobilized by the consequences of industry-wide commercial success and that participation in commercial success appears to risk authentic AP practice.

These tensions are made all the more complex by the particular contribution Eleanor made to the babywearing community/industry.

In her usual self- and business-deprecating fashion, Eleanor described her unique use of "African" fabrics: "I'm not saying that what I was doing was so well known but I was the only one making African print slings." Later, she explained why she decided to use such fabrics:

> 'It's funny because I think that's one of the reasons why I started doing the babywearing thing and it's funny because I say that we don't see ourselves so we don't identify with it but the minute we do put ourselves in it we're still not interested in it because we assume that with it being a black person then it's of poor quality. We only accept when it's a white person doing it. So it's a catch, it's a double-edged sword 'cause one of the reasons why I wanted to have this kind of movement, as it were, of babywearing and I took it on because I started using African prints with my slings and stuff [was] because I wanted to bring it back to where I know I originally saw it from, where I grew up watching it from and, and kind of pay homage to that.'

The apparent contradiction between the 'anticonsumer ethos of natural parenting' (Russell, 2015, p. 1148) and the commercial success that necessitates safety legislation has been examined elsewhere, with other natural parenting-related consumption. This contradiction reveals the individualist nature of these philosophies, which resist dominant narratives of patriarchy, consumerism and technology but in limited ways and only for individual mothers and families (Bobel, 2002, 2008). The distinction here is in Eleanor's deployment of an individualist parenting philosophy for the purposes of community development. Eleanor participated in the babywearing community by making slings that not only "pay homage to" and reassert the African origin of babywearing but that specifically targeted black mothers. Yes, she evoked an old stereotype about black communities 'failing to support their own' but she persisted nonetheless, talking to black women about babywearing even when she was no longer able to sell them her slings. Eleanor's commercial viability was second to the important work of promoting AP in the black community.

Back to Africa?

While Eleanor's construction of babywearing as African grounded her promotion of the practice among her black peers, framing babywearing in this way had other, unexpected implications for how value was assigned to AP expertise and who was widely understood as the source of that expertise. As the controversial *TIME* magazine cover story indicates, AP is widely recognized as the invention of William (and to a much lesser extent, Martha) Sears, a US paediatrician. The Sears' themselves frame AP in a personalized way, explaining in their book that their take on the philosophy is developed from their own experiences as parents as well as 'observing moms and dads whose parenting choices seemed to make sense and whose children *we liked*' (Sears and Sears, 2001, p. ix, emphasis added). Bolstering this personally informed construction of AP, the Sears' make regular references to the practice's 'primitive' origins (2001, p. 62), and babywearing represents the most obvious example of AP's habit of drawing evidence from 'traditional societies' (Green and Groves, 2008, p. 523). The Sears' babywearing chapter begins with the citing of the 'various cultures around the world who have carried their babies in different kinds of slings and shawls' (Sears and Sears, 2001, p. 65). Such anecdotal references are meant to lie alongside and work together with the Sears' wider claim that AP, and babywearing in particular, is natural, ancestral and the way that parents *would* be carrying their babies if not for the intervention of '"experts"' (2001, p. 65). The Sears' sarcastic dismissal of 'experts' does not undermine their own expertise, which draws from 'nature', 'science', the irreproachable experience (Murphy, 2003) and, of course, primitive culture.

In the very same babywearing chapter, William Sears (he identifies himself explicitly here) tells a story he has relayed elsewhere, in the Sears' *The baby book* (1993), a rather more comprehensive and less overt (albeit most certainly *covert*) guide to AP. He describes attending a conference with 'parents from all over the world' and standing next to 'two women from Zambia' carrying their babies in slings made of fabric that matched their 'native dress' (Sears and Sears, 1993, p. 263; 2001, p. 67). When he asks the women why 'parents in their culture' carry babies this way and the women respond that it is easier for mothers and good for babies, Sears interprets for the reader: 'Women in their culture don't have the benefits of books and studies about mothering hormones. What they have is centuries of tradition' (Sears and Sears, 1993, pp. 263–4).

Such a rendering of African parenting positions African women as unthinking, driven to follow a 'cultural script' (Green and Groves, 2008, p. 523) and contrasted against the discerning, entrepreneurial citizens (Murphy, 2003) at whom the Sears' numerous published works are directed. This version of African parenting robs African women of the moniker 'scientific' and the accompanying social prestige such a description of one's knowledge carries, while also serving to elevate the Sears' social standing at the expense of monolithic 'African women'. The babywearing advice offered by the Sears' draws on this 'natural', instinctive African knowledge but then is reinforced by reference to scientific studies that claim that carried babies 'cry less' and 'are more connected' (Sears and Sears, 2001, pp. 71, 75), producing a kind of 'scientifically natural' hybrid. This combination of science and nature has only intensified as babywearing has grown in popularity alongside the wide variety of slings now available. In such a scenario, mothers are increasingly expected to turn to experts, such as the Sears', to learn how to perform this purportedly 'natural' activity, while still maintaining responsibility for any (negative) outcomes (Russell, 2015).

The construction of babywearing as both scientific and natural was similarly evoked by participants in the current study, with some also conflating 'natural' and 'African' as the Sears' do. Eleanor already explained that she used "African" fabric in her sling making as a way to "pay homage" to the African origins of babywearing, but, in the following quote, more explicitly linked the practice to both 'nature' and African women:

> 'I grew up … watching African mums carry their children, it's something that always stood out to me like it does with everyone else. It's like something I always thought that was a normal and most natural thing to do and detaching yourself from your child just didn't seem normal to me….'

Eleanor entangled the normal, the natural and the African in her construction of babywearing as originating in Africa. In some ways, her account of the practice echoed the Sears' description, "that always stood out to me *like it does with everyone else*" (emphasis added), plainly captured William Sears' attraction to the two Zambian women. As she expanded on this African view of babywearing, however, Eleanor challenged the Sears' retelling of the story of African babywearing in a way that eclipsed African women's expertise. Seen through Eleanor's perspective, William Sears' interpretation of the women's babywearing knowledge is appropriative and signals the wider 'loss' black people experience as they lose touch with their 'true' culture:

> '… babywearing is a concept that's been happening for decades, for centuries especially in African cultures, South America and those places. They … put in place this contraption which is a pushchair, a pram … what was the

reason? To make money? Because it wasn't helping anyone really and then they try to make you feel like that was alleviating me of the burden of carrying your child. When they do something like that they're making money, we as West Indians or whoever adopt that culture and because it costs money to do it, there's that class thing now. If you've got a sling, you're poor, if you got a pushchair, you're rich. But now they spent, like, 20 years doing research, scientific research, into babywearing and the benefits of it, to now, they're saying, proving that slings are better for your baby than pushchairs. But they know that, they've got the information, they've done the scientific clinical research but we as black people that have been doing it for centuries, we don't know nothing about it.'

Eleanor's critique of the black community's loss of babywearing practice (and other 'natural' parenting practices) is both raced and classed and provides important context for her objection to the professionalization and commercialization of sling making. The shift from a babywearing community to an industry echoed Eleanor's critique, where the benefits of safety legislation and "scientific research" are not felt by the communities from which these practices come. The consequences for black (and racialized) communities are vast. The distancing from nature, characteristic of modernity and progress, is racialized; the loss of nature has simultaneously been a loss of culture not only for Africans but for the black diaspora. In turn, the resurgence of interest in babywearing operates as both the scientization of what should be a natural activity and an appropriation of African traditions. The experts that emerge from such a coalition are inevitably white, middle-class and Western. As Barbara explained:

'[I'm] very conscious of this sort of split where it's, like, yeah, you know, there's African mothers carrying their children 'cause that's what they've always done and it makes sense and ... there, I don't, my family are from ... [the Caribbean], they don't have that heritage, I don't have an auntie or someone to teach me how to do it, so, kind of, my option is to access like the sling library and so on which tend, from my experience of it, tends to be white, middle-class mums ... and just kind of feeling like it's weird this, like, yeah, kind of split in a way.' (Barbara, 38, one daughter aged 12 months, interviewed in the UK)

The loss of cultural expertise is felt acutely in the distinction between Africa and the Caribbean. The women readily claimed babywearing as African but named the Caribbean as a site at which the practice was rejected. The authentic expertise, then, associated with babywearing was decidedly African. The turn to Africa as the source of a kind of authentic blackness (expressed here in African ownership of babywearing) echoes sociologist Tracey Reynolds' (2005) findings in her study of Caribbean mothers living in the UK. Reynolds described visiting her interviewees in their homes and finding African 'cultural artefacts' (2005, p. 89) and suggested that this was an indication of the mothers' investment in a 'transatlantic black consciousness' (2005, p. 90) underlined by an imagined Africa. For Barbara and Eleanor, this imagined Africa featured as a type of unadulterated source of parenting expertise where black women's claims on good mothering are assured. Although like the Sears', they risked homogenizing Africa and African women, their claims served a different, oppositional purpose that complicates the simplistic story of good mothering on which intensive mothering and AP rest. This resistive image of a black and African AP was a common thread in the interviews of those mothers who identified themselves in some shape or form as attachment parents and signalled a complex and thus far unexamined image of AP.

Conclusion

The difference between engineered and loose carriers, between easy-to-use BabyBjorns and difficult-to-master sling-type carriers, is yet another indication of the unique place AP occupies in contemporary parenting culture. Babywearing as an alternative to using a pram or pushchair has clearly entered the mainstream, with international organizations and advocacy campaigns such as International Babywearing Week organized by Babywearing International, celebrities using a variety of baby carriers (and sparking controversy, such as the 2018 Twitterstorm in response to a photograph of actor Daniel Craig wearing his newborn daughter) and public health bodies including baby carriers among their list of recommended equipment for infants. However, there is always *more* that attachment parents do beyond the norms of what is accepted as appropriate parenting behaviour: more breastfeeding, more attention, more physical proximity. Babywearing, particularly the use of slings that require that much more practice, research and preparation, is another avenue for this 'more' and further, it is a visible and public way to display AP, to model it for 'the next generation' (Sears and Sears, 2001, p. 80).

This further encapsulates AP's occupation of a unique status in contemporary parenting culture. By pushing for this 'more', AP's expansion of the appropriate parenting sphere risks disrupting the delicate balance demanded of mothers by neoliberal rationalities to act as both ideal mothers and ideal citizens. Women must manage the contradiction of intensive mothering by, for example, breastfeeding but not so much (or so publicly) that it hinders their ability to return to paid work. Risks associated with AP practice are heightened for black mothers, whose capacity to perform both good mothering and good citizenship is suspect. However, engagement with this philosophy can also offer a unique path through these contradictions. As Eleanor demonstrated, for example, interest in babywearing and AP opened up a community with which she could identify, especially as she dealt with the financial and social consequences of removing her children from mainstream education. This community was both African and AP-orientated; for Eleanor, the two cannot be separated in order to understand her maternal practice. Babywearing offers a useful example of this African AP but can lapse into homogenized constructions of Africa that reinforce rather than challenge racial stereotyping. That AP is always both resisting and perpetuating dominant ideas about ideal parenting and citizenship is especially evident when attention is paid to the philosophy's gendered effects, particularly its starkly uneven demands of mothers and fathers, as the next chapter examines.

PART III

Dividing Parenting Labour

7

Negotiating Parental Leave Policies in Britain and Canada

With 'birth bonding' and breastfeeding among its tools, and its explicit naming of mothers as primary caregivers (Sears and Sears, 2001, p. 5), AP presupposes and reinforces women's biological responsibility for the work of childrearing. Like much contemporary parenting discourse (Lee, 2018), AP assumes cis women as the only possible and appropriate parents and idealizes a biological relationship between mother and child, reinforced by parenting practices that ostensibly work to strengthen such a relationship. Despite its name suggesting it may be equally available to fathers, AP particularly identifies mothers' bodies as a site through which 'good' parenting may be enacted. These gendered beliefs about appropriate caregivers (evident in the ideology of intensive mothering that informs contemporary parenting philosophies) shape and, in turn are shaped by, policies and legislation that govern the experience of childrearing. Perhaps the most prominent among these policies is parental leave.

Parental leave has attracted a great deal of public and scholarly attention, with feminist scholars in particular delineating the gendered patterns in leave taking and criticizing the gendered logic in legislation in order to devise new, gender-equitable approaches (Doucet, 2009; Macdonald, 2009). These gendered patterns cannot be challenged solely through legislative changes. The persistence of these patterns is linked to the dominant ideology of mothering (Macdonald, 2009) that requires mothers to take the greatest responsibility for their children's wellbeing and is embraced by mothers and policy makers alike. AP represents one significant embodiment of this ideology. In its emphasis on breastfeeding, babywearing and other parenting techniques that centre the maternal body, AP aligns with the underlying message of parental leave legislation that stresses the importance of the early years of an infant's life and mothers as uniquely suited to perform care during this period. However, as the chapters in Part II demonstrate, the black mothers interviewed for this study negotiated and deployed AP in ways that both affirmed and undermined these ideals of good mothering. These mothers' management of parental leave is similarly complex, revealing the raced and classed dimensions of parental leave legislation, and through their narrative negotiations with leave and AP, convey a uniquely intersectional experience of motherhood. This chapter discusses the divisions of parenting labour shaped by parental leave policies and adherence to (or rejection of) AP. First, it shows the maternalist logic that informs seemingly gender-equitable policies in both the UK and Canada and how this manifested in the mothers' use of leave in complex, class-influenced ways. Second, it considers the different purposes that parental leave is meant to serve and shows that the often competing aims of the policy have classed and gendered effects. These effects, and the consequences they have for the division of parenting labour, are brought into view by centring black mothers' experiences, always drawing attention to the intersection of race, class and gender in contemporary parenting culture's ideas about good parenting.

From maternity leave to parental leave (and back again)

The dominant narrative that describes paid parental leave policies throughout the globe defines such policies as a marker of the state's investment in gender equality (Baird and Cutcher, 2005; Ray et al, 2010; McKay et al, 2016). Although they are named 'parental' leave policies, they are widely understood to enable *women* to strike the balance between work and family and protect women's place in the labour force. This is true in both countries in this study: in Canada, the full entitlement of 52 weeks is only available to mothers, with fathers entitled to 37 weeks (Evans, 2007). In the UK, shared parental leave was introduced in April 2015 and entitles fathers to up to 50 weeks of leave, but only if mothers are willing to 'share' (O'Brien and Twamley, 2017). The evolution of paid parental leave policies also reflects this pattern, benefitting particular groups of women (and men) at the expense of others. For example, in Canada, the 2001 expansion of parental leave to 35 weeks took place in the context of neoliberal cost cutting that reduced the number of people eligible for unemployment insurance and a range of other benefits (Evans, 2007). Some have suggested that the surplus created in the Employment Insurance (EI) fund as a result of these cuts needed to be spent in a politically agreeable manner, resulting in the parental leave expansion, a programme of benefits that has largely served women from higher-income groups (Evans, 2007; McKay et al, 2016). The histories and characteristics of these policies deliver a consistent message: the purpose of parental leave is to protect the employment prospects and enable early years parenting by *women*.

The gendered nature of parental leave policies and practice is contradicted by widespread rhetorical support for involved fatherhood and equitable sharing of childrearing duties (O'Brien and Twamley, 2017). While some scholars might argue that the intensification of mothering that characterizes contemporary notions of appropriate childrearing are being extended to fathers (Shirani et al, 2012), that parental leave policy continues to be constructed around women's 'needs' suggests otherwise. This is particularly evident in the UK's much-heralded introduction of shared parental leave, which extends 50 weeks of leave to fathers but only when transferred by the mother. The 'maternalist design' of this policy reflects the dominance of intensive mothering ideology (in the belief that mothers are primarily responsible for the wellbeing of children) and shapes the decision-making practices of even those couples who aim for a more equitable division of leave and childcare labour (O'Brien and Twamley, 2017, pp. 163, 172). For the black mothers I interviewed, maternalist logic weaved in and out of their narratives, producing a wide range of responses to the prospect of sharing leave with their partners. Some expressed an ardent claim on parental leave as belonging to the mother:

PH: 'Would he have stayed home with her, do you think, if you had qualified, for example, for this new shared parenting?'
Gloria: 'No.'
PH: 'No?'
Gloria: 'No. No, I don't think he would. Actually, I don't think I would have wanted him to, really. It's my time.'
PH: 'So you see it as your time to kind of bond with her?'
Gloria: 'Yeah, to be a mum and it's quite nice actually, I've got time to, you know, take care of him a little bit more and, you know, make sure he's got clean clothes [chuckles] and there's food, like a decent meal cooked and so I'm enjoying my time being at home, being a mum, being a wife and … it just feels … yeah, I don't think he would have done, I think he's quite traditional in that role, it's his role to take care of us so.' (Gloria, 34, one daughter aged eight months, interviewed in the UK)

Gloria's claim on parental leave expands the work of mothering to include other 'womanly activities' (DeVault, 1991, p. 95) such as laundry and the provision of "decent" meals. That she took greater responsibility for childrearing is part of a wider distribution of roles in the household, where motherwork is entangled with wifework, an entanglement that requires subordination to her husband's vision of the appropriate division of duties. While she stated that she was enjoying this time at home, her description of her husband rather than her family as traditional ("*he's* quite traditional" rather than "*we* are quite traditional") suggests a division of labour that organizes women's caring work in service of men (DeVault, 1991). Gloria's ownership of this time was thus only made possible by her agreement to relieve her husband of not just childrearing duties but also the tasks and activities associated with sustaining a household.

In Patricia's case, the Canadian (or rather, Ontario) parental leave system provides several weeks of leave available to either parent and has done so since parental leave was introduced in 1990 (Marshall, 2008). Men's entitlement to parental leave is independent of their partner, and in most provinces, parental leave can even be taken by both parents at the same time but for a shorter period and provided that the family can afford the reduction in income. Despite the seemingly more equitable logic that informs Canadian leave policy, Patricia still viewed this leave in gendered terms. Due to unexpected job loss, her partner had managed to spend an extended period at home with both children in their early years but Patricia recoiled at the notion of officially sharing leave with him: "I didn't wanna give it up, I was just like, 'I'm not giving you my year, this is my year.'"

Gloria and Patricia's claims on parental leave as belonging to them as mothers reflects the maternalist logic expressed in policy making, employers' attitudes and popular discourse. Each woman's decision is also an invitation to more closely reflect on the intersection between race, class and parenting ideology. Gloria and Patricia came to the conclusion that parental leave is for mothers from different positions: Patricia was keen to embrace AP, especially as it represented good parenting. She viewed her approach to parenting as unique among the black, working-class community in which she lived, as she reluctantly explained:

'Unfortunately ... the majority of, I guess the people with black backgrounds, um ... they, for me, it's not about ... raising their children in ... how do I describe it?... Now not a lot of black people that I would think anyways would go to these programmes, I'm usually like the only one, right? … and again and I think it might be because of what the generation did before and before and before and they won't see that there's need for change if there is change needed…. I do a lot of these that I don't think a lot of black people would do.' (Patricia, 41, two daughters aged six and three years respectively, interviewed in Canada)

Her commitment to good parenting, including attending parenting classes and reading parenting literature, was confirmed by her description of the 52 weeks of parental leave as 'her year', both reinforcing the belief that mothers are uniquely suited to childrearing and undermining the assumption that racialized, poor mothers are uninterested in the wellbeing of their children. Patricia's ownership of the year signalled her occupation of the good mother position regardless of class and racial stereotypes.

For Gloria, while her style of childrearing was emphatically *not* AP, she still prioritized spending time with children during "the most important years, between now and seven" and recognized how her particular socioeconomic position enabled her to stay at home:

'I always said I wanted to go to a certain level in my career before I had children. And I got there a few years ago so actually I was quite happy to take a step back. But I don't know … perhaps if I was younger I might want to go back [to work] … and then I suppose there's the financial aspect, if we weren't that little bit older perhaps we wouldn't be in a such a good financial position so I would have to go back to work.'

Gloria's explanation echoes Fox's (2006) findings that link career achievement with the 'general sense of accomplishment and confidence' required to mother intensively (p. 250). As Fox argues, this sense of career satisfaction is most likely linked to class, creating the circular conditions where the standards of good parenting are framed according to the experiences of those with the resources to meet them. Gloria herself recognized this circular logic (as discussed in Chapter 4) and concluded that regardless of particular parenting choices, "actually it's best to be middle-class".

Gloria's confidence in her parenting choices cannot be separated from the security afforded by her "good financial position". Nor can this hard-won financial position be separated from her sense that her experience as a black mother is no different from that of her white counterparts:

> '[My mum] was determined that we were gonna do, be much better, give us a better start than she had in life. 'Cause they always strived to better themselves ... but then that's not the same throughout my whole family, you know ... so I'm not sure if that *is* a cultural thing or that is just ... what my parents have instilled in me. And I'm not sure to think about it ... am I a different type of mum to my sister-in-law, who's white and has two children? Not ... I don't know. I don't think so.'

Gloria and Patricia's maternalist claims on parental leave were generated through their own unique sense of what good motherhood entailed, each shaped by classed positions that produced particular ideas of blackness that result in the effacing of race for Gloria and a more explicit naming of the constraints race can inflict for Patricia. Their employment of these maternalist claims on leave is one strategy for asserting themselves as good mothers, both seemingly against families and communities that do not necessarily share their parenting values, but utilizing AP in different ways. For Patricia, it was through attachment-influenced parenting that she was able to distinguish herself as a good parent, whereas for Gloria, being a good parent was, paradoxically less focused on instantaneous and continuous responding to a baby (Fox, 2006). In Gloria's narrative, priority lay in the fulfilment of an idealized femininity that centres wife- and motherwork.

Notisha's claim on parental leave introduced the fear of wider consequences for women's careers. While they travelled different journeys to get there, Gloria and Patricia's claims on leave were indisputable and provided no room for fathers except in the fulfilment of the role of financial provider. In Notisha's narrative, these roles were in flux:

> '[My husband] didn't take any with both of them and he was fine with that, he, um, I asked him if we wanted to do it and he said ... I think that, and it could be just him, you know, wanting to be the provider [chuckles]. He was all, "No, no, I'm good" so ... so, then I was like, "Well, I'll take the year, I have no problem with that" [chuckles].' (Notisha, 34, two daughters aged three years and one year respectively, interviewed in Canada)

Her account suggests that the decision was made after a discussion of sorts, rather than an unequivocal maternal claim on all parental leave. However, the language she used indicates some ambivalence about the proper division of parenting labour. Earlier in the interview, Notisha was keen to emphasize her partner's commitment to childrearing, describing him as "very involved" and the sharing of their duties as "fairly balanced". However, the image she constructed of him in their conversation about parental leave suggests a more traditional outlook in which he plays the role of financial provider. This ambivalence was also evident in the way she represents the conversation: "I asked him" suggests that parental leave is indeed a mother's possession that she might gift to her partner, whereas "if *we* wanted to do it" (emphasis added) could signal shared ownership. Notisha's ambivalence about parental leave is reflected not only in previous studies of Canadian couples sharing leave (McKay and Doucet, 2010) but also in the broader scholarship on parental leave in general, as scholars struggle to capture the competing purposes parental leave ought to serve (Galtry and Callister, 2005; Doucet, 2009). However, this was contextualized by Notisha's wider commitment to AP, as revealed in the rest of her interview, a commitment that allowed her to resolve this ambivalence. By prioritizing AP practices, particularly breastfeeding, Notisha retreated to a traditional division of parental leave where she happily "takes the year". This retreat was apparent even in the critique she offered of parental leave, as she pointed out the negative effect parenting often has on working women's careers:

'… last year I remember hearing on the news that, um, you know, women, some women, well, if you're a mother and you're working in the corporate world, your career will most likely be stagnant because you can't put in the work and maintain your family life, you know what I mean? And you might be held back in your career and of course, it's obviously not for everyone or the case in every family but for a majority they may not go as far in their professional career because they have children. And because they have to carry on those two things. And I think that's, I mean, I think it's true, um, I think it's partially true in my case as well. And I mean, my husband and I we have those conversations because with … I mentioned to you briefly, that with [my oldest daughter], I had, you know, I went through a mental health issues phase, right? Where I'm just like, "Oh, my gosh, I wanna work but I can't." And part of that was, you know, I'm on Facebook or whatever and I'm seeing colleagues that don't have children, they're progressing, you know, they're climbing up the ladder and I'm like, "Well, when I go back to work I'm gonna be in the same place where I was."'

Notisha suggested that this negative impact on career prospects is not felt by her husband because "he doesn't have to take time off". In this throwaway comment, Notisha revealed the persistence of gendered approaches to childrearing, particularly as they are expressed in AP, and its effects on a seemingly egalitarian parental leave policy. Although earlier in the interview she suggested that it was possible for parental leave to be shared, the reality of her experience and those of her friends indicates that leave is for mothers and that by succumbing to this maternalist orientation, the policy fails in its stated effort to protect women's careers and earning potential. In this failure, however, the policy opens space for the mothers in this study, especially those who identified as attachment parents, to perform good motherhood. After all, mothers who do not take all the parental leave available can sometimes attract suspicion for failing to fully embody good motherhood (McKay and Doucet, 2010; Christopher, 2015). To *not* claim this leave, then, could create greater risks for these mothers' already precarious hold on good motherhood.

Notisha's quote also captures the cultural contradiction sociologist Sharon Hays (1996) described in her articulation of intensive mothering's emergence just at the point when economic productivity is the standard by which *all* women are measured. This contradiction has wide-reaching effects on mothers' health and wellbeing. For Notisha, her career aspirations represented a conflict with her dedication to her children and her employment of a parenting philosophy as labour-intensive as AP. Given her partner's expressed desires about parental leave, it appears this conflict cannot be resolved by his greater involvement, an arrangement she purported to have "no problem with" and leaving her with little choice but to cede to the appeal of good mothering and the higher maternal responsibility it required. The tensions Notisha experienced between the appeal of good motherhood and the desire to advance her career are echoed in the broader scholarship on intensive mothering but strike a particular chord for black mothers whose motherhood has long been defined by the negotiation of combining paid work and mothering (Collins, 2000; Reynolds, 2005).

Parental leave in Britain and Canada

This differential experience of parental leave is expressed in sociologist Anita Harris' (2004) argument that, contrary to declarations that the state has abandoned mothers altogether (Orloff, 2006; Stephens, 2011), financial support exists for a select group of women whose 'appropriate participation in the workforce' grants them rewards in the form of 'temporary baby bonuses or maternity leave', rewards that exist only for those women who 'enact motherhood in the correct ways, that is, juggled with a good job at a later stage in their career' (Harris, 2004, p. 73). Harris describes the simultaneous promotion of middle-class, stay-at-home motherhood and the demand that poor and working-class mothers leave their children to take up poorly paid, low-status employment as a 'class-inspired ideological reversal' (2004, p. 73). I suggest that these contradictory directives are also underlined by race; black women in Canada and Britain are more likely to experience poverty and unemployment than their white counterparts. Even for those women who attain middle-class status, stereotypes about black women's capacity to work (Reynolds, 1997, 2001) and controlling images that devalue their motherhood (Roberts, 1991) inform black women's experiences of mothering (Blum, 2011; Lareau, 2011).

Harris' assessment of maternity leave as a reward for middle-class women is evidenced by consistent findings in the UK and Canada that access to and length of parental leave is constrained by earnings, family income and type of employment (Evans, 2007; O'Brien and Koslowski, 2016). In sum, middle- to upper-class women are more likely to access maternity and parental leave and their leaves tend to be longer and better paid. These findings are made more complex when race is considered. Among the few studies that examine the intersection between race and parental leave in the UK and Canada, findings have suggested that race shapes eligibility, awareness of policy provisions and how people experience and define their leaves (Christopher, 2015; O'Brien et al, 2017; Twamley and Schober, 2019). In the US, Manuel and Zambrana's (2009) quantitative, intersectional study of the Family and Medical Leave Act of 1993 (FMLA) makes two important contributions to scholarship on race and parental leave, first, by contextualizing the development of FMLA alongside wide-scale (racialized) welfare reform in the US, and second, by drawing attention to the complex interaction of gender, race and class in leave-taking patterns. Using longitudinal data, the authors found that, among factors such as marital status, education and access to maternity benefits, race and socioeconomic status strongly influences the length of leave taken. Manuel and Zambrana's analysis revealed that 'higher income middle-class Black women' take shorter leaves than white or Hispanic women of a similar class and income group (2009, p. 139).[1] I suggest that the rate at which maternity and parental leaves are paid in Britain and Canada might explain similar class and racial disparities. Table 7.1 summarizes these benefits, as at March 2017, the time of the study.[2]

While the Canadian government's 2001 decision to expand parental leave from 10 weeks to 35 weeks is often applauded as an indication of the state's commitment to gender equality and early years development (Evans, 2007), moves to extend parental leave tend to benefit the same group of middle-class women for whom such leave seems to have been designed in the first place. Evans speculated that because women of colour 'experience particular difficulty in meeting the qualifying period for "regular" EI benefits' (2007, p. 122) they likely struggle to qualify for maternity and parental leave benefits, which are sourced from the same EI fund. In a study of couples' decision-making around leave, McKay and Doucet (2010) suggested a similar conclusion. They described their participant pool as largely 'white, middle-class dual earners', which they frame as a reflection of the 'population that qualifies for parental leave benefits' (p. 304). While, in the current study, on the whole, the interviewees living in Canada described the benefits available to them positively, especially when contrasted with provisions in the US, not all participants were able to have the parental leave experience they would have liked:

> 'I feel like something they really need to consider is giving ... partial because I had like, 400 and something hours but you need 600 so ... I need 600 to get a whole year but I have 450, why can't I at least get six months of parental leave kind of thing? That's what really upset me and I think that they should consider ... they shouldn't be "at 600", it should be ... this is how much you qualify for because of the number of hours you have which is ... your EI ... it depends on the hours you have, how much time you get paid for or something so that's what I think should change.' (Olive, 28, two sons aged three years and two months respectively, interviewed in Canada)

Olive's example demonstrates the importance of distinguishing between 'availability and use' (Baird and O'Brien, 2015, p. 206) in examinations of parental leave policies and their gendered effects. Indeed, the

Table 7.1: Parental leave in Britain and Canada (Ontario)

	Britain	**Canada (Ontario)**[a]
Maximum length	52 weeks	54 weeks
Weeks available to mother only	Two	17
Weeks available to father	50	37
Benefit	90% of weekly wage for first six weeks (no cap) £139.58 or 90% of weekly wage (whichever is lower) for 33 weeks Unpaid for 13 weeks	55% of weekly earnings for whole period, aside from two-week waiting period (cap of $537 per week) Low-income families qualify for a benefit that increases wage replacement to 80%
Eligibility	Continuous employment for 26 weeks[b]	600 insurable hours in the previous 52 weeks (benefit)
Average taken by mothers	39 weeks (2008 data, Chanfreau et al, 2011)	43.6 weeks (Outside of Quebec, 2010/11 data, Findlay and Kohen, 2012)

a The benefits paid to parents are part of EI, a federal programme (with the exception of Quebec, which has its own), whereas the leave entitlements are determined by individual provinces. The entitlements for Ontario are shown here because all participants interviewed in Canada lived in this province. Quebec's programme is unique and is particularly effective at increasing fathers' take-up with its use-it-or-lose-it policy. However, given that none of the participants living in Canada lived in this province, I have not included details of its policy here.

b This is the requirement to be eligible for Statutory Maternity Pay (SMP). To qualify for Maternity Allowance, which amounts to slightly less than SMP, the individual needs to have worked for 26 out of the previous 66 weeks and earned at least £30 per week in 13 of these weeks. The distinction between SMP and Maternity Allowance offers self-employed and underemployed women access to maternity benefits.

phrasing of this distinction reflects the two ways that parents might find themselves barred from enjoying the parental leave benefits offered by their governments. Either parents are not eligible for parental leave, as in Olive's narrative, or they are eligible but cannot afford to take any or as much parental leave as they would prefer, as reported by Florynce ("I wanted to take a year but financially it's just not really an option"). That these two examples are sourced from women living in Canada and Britain respectively, reflects a key difference between the two countries' policies. While parents in Canada might receive more in benefits over

52 weeks (depending on whether their individual employer offers a non-obligatory top-up), Britain's less stringent eligibility criteria means that more women qualify for benefits in the first place.

While the mainstream narrative about Canadian parental leave provisions emphasizes the 52 weeks available to parents, the stories of women like Olive, who represents the one third of all mothers excluded from accessing parental leave benefits (McKay and Doucet, 2010), demonstrate the policy's uneven effects and thus, the barriers social class and low income can create to accessing good motherhood. As Olive suspected, these are not the women policy makers have in mind when they propose extending parental leave to 18 months, introduced in late 2017, fulfilling a Liberal campaign promise: "'Cause maybe they'll extend it but then they'll maybe raise the hours that you need to qualify.... So that's not helpful anyway."

The extension of parental leave further complicates the complex balancing act leave policies are attempting to achieve. Longer leaves are associated with reductions in women's long-term earning potential (Galtry and Callister, 2005), thereby encouraging women's economic dependence on men to ensure the stability of family income. While such a campaign promise reinforces the Liberal image of family friendliness, in reality, it becomes yet another mechanism through which middle-class, financially privileged women are rewarded for their motherhood, particularly that which is supported by men, while a message encouraging economic productivity at all costs is directed towards poorer women, and in this distinction, good motherhood is only available to those women who can afford it.

What is parental leave for?

The various and competing goals of parental leave frame the strategies that black mothers use to claim good motherhood. Is parental leave necessary to enable women to recover from birth? To ensure that children receive the one-on-one maternal care that they ostensibly require? To protect women's newly (for some) acquired positions in the paid workforce? To encourage fathers to play a more significant role in childrearing? The examination of such questions reveals the complexities and contradictions of state policy that is pressed into affirming social justice goals such as gender equality while attempting to minimize disruption to the economic productivity centred in neoliberal governance. These questions also capture the different ways the participants managed the division of parenting labour in their households as they negotiated classed expectations about which mothers ought to stay at home, minimizations of fathers' roles and the importance of the body in signalling good parenting, each informed by diverse investments in AP.

Staying at home

The increasingly dominant early years narrative (described in Chapter 3) has resulted in a shift in the purpose that parental leave is meant to fulfil. From ensuring women's continued attachment to the workforce, parental leave is now framed by increasingly frequent references to 'the wellbeing of the child' (Marshall, 2008). There is tension between a recognition of the 'importance of female employment "activation"' (O'Brien and Twamley, 2017, p. 164) and a belief that experiences in the first five years of a child's life have a transformative (and in some narratives, permanent) effect on their future development. This tension has facilitated the provision and extension of (mostly) paid parental leave that a growing number of women employed precariously are nevertheless unable to access or afford. This classed extension of parental leave occurs simultaneously with the British practice of extending free childcare provision for children aged three years and older (as well as offering provision for younger children in families that receive certain state benefits, the implication being that such children are better served by external childcare and economically productive parents [see MacLeavy, 2011]). This tension reveals the classed underpinnings of parental leave policies that are often overlooked in the celebrations of Britain and Canada's 'generous' offerings.

They also obscure the racial implications of pitting women's ability to participate in the paid labour force against the developmental needs of their children. These arguments have rarely been sufficient to protect black children from the purported dangers of growing up with a mother who works outside of the home. The construction of black children as disposable (Giroux, 2006), as already failed citizens, is entangled with the belief that black mothers have always been capable of work. This entanglement, along with the racialization of welfare, informs the repeated, cross-party decisions to reduce the point at which a mother on benefits must begin seeking employment to prevent the loss of those benefits. For example, in the UK, the 'age limit for unconditional support' for lone parents has decreased under both Labour and Conservative governments (Campbell, 2008, p. 465), a change that determines which parents are understood as best suited to staying home with their children and frames benefit-claiming parents' interactions with the state. In Florynce's case, the end of the traditional parental leave period (12 months) was marked with frustration as she required access to welfare benefits to continue staying at home with her son but was met with an inducement into paid work:

> 'I mean, with my son, I was home for the first year and then I went to train to be a teacher. I would have loved to have stayed [home] a bit longer but actually I was just sort of frustrated with the system. I remember at one point I was claiming Income Support and I had to go for some sort of review and they went and, you know, they'll question me about when I'm looking to go back to work. And I'm thinking, my son is just one, if I want to stay at home until he's five I'm allowed to do that. I'm allowed to do that as well and claim a benefit until he's five. I think at the time it might've been seven or something, um, and prior to that it was 12 under the Labour government, which is probably, maybe a bit steep. But the point is, you know, that support just isn't there.' (Florynce, 29, one son aged six years and one daughter aged six months, interviewed in the UK)

The persistent pressure exerted on benefit-claiming parents to seek work is at odds with the stay-at-home parenthood that is promoted by parental leave policy and indeed, AP. As Florynce reported, she experienced this pressure when her son was only 12 months old, during the apparently crucial early years when popular parenting discourse demands close, maternal–child bonding and attachment. The coexistence of such policies is further evidence of the contradictory messages aimed at middle-class mothers and those who are working-class and racialized. While the former is viewed as capable of good mothering and is overtly supported in this endeavour by paid parental leave, the latter is subject to ever-more coercive encouragement to pursue good citizenship through economic productivity. Florynce described an attempt to resist this encouragement, to access stay-at-home motherhood even as state employees and cultural attitudes framed this kind of motherhood as unsuited to 'scroungers'. Even as Florynce criticized this raced and classed contradiction, she also conceded to its underlying logic (an age limit of 12 years is "probably, maybe a bit steep") that there is a point at which mothers ought to end their reliance on benefits and return to the workforce. This concession demonstrates the tensions that black mothers negotiate as they attempt to challenge both prescripts of good mothering that exclude them and discourses of idealized citizenship and economic productivity.

A child-centred justification for the existence of parental leave is belied by Florynce's description of her thwarted access to benefits. Although focusing on children may appear to be neutral in that children are centred regardless of their socioeconomic or racial location, the dominant constructions of black childhood reveal the limitations of a child-first approach to policy making. Even if a racially and socioeconomically neutral interest in children's wellbeing were possible, because such a framework is produced by a political rationality that situates responsibility in the hands of individual parents, particularly mothers, a child-centred approach merely highlights the great expanse of needs and goals for which women are ultimately responsible. A child's physical, cognitive and emotional needs as well as the likelihood that they will be healthy, productive, well-disciplined citizens in the future are predicated not only on mothers' 'investments' of time, energy and resources but the intensity of such investments. Like recent shifts towards focusing on addressing 'child poverty', the larger context in which a child lives and the experiences of adult family members, in this case, mothers, are erased (Brah and Phoenix, 2004).

The introduction of a focus on child wellbeing within the context of economic restructuring that seeks to reduce the state's welfare provisions and expand its punitive arm (Wacquant, 2012) results in the identification of individual policies or programmes as the solution to persistent inequities rather than wholescale structural change. That I single out AP or parental leave is not to suggest that either practice is inherently problematic but rather reflects their capacity to be deployed in ways that serve a neoliberal agenda, particularly as interest in these activities can be read as indicative of the state's progressive orientation without requiring much material investment. Black mothers' attempts to claim good motherhood under these circumstances are fraught with contradictions as they attempt to value 'disposable' children (and demand the right to stay at home with them) through the very mechanisms that render them failed citizens. These contradictions have a similar effect when considering how the women negotiate the role fathers play in their claims on good motherhood.

"Little details" and gifts: fathers' roles and responsibilities

Despite a growing interest in the contribution fathers can make to good childrearing, the primary responsibility for parenting remains a woman's concern. Tensions emerge from this simultaneous encouragement of active fatherhood and the pressures exacted on women to mother intensively, tensions exacerbated by practice of AP. Of the 19 women interviewed for this study, only three reported that they divided childrearing evenly or "fifty-fifty" with their partners, while the remainder described a distribution of parenting labour that left most of the responsibility with the mother. When I asked Barbara, for example, how parenting was divided in her household, she answered that it was "fairly evenly split" but "mum's in charge". Olive responded to the same question by calling herself "the first responder":

'... when he was smaller I never left him with his dad to like go out and give him a bottle and like, "You can feed him." Like I usually took him with me all the time like I, especially 'cause I was breastfeeding I didn't wanna pump and leave him, you know? If like I couldn't take him with me I wouldn't go. Yeah. It was never like he wouldn't be there, like he would if I asked him to but at the same time we kind of both, I know, even though it was never discussed.... It's like he has fun with his dad and when he needs stuff I'm the one who does it.' (Olive, 28, two sons aged three years and two months respectively, interviewed in Canada)

Olive's division of parenting duties in her household reflected her commitment to AP practices, particularly breastfeeding, and captures the correlation between AP and heightened maternal responsibility and labour. This correlation is reinforced by the fact that of the 19 participants interviewed, there was only one clear exception to the trend of mothers taking greater responsibility: Claudia, who rejected AP as "a bit strange". When asked to describe the division of parenting duties in her relationship, Claudia named herself as the "provider" and her partner as the "caretaker".

While men's exemptions from parenting duties have often been explained as a result of their apparently biological inability to parent 'appropriately', the women I interviewed did not invoke this logic. Instead, underlying many women's descriptions of their superior maternal expertise was the suggestion that men are 'just different'. Although male 'difference' was not always necessarily expressed as a negative characteristic, the women's articulation of 'difference' resulted in the participants feeling obliged to claim primary responsibility for parenting in their households. Like Olive, Rebecca saw herself as responsible for what is necessary, while her partner provided the "fun":

'I think nature probably designed that way for a reason because I think [chuckles] imagine if both parents were

just like mommy, then our kids would never take risks ...
they'd probably be in bubble wrap until they're 20. So,
I think nature purposely designed it that way 'cause when
I look at how she is with her dad, he'll throw her up in the
air and I'm like, "Oh, my god, what are you doing?!" He's
like, "She's fine." And I think they need that balance, you
know what I mean? Otherwise, I'd be holding her hand
and shadowing her everywhere she went whereas he's like,
"No, just let her try it on her own, she has to fall." I'm
like, "What?! My child has to do what? No." But it's good,
right? So ... we need a balance ... it's, it's good that we're
around because then we pay attention to all the details and
so on ... she has to put sunscreen on and we remember
those little details and then they kind of take care of the
okay, the riskier, "gotta try it out" kind of stuff, you know
what I mean?' (Rebecca, 38, one daughter aged 13 months,
interviewed in Canada)

Rebecca's description of the distinct roles mothers and fathers play
is predicated on "balance". Although she assigned the "riskier" and,
arguably, more enjoyable activities to fathers, her division of labour does
suggest that each parent has an equal part to play in the development
of a well-rounded child. The suggestion that children *need* the unique
input fathers can provide facilitates fathers' more active involvement
in childrearing. And yet, Rebecca's naming of the "little details" that
mothers ought to manage suggests a responsibility for the 'mental
load', the 'planning, scheduling, negotiating and problem-solving
work' required for running a family (Owens, 2018; Daminger, 2019).
This responsibility to do the "stuff" that's needed, to use Olive's words,
is heightened in a context where parental decision making involves
reading, research and evaluation, let alone the embodied requirements
to babywear all the time or breastfeed on demand. These "little
details" suggest a greater responsibility for the basic, everyday burden
of childcare, while fathers take care of the more superfluous, "fun"
aspects of childhood, even (and perhaps *especially*) when couples are
seemingly egalitarian. This is evident in Rebecca's own account of
her parenting practice, where, although her husband's work schedule
allowed him to carry out a significant amount of childcare, decisions
over when to stop bedsharing, for example, were still primarily hers.

That an imbalance in the division of labour is centred on an
archetypal AP activity is evidence of the philosophy's promotion of
maternal responsibility. If the women claim primary responsibility

for the rearing and successful development of their children, they can claim good mothering, despite the ways their race and/or class location might impede such an assertion. However, this sometimes comes at the cost of displacing fathers, who are framed as lacking the specialized maternal expertise called for by all parenting philosophies in a context dominated by intensive mothering but especially by AP. Having located the maternal body as the site of an array of 'essential' childrearing activities, AP enthusiasts position fathers as helpers or assistants to the process of raising children. At best, fathers can hope to replicate the 'natural' bond understood as already established between mother and child by engaging in the occasional bout of babywearing or skin-to-skin contact, but ultimately, it is the mother–child relationship that is foregrounded. As the Sears' explain:

> Attachment fathering makes attachment mothering easier. Dad's knowledge of his baby helps him understand how important Mother is to baby, and this motivates him to create a supportive environment that allows Mother to devote her energy to the baby. An attached father is also ready to take a baby handoff from Mom when she is tired or needs a break. (Sears and Sears, 2001, p. 143)

The Sears' summarize this division of labour as 'sharing the baby duties' (2001, p. 143) despite the clear implications of the advice to fathers to be available to take care of their children *only* when their partners are 'tired or need a break'. This advice reflects widely held beliefs about the proper role of mothers and fathers and has long informed parental leave policies, which, despite various changes and adaptations, have remained maternalist in their orientation. In this convergence of interests, both AP and existing parental leave legislation leave room for a black practitioner of AP to claim good motherhood, obscuring the risks associated with taking on a greater burden of childcare labour and diminishing fathers' contributions (Hill, 2004).

Even when parental leave is constructed as ensuring fathers' contributions, it still results in greater pressure and an intensification of duties for mothers. As suggested by Notisha's description of her parental leave-sharing conversation and as both Fox (2009) and O'Brien and Twamley (2017) report, the low take-up of parental leave among fathers in Britain and Canada means that when fathers *do* take parental leave, the arrangement is framed as a gift exchange: 'the woman "gives" her husband the opportunity to take [parental leave], and he "gifts" her father involvement by taking it' (O'Brien and Twamley, 2017, p. 173). In this context, the responsibility to ensure that a child has access to all the necessary experiences for optimal growth remains with the mother. The father's involvement is an item she has had to procure through the relinquishment of her legal and culturally encouraged entitlement to a lengthy maternity leave. Further, this exchange is not complete. The mother's acceptance of the 'gift' of fatherly involvement requires further action in the form of 'gratitude and praise' (O'Brien and Twamley, 2017, p. 179). Whether fathers accept the gift of parental leave or not, it is mothers who must offer it, as Notisha offered leave to her husband, and in the UK context, it is the mothers' employment history that enables the father to accept such a gift in the first place.

This gift exchange directly maps on to the division of parental labour described earlier, in which fathers are necessary but only in so far as they provide the lighthearted, 'fun' side of parenting, while mothers take responsibility for everyday care. In turn, this contributes to a trend in leave taking in which mothers take the bulk of parental leave in the first months of a child's life, while fathers take the final months of eligible leave (McKay and Doucet, 2010). This pattern was identified, and rejected, by Tracey in her objection to sharing parental leave:

> 'I just wouldn't let him [chuckles]. He still asks, like, "Can I do it?" It's like, "No, you can't." Especially now 'cause … the first six months are so hard, so he's gonna do all the fun part? I don't think so. It's not gonna happen.' (Tracey, 31, one daughter aged five months, interviewed in Canada)

The hard work of early infant care involves the three tools the Sears' and AP enthusiasts identify as markers of AP: adjusting to disrupted, and in some cases, a lack of sleep, purportedly solved by bedsharing; learning how to entertain a new baby and keep them safe while accomplishing other necessary household tasks like cooking and cleaning, enabled by babywearing; and the process of feeding, which, for Tracey, involved many weeks of concerted effort and practice to achieve the successful breastfeeding relationship she so valued. When this hard work is assigned to mothers, as the philosophy of AP and the state's investment in policies such as 'breast is best' encourages, fathers are free to enjoy the 'fun' parts of early childrearing, especially when they take parental leave once a child's sleeping, playing and feeding schedule have been established. This is not to suggest that mothers are incapable of enjoying these everyday activities; many participants reported, for example, that they loved their parental leaves for the time it gave them to bond and have fun with their children. Nor does failing to share parental leave automatically assign fathers 'fun' activities, as Notisha reported.[3] I suggest that even when men's contribution to childrearing is viewed as essential, whether it is to fulfil the requirement for 'fun' or to give mothers a break, as the Sears' propose, the responsibility for ensuring such a contribution remains with mothers. In this way, whether mothers use all the parental leave or split it equally, they remain the "first responder", to use Olive's phrase, culpable both when fathers take parental leave and when they do not. While this construction of parenting labour, between fun and responsibility, can contribute to black mothers' attempts to claim good motherhood, it requires mothers to carry a great burden, especially on the body.

The gendered logic of dividing parenting between fun and the everyday underlies parental leave policy itself, evident in Additional Paternity Leave, the precursor to the current Shared Parental Leave in the UK, that entitled fathers to share only the remaining 30 weeks after mothers had taken the first 20. This is arguably a characteristic of Canadian parental leave policy if one interprets the breakdown of 15 weeks of maternity leave and 37 weeks of parental leave as suggesting that mothers take at least the first few months of leave while fathers are entitled to the months that follow. Margaret reported that she and her husband had shared parental leave in this manner:

> 'My husband took three months off for pat leave actually, so my daughter was nine months old when I went back to work and then he did nine months to a year. So very much hands on as well. 'Cause he wanted to kind of be there and he realized how hard it is and I'm glad he realized, he's like, "Next time you can take the full year."' (Margaret, 28, one daughter aged 16 months, interviewed in Canada)

Given the low uptake of parental leave among fathers in Canada (a 2013 study reported that 30.8 per cent of fathers 'claimed or intended to take' parental leave [Lero, 2015, p. 2]), Margaret's husband's use of parental leave was outside of the norm and demonstrated the long-term impact leave taking can have on attitudes towards childrearing. Margaret was clearly proud of his (implicitly unique) status as a "hands on" father and his recognition of the hard work of parenting. However, the conclusion they both drew from the experience of sharing leave is that she ought to take the full year of leave with their next child, suggesting an unexpected retreat towards a more traditional division of parenting labour. Having given him the gift of parental leave, Margaret's husband rewarded her with recognition of the difficulty of childrearing but did so in a manner that suggested her taking greater responsibility for it. The explanation for this unexpected retreat to tradition might be located in the body, both fathers' and mothers' bodies, especially the latter's broader cultural recognition as the site of good parenting.

"Staying healthy for you": fathers' bodies

Putting Margaret's comments in the larger context of her interview introduces another dimension to the competing bodily agendas of neoliberal citizenship: the enactment of good fatherhood through the body. Perhaps inseparable from 'fun' and financial provision, fathers' responsibility to the family may also be expressed bodily. After she described the pressure she felt to ensure that she make the time spent with her daughter 'count', I asked Margaret if she thought her husband felt the same way:

> 'No, like he definitely values time with her but his priority is to stay healthy ... he'll be around for her because he's aware, he's very healthy but he's aware of the fact that his grandfather died at a young age from ... a heart attack. But he was a heavy smoker and drinker, his grandfather, great grandfather so it's kinda different 'cause he's quite healthy but he still has that on his mind ... he doesn't wanna leave us, you know, before his time. He's eight years older than me and you know, statistically women outlive men so he's very conscious of all those things so this is why, you know, he's like, "I'm staying healthy for you guys, I'm staying healthy for her and for you" so it's smart and I wanna do the same 'cause then ... I wanna be around. I wanna be doing the right things too but I just have that, more guilt than him.'

His commitment to staying healthy gave Margaret's husband licence to attend sports activities that necessitated time away from their child. His concern for his physical health may arguably be tied to wider beliefs that link good fathering to financial provision. The imperative to be healthy expresses neoliberal values, especially as health is linked to the capacity to be a productive worker (Peterson and Lupton, 1996; Ayo, 2012). In this way, Margaret's husband's commitment to his health served dual purposes, allowing him to fulfil both good father and good citizen roles. However, the "guilt" Margaret experienced constrained her ability to do the same. While mothers have not been able to escape pressure to remain healthy themselves, especially as their health is linked to that of their children (Peterson and Lupton, 1996; Lee and Jackson, 2002), there is little room in dominant maternal ideology for mothers who take time for themselves to go to the gym or take a yoga class. When mothers do carve out time for such activities they experience the guilt Margaret named. Mother guilt and blame characterizes the narratives of many mothers who accept intensive mothering as ideal (Elliott et al, 2013) and has intensified in a parenting policy context that emphasizes the brain-shaping importance of parent–child interactions (Gillies et al, 2017). As the range of decisions parents are expected to make becomes ever more detailed, so the significance with which such decisions are invested is heightened and so the stakes are raised, particularly for black mothers.

"He doesn't have a boob, so …": mothers' bodies

The introduction of shared parental leave initiatives in the UK and use-it-or-lose-it paternity leave in Canada is often couched in the language of gender equality, regardless of the actual results of such policy changes. These tensions are heightened by adherence to AP, given its emphasis on embodied parenting activities as essential for children's wellbeing. This promotion is centred on the *maternal* body, resulting in women performing even those activities that could be easily carried out by fathers, such as babywearing and bedsharing, and performing them in such a manner that can preclude fathers' involvement. In this context, women's accounts portray their bodies as both sites of immense power and as an instrument of accessing good motherhood as well as the site at which the constraining effects of racial ideologies and mothering discourses are felt.

The body has been the primary site through which black women have experienced gendered and racial ideologies and oppressions. Black women's reproductive capacity, in particular, has been framed as either a source of profit, as during slavery, or as a threat to the whiteness and wellbeing of Western nations, as expressed in ongoing practices of sterilization abuse (Roberts, 1997a) and immigration detention (Tyler, 2013). The belief that black women are more 'bodily' than their white counterparts (Firth, 2012) is an expression of the same logic that constructs black women as closer to nature and therefore more likely to (unthinkingly) practice AP. It is this vision of black womanhood that the Sears' evoke in their celebrations of 'primitive' cultures that, uncontaminated by the West, have managed to sustain their superior parenting practices. While this vision strips black women of their subjectivity, the potential to turn this narrative on its head and (re)claim AP as African can protect black mothers from these dehumanizing impulses. However, such claims on AP are often made through mothers taking greater responsibility for childrearing, apparently deeming a less equitable division of labour as an appropriate price to pay for this protection.

This is true of Olive, who, as described earlier, referred to herself as a "first responder" and through her prioritization of breastfeeding had rarely left her sons in the sole care of their father. Tracey, as discussed earlier, offered another example:

PH: 'Did your husband take any of the parental leave? Did you think about doing that?'
Tracey: '[Chuckles] We did and, uh, if I would've let him he probably would have [laughs] but I didn't let him.'
PH: 'Okay [chuckles]. And what motivated that, what was the decision making around that?'
Tracey: 'Um, well, I think, number one he doesn't have a boob so he can't feed her so....'

Tracey's description of the decision making in her household demonstrated the concentration on women's bodies that AP and other mainstream parenting philosophies encourage and therefore complicate and in many cases, contradict, the expressed aim of parental leave policies (Doucet, 2009). In Tracey's case, the prospect of sharing the responsibilities of parenting their infant daughter was subordinated to the need to breastfeed successfully. Situated in her broader investment in AP, this prioritizing of breastfeeding prevented a more equitable division of labour. In the overlap between AP and intensive mothering, mothers' bodies are foregrounded and thus their labour is viewed as essential to the current and future wellbeing of children. That such a goal (the wellbeing of children) is subordinated to a broader aim of gender equality is unsurprising in a postfeminist context. If the work of feminism has been completed and women's parenting decisions are framed as individual choices, black women's embrace of AP can only be read through its anti-racist effects and the pathway it provides to good motherhood, rather than as a potential source of overburdening.

As Tracey's declaration that "he doesn't have a boob" suggests, the message that 'breast is best' reinforces this overburdening. The moral impetus to breastfeed in a neoliberal context reinforces the belief that mothers 'own' parental leave (McKay and Doucet, 2010), allowing the need to decide how parental leave ought to be shared to become another manifestation of the primary responsibility women possess for maximizing the wellbeing of their children, as captured by Notisha and others. This responsibility is intensified further for black mothers for whom decision making around parenting techniques is invested with vital importance. The choice to breastfeed or formula feed is entangled with the requirement not only to ensure the production of a healthy, economically productive future citizen but also to protect the child from the health disparities, educational exclusion, employment discrimination and other consequences of a systemically racist society.[4]

If the promotion of breastfeeding contributes to mothers being more likely to take the leave during the first months of a child's life, as McKay and Doucet (2010) found and Margaret and Tracey's accounts attest, this reinforces the belief produced by mothering and gender ideologies that the reason mothers take greater responsibility for childrearing is that they are 'naturally' better at it. Research has found that for first time parents, the early experiences of childrearing determine the pattern of division of labour in the future (Fox, 2009). Due to prioritizing breastfeeding and the maternalist orientation of parental leave, it is mothers who are more likely to spend time caring for their children during those first few months, developing parenting skills that fathers do not. In such a scenario, mothers develop confidence about their capacity to perform the work of childrearing, while fathers, who fail to share in these experiences, become less and less likely to develop the confidence to claim primary parenting responsibility in the same way. Jayaben referenced this phenomenon when she reported that as her daughters grew older (they were aged three and six years at the time of the interview), her husband felt more comfortable asserting his parental expertise rather than relying on Jayaben to determine the appropriate course of action. Even noting this shift, Jayaben still claimed primary responsibility for not only caring for the children but determining the kind of childrearing she and her husband employed:

> 'Well, I think as they get older ... and as we both become more comfortable in our role as parents ... he's gained confidence in saying, "Well, I think this is what the girls need or this child needs this or I think this approach will be better" so that is changing. But I think when they were very, very small, particularly when they were so physically attached to me, quite literally, I think that he would defer

to whatever I thought was necessary.' (Jayaben, 44, two daughters aged six and three years respectively, interviewed in the UK)

The children's physical attachment to Jayaben required her husband to "defer" to her greater authority, demonstrating the significance of breastfeeding promotion and the consequent effect it has on the division of parenting labour both in the early years of a child's life and in the years that follow. Although Jayaben's narrative reveals how patterns of childrearing responsibility can change as children age, it also suggests the tensions between breastfeeding promotion and parental leave legislation that purports to encourage fathers' involvement. Her children's attachment was a necessary condition of successful breastfeeding and it is that attachment that state parenting advice names as a marker of good motherhood.

Conclusion

While acknowledging that fundamental changes in workplace culture, gender ideology and the provision of state support for citizens are required for long-lasting change in unequal divisions of labour in families, what kind of parental leave policy can be implemented immediately, as a means of achieving these wider goals? The solution proposed by some feminist scholars hoping to address mothers' disproportionate use of parental leave and its long-term consequences is to assign each parent six months of leave that cannot be transferred (Gornick and Meyers, 2009). However, such a policy would be limited by the dominance of particular kinds of parenting techniques growing in popularity among the public and promoted by the state (Macdonald, 2009). In the context of 'breast is best,' for example, how might this policy accommodate the recommendation that mothers ought to breastfeed for up to two years? As the accounts of the women in this study suggest, splitting parental leave evenly between heterosexual couples ignores not only the actual 'differentially embodied experiences' of mothers and fathers but also, and perhaps more crucially, parents' *beliefs* about what those differences mean (Doucet, 2009, p. 92). For feminist advocates of egalitarian leave policies especially, the tension arises from the effort to accommodate both the choices of the mother whose belief in the importance of breast milk requires her withdrawal from the labour market for an extended period of time *and* the larger effort to improve women's position in the workforce.

Changes to parental leave policies are necessary but not sufficient, especially considering the absence of state-funded childcare, the gender *and* racial pay gap, the 'long hours culture' (Gray, 2006) and a general belief that such problems ought to be solved by individual enterprise. Scholarly research can only have a limited effect on policy making, given the gamesmanship that characterizes contemporary politics (Galtry and Callister, 2005), but the promotion of equitable parental leave policy can only be successful if carried out within the context of, among others, demands for a reduction in the average working hours (Gray, 2006), the introduction of state-subsidized childcare (Gornick and Meyers, 2009) and the dismantling of a gendered, racialized and classed labour market that differentially determines how parents access and experience parental leave in the first place. When it interacts with dominant gender, racial and parenting ideologies (which are themselves gendered and raced), leave can operate as a policing mechanism, offering another avenue through which mothers can be scrutinized for failing to make the appropriate choices expected of a good mother.

These moments of judgement can have damaging effects on efforts to divide parenting labour more equitably (McKay and Doucet, 2010). The persistence of paid parental leave policies (and in some cases, their expansion) might appear to some scholars as a departure from or contradiction of neoliberal efforts to promote individualism and centre the market (Baird and O'Brien, 2015). After all, neoliberalism assumes a reduction in state spending, particularly in areas broadly defined as 'welfare'. However, the 'neo' in 'neoliberalism' marks the emergence of a new kind of state, a 'Centaur-state' that 'uplifts' at the top and 'castigates' at the bottom (Wacquant, 2012, p. 74). Building on Harris (2004), this suggests that the purpose of parental leave policy in a neoliberal context *is* the production of two messages, the first designed for white, middle-class mothers, for whom the poorly paid parental leave provisions can be topped up by individual employer agreements and the support of a well-paid spouse. For such women, the message suggests that staying home with one's baby is essential for their optimal development. The second message is targeted at women in low-paid, low-status work and in some instances, racialized women who, because of barriers such as institutionalized racism and sexism, find it difficult to meet the requirements to access EI benefits in Canada (Evans, 2007) or experience a wider wage gap than their white counterparts in the UK, shaping the extent to which a 90 per cent wage replacement will be a living wage. For working-class women like Olive and Florynce, the experience of parental leave is short due to its unaffordability. Like Florynce, whose interactions with the British benefits system drove her to return to work and Patricia, who was told to consider lost "benefits" if she quit her job to look after her child full-time, some children are framed as being best served in an institutionalized childcare setting. That the state's investment in parental leave pay is motivated by the 'business case' (Baird and O'Brien, 2015, p. 213) is evidence of both the market-centred logic that governs neoliberalism and of the role social policies play in the production of new kinds of citizens (Polzer and Power, 2016).

The mothers interviewed for this study attempted to navigate this scenario in different ways: some used the maternalist design of parental leave to claim this time as their own, others asserted male 'difference' to narrow their partners' parental role and responsibility, while others cited the bodily demands of AP to explain their primary responsibility for and investment in childrearing. Each of these attitudes is best understood when contextualized in this particular sociohistorical moment as women confront both heightened pressures to mother intensively and repeated reminders to take (financial) responsibility for their children. Within the limitations set by a maternalist parental-leave policy orientation, even as it appears to be egalitarian, these mothers negotiate contradictory messages about what good parenting ought to entail, reflecting their particular intersectional social locations and deploying AP to claim and explain their good mothering.

8

'Staying at Home' or 'Choosing to Work'

The effort to balance work and family is one of the defining features of contemporary parenthood. For women in particular, the conflict between staying at home or working outside of it has inspired much scholarship, policy and public debate, most vividly captured in the prevailing 'mommy wars' discourse (Douglas and Michaels, 2004; Dillaway and Paré, 2008). According to this discourse, women's 'recent' entrance into the paid workforce has thrown up a variety of as yet unresolved obstacles that women must overcome in order to meet both their economic responsibilities as good citizens and the requirements of *raising* good citizens. In her discussion of intensive mothering, Sharon Hays (1996) points to the inevitable contradiction such an intensification of childrearing requires: how can mothers do both? Parental leave policies appear to be one strategy to enable mothers to manage both but as the discussion in Chapter 7 describes, assessing the effectiveness of such a strategy requires attending to the complex intersection of race, gender, class and dominant parenting ideologies as they shape and constrain policy making and individual parents' experiences. Indeed, the very question itself, and the suggestion that it is a new dilemma, is extrapolated from the experiences of white, middle-class women. Historically, from slavery through colonialism and into the postwar period, black women have been 'socially positioned as workers' (Reynolds, 2001, p. 1049) and have had little choice but to balance work and motherhood for generations.

But how do contemporary mothers negotiate this legacy? Historical representations of black womanhood continue to inform black women's mothering, including both experiences and perceptions of it, with their capacity for work framed as neglectful, whether in their inability to find work and provide for their burdensome children or their emasculating prioritization of work over family (Reynolds, 1997, 2001). Today, women confront both heightened pressures to mother intensively and repeated reminders to take (financial) responsibility for their children. These injunctions are intensified for black mothers thanks to a historical legacy that excluded them from the boundaries of good motherhood precisely *because* they participated in paid work. That mothers might zealously conform to dominant models of good childrearing or resist this model by an equally ardent commitment to economic productivity and good neoliberal citizenship is evidence of the lasting effects of this legacy. However, these pressures may also offer opportunities for negotiation, rejection and reshaping of black motherhood. AP in particular, with its claimed link to Africa and emphasis on the transformative presence of mothers, offers one pathway, constrained by the intersection of race, gender and class, to navigate this dilemma.

In this chapter, I focus on the narratives of two mothers living in Canada: Rebecca and Olive. Although the women chose 'opposing sides' in the mommy wars discourse, with Olive choosing to stay at home and Rebecca opting to return to work, their narratives are more complicated than such a simplistic dichotomy suggests. Using black feminist theory, particularly its emphasis on black women's capacity for self-definition, I argue that the experiences of the two black mothers described here signal the complexity of contemporary black motherhood and the different, seemingly contradictory, ways that a popular parenting philosophy like AP can be utilized to bolster a claim to 'good' motherhood.

Black feminist self-definition

One of the central tenets of black feminist thought is recognition of the 'controlling images' created to disparage black womanhood that work to frame racism and sexism as 'natural' (Taylor, 1998; Collins, 2000; Norwood, 2013). Black feminist theory does more than catalogue oppression; its project is concerned with the work black women do to respond to these oppressions. Self-definition is the phrase black feminist scholars and activists have given to ideas of self that challenge and transform the hegemonic constructions of black womanhood expressed in controlling images.

Controlling images emerge in and reflect the social context in which they are developed, from the slavery and post-emancipation era Mammy (Collins, 2000) to the 'angry black woman', popularized in our current postracial context (Springer, 2007). The 'angry black woman' is a particularly effective stereotype in these times, building on the belief that racism is no longer a serious concern and castigating those who 'play the race card'. This image has appeared in a variety of arenas from politics, where representations of Michelle Obama frame her as angry and militant (Guerrero, 2011), to reality television where black women's disproportionate anger is linked to moral and sexual excess and the 'realness' of the medium is particularly adept at reinforcing dominant images of black women's lives (Ward, 2015).

Against these images and the policies and wider culture they inform, black women endeavour to assert themselves as fully human subjects (Samantrai, 2002). This is not to suggest that black feminist theory calls on black women to create flawless and narrow visions of black womanhood, nor does it discount the structural barriers black women face as they develop their subjectivities. Black feminist thought instead suggests tools with which to unpick the tangle of contradictions that shape both controlling images and the self-definitions black women create to oppose them. These contradictions lie, for example, in negotiating the ethics and politics of authenticity. How can we criticize depictions of black womanhood, especially those featured on reality television, without invoking a politics of respectability (Ward, 2015) that suggests that 'respectable' behaviour is the most appropriate method for overcoming oppression? On the other hand, how do black women express an affirmative sense of self against dominant constructions of black womanhood while refusing the burden of representing an entire community?

Black women's attempts to untangle these contradictions are not easily resolved, nor can they be with, for example, one single image of authentic black womanhood (indeed, black feminist theorizing specifically demands capturing the diversity of black female experience [Reynolds, 2002; Massaquoi, 2007]). Self-definitions need not be perfect and may not always cohere neatly or may sometimes reflect problematic politics, but that they exist at all is evidence of black feminist consciousness and resistance (Lawson, 2002). Just as controlling images do, these self-defined images emerge in response to the specific context in which they are forged and, for the purposes of this book, can speak directly to and shape black women's experience of motherhood, directing them towards or away from philosophies such as AP. Olive and Rebecca's narratives describe just this navigation, both drawing on AP to craft self-definitions that assert their good motherhood in the face of raced and classed constraints on their childrearing. Rather than consider whether one or the other is the correct or 'authentic' image of black womanhood, I consider instead how the experiences of these two women reveal the different paths black mothers travel as they negotiate constraining discursive constructions, especially as they are informed by social class and citizenship.

Olive

Olive, one of the few participants to describe themselves as working-class, was strongly committed to AP. When we met for the interview, she had just given birth to her second child two months before and brought him and his three-year-old brother along to our meeting. Having arrived at the interview wearing her youngest son in a fabric sling, there was no doubt whatsoever about her preferred style of parenting. While she was not sure that she adhered to AP criteria she had read about online "a hundred per cent", she described loving babywearing, bedsharing and, of course, breastfeeding:

> 'Oh, breastfeeding's very important to me. I'm not, I don't even like the idea of giving them formula. Like you don't know what's in there, right? So for him [referring to her older son] I breastfed him until I found out I was pregnant with him [referring to her youngest son] so he was already past two years when I was still breastfeeding him. And I wasn't gonna stop, it was, I feel like it was more of a comfort thing 'cause he only did it as soon as he woke up and then before he went to bed, like he was eating a long time ago and he ate properly so ... but again it was like the bonding and just the, just being there for him kinda thing. Yeah, and so I'm hoping that he will breastfeed for a very long time, yeah, I don't wanna give formula.' (Olive, 28, two sons aged three years and two months respectively, interviewed in Canada)

Olive's preference for this style of childrearing stressed the importance of bonding, being led by her children and their needs and desires and her ability to do "everything" for them. It was not enough to breastfeed; Olive's version of AP required her to take almost complete responsibility for the raising of her children, eclipsing even their father whose role was reduced to "fun" and support for her own responsibility as "first responder". But for Olive, this all-encompassing responsibility was just a stage in her children's development, necessary and crucial but temporary and thus "worth" the "sacrifices" necessary to make her parenting approach feasible.

At the time of our meeting, these sacrifices were largely financial. After taking "the full year" of maternity leave available after the birth of her first son, Olive briefly returned to her job before realizing that she would prefer to stay at home with her child. As she described it: "I was like, 'I just wanna be with my son, I need him! I need to be there for him!'" By the time she was pregnant with her second child, Olive had returned to work, in a minimum wage job that allowed her to bring her older son to work. However, the flexibility the job offered had other consequences. Olive was ineligible for paid parental leave because she had not worked the required 600 hours in the 12 months prior to the birth of her second son. She chose to stay at home with her sons despite the absence of this financial support because she so valued the time spent with her young children. Her dedication to AP and the vital importance that the philosophy assigns to the early years of childhood allowed her to resolve the tension between work and stay-at-home parenting that features prominently in popular discourse about motherhood (and in all but one interview):

> 'I think it's worth the sacrifices that I'm making to have this lifestyle. Which is hard … I could be at work just making money … my sister's more career-oriented and for her it's … "Oh, why don't you go back to school so you can do something that makes more money? You have two kids now." But … I'm going back to school, I'm working to support my kids and then … they've grown up and I have missed everything … what is that? What am I gaining out of this? Do you know what I mean? Maybe one day I'll do that, maybe once they're past a certain stage but when they need me the most I'm not gonna go try to do something to sup-, to be with my kids in the end, you know what I mean? Be there now and do something else later when they don't need me all the time.'

Olive's belief in the importance of this "certain stage" overruled any injunction to participate in the workforce. Olive did not seem at all concerned about what might come after this "certain stage", what this "something else later" might be, other than an interest in homeschooling her eldest son, arguably elongating the developmental period when her children "need [her] all the time". Indeed, this "something else later" paled in significance compared with the kind of parenting she could offer her children in the early (and apparently crucial) years of their development, a style of parenting that required her to forgo paid employment. While traditional (white) feminist theorizing might read this preference for staying at home as an indication of conformity to patriarchal oppression, I suggest that, given the predominant images of black motherhood as pathological and financially reckless so deftly captured in the Shanesha Taylor story (see Chapter 3), there is something radical in Olive's insistence on her children's needs and in her positioning of herself as being ideally and exclusively suited to meeting them.

Olive's experiences are shaped by a complex interaction between race, social class and parenting philosophy, as Olive herself recognized. When I asked if AP was popular in her neighbourhood, she demurred:

> 'I definitely think it's like maybe a cultural thing. I don't know, I don't know. But I know it's like this area, it's mainly like black people, they do have baby programmes but they are different than the ones I've gone to that aren't in this area that are more like, um ... more white people that are staying home with their kids doing that different, like, mommy and baby groups and all of that. So I feel like maybe that's the difference. It's like they, when you can afford to stay home kind of thing, you know what I mean?'

Olive recognized the entanglement of race and class that made stay-at-home parenthood possible for some Canadians and described a kind of circularity that meant that information about apparently superior parenting practices was only offered to those with the resources to meet its demands. Olive responded to this conflation of race, class and ideal parenting behaviour by turning it on its head, by rejecting the assumption that as a resident of her neighbourhood, she would be uninterested in "mommy and baby" groups and would put "her kids in daycare". Instead, she chose stay-at-home motherhood, an occupation she felt most closely aligned with her parenting philosophy ("In my heart I am [a stay-at-home mother]"), even as financial pressures meant that a return to paid work was likely.

Through Olive's experience, the mommy wars can be reread as the expression of two contradictory views of ideal motherhood that 'sort [mothers] into those who ought to stay home and give their children the benefit of their time and attention, and those who ought to work, and give their children the benefit of enriching activities' (Macdonald, 2009, p. 425; Harris, 2004). As Olive described, these views of motherhood are intrinsically raced and classed, framed by popular beliefs that equate blackness with failed citizenship, thus making black women unsuited to the work of raising their children and nevertheless deeming those children irredeemable and disposable. Viewing Olive's determined stay-at-home mothering through this lens challenges these constructions of blackness but comes at the cost of relieving women's care burdens and, without a supportive state apparatus, risks exacerbating black women's already disproportionate rates of poverty and unemployment. My aim here is not to reduce Olive's mothering to merely the expression of apparently revolutionary opposition to raced and classed stereotypes but to note the complexities of her maternal practices, to depart from critiques of mothering ideologies that frame mothers, particularly marginalized mothers, as victims of circumstance and oppression. The bargain Olive made, exchanging financial security and a shared burden for dedicated, exclusive mothering, is both coherent and disruptive; it both undermines and accords with neoliberal rationality in ways that can open space for alternative and resistive enactments of mothering.

Although Olive acknowledged the difficulties associated with AP practice, both emotional and financial, she remained committed to the philosophy, believing that the price was worth it:

> 'I'm … really struggling by making this choice in the way … I'm sacrificing a lot of things like even just fixing my car and stuff that I could do if I just put my kids in day care and went to work. I'm giving up those things because being with them is more important to me … they're never gonna be the same age again….'

Work was secondary for Olive, especially while her children were young. The importance of building a bond during the early years was worth both giving up or compromising work and taking greater responsibility for childrearing. As a working-class woman, Olive's rejection of financial stability and sustained economic productivity is radical in such a context but is not the only way to counter intensive, neoliberal pressures on mothers, as Rebecca's account captured.

Rebecca

I met Rebecca on her lunch break, six weeks after she had returned to work following a 12-month maternity leave. By her own admission, her family was still adjusting to the "big transition", both in terms of what it meant for the routine she had developed while home with her now 13-month-old daughter and parental leave's impact on her career. Like Olive, Rebecca seemed tentative at first in her claim on

AP but as she described her own practices, alignment with AP tenets became apparent:

> '... from what I understand it to be it's kinda more about, like sort of feeding on demand and kind of being more available. And I guess I wore her, like I was a big, a very big promoter of wearing her. So when I was on mat leave, that was a big thing for me, having her in a carrier and having her close to me a lot, responding to her cries, that kind of thing. So I guess I would say that I am, like we co-sleep, we've been doing that since she was born.' (Rebecca, 38, one daughter aged 13 months, interviewed in Canada)

Rebecca also prioritized breastfeeding and as is often the case in attachment parents' accounts, the individual tools of AP practice reinforced each other, with Rebecca's continued feeding reinforcing bedsharing and vice versa. These practices also reinforced a gendered division of parenting labour ("my husband sleeps in the other room because she still feeds at night") that resulted in the couple dividing the work "ninety-ten" in the early months of their daughter's life:

> 'I think the main discussion we had was around the co-sleeping 'cause that was a big change. So in terms of him having to sleep, 'cause he's very sensitive about his sleep and stuff, so for him it meant that he'd have to sleep in the other room, for sure. So from the time she's been born I've been kinda doing the night-time work.'

Since Rebecca's return to work and its accompanying sense that her daughter didn't "need" her as much "*all* the time" (original emphasis), the division of labour had shifted but Rebecca maintained her position as decision maker and her reluctance to sleep train remained a "bone of contention" with her husband that echoed Rebecca's own internal conflicts about the merits of AP:

> '... that's one of the things I find with the whole attachment parenting approach like I find ... you end up making so many decisions that are baby-centred. So it's almost like you go too far, maybe it's *my* thing in that I've gone too far in that direction where I've made everything sort of baby-centric as opposed to taking into account the whole family, in terms of having a balance. 'Cause I'm sure for

him, it's no fun, like your wife's not there anymore, basically like she's off in the other room and you've kind of been relegated to the guest room or whatever in favour of baby so that can't be easy, right?'

Despite these struggles, Rebecca remained committed to the bond and emotional development she believed parenting in an attached manner could facilitate. Although before having her daughter she had not intended to breastfeed for more than six months and envisioned returning to work after nine months, her experience, particularly the very early weeks with her newborn daughter, led her to re-evaluate her plans. While a 'long' maternity leave had allowed her to give her daughter this early attention framed as essential in dominant mothering ideologies, it did not entirely eliminate the contradiction between work and family. Our conversation was punctuated with her concerns about adjusting to life as a mother working outside of the home, particularly the pressure to succeed in both arenas of work and home. This tension between a dedication to work *and* AP manifested in her response to the question, "If money was no object, would you stay at home?":

'No. I don't, I don't … I think it's good, yes, like I can see why mums do it and stuff … I think it's great for kids and stuff to have that constant support and so on but I don't know, I think mentally I'd go bananas because … I feel, I don't know, it's like you know our minds need stimulation and that kind of stuff? …Well, I guess my mind does anyways, I should say, 'cause … everybody has different goals and stuff like that and that's not to say that for a stay-at-home mom it's not stimulating … they can find other activities … maybe they find their stimulation in other activities and so on but yeah, I don't think for me, it would. And I think part of the pressure for me is you know, being a black woman and being an immigrant as well at the same time … I sacrificed so much to come here and do my Master's … I gave up my whole awesome life I had at home to come here … I got a full scholarship and stuff but I gave all that up to come here, to study, you know, and I'm so grateful that I have the position. When I see how there are other people who have to clean, people who are way more qualified than me are just out there cleaning and that kind of stuff or working as a cab driver … I feel like I've done so much to get this far and I think for my daughter, I want her to see that you know what? These things are possible 'cause I guess I'm also very mindful of the, the race aspect of things ... you know what I mean? When she looks around her world and stuff she sees, she's gonna see mostly Caucasian people you know what I mean? And I don't want her to look and feel well ... I'm sure mentally it's gonna be like, "Well, why is my mom different from everybody else's?", you know what I mean? And I, and I, and you know there's this kind of ... I guess I've kind of always felt like, you know, as a black woman it's almost like you're kind of at the bottom of the social ladder to some extent, regardless of education and that kind of stuff, socially, it feels like you're a little bit below so I don't want her, so it's almost like you have to try that much harder to kind of ... so I feel ... if I were to stay home now it would be kind of like a, I don't know, I'd be throwing everything away somehow and I don't want her to ... I want her to see that "Okay, you know what, here, yes, my mom looks different but you know what? She's educated and she works", you know ... those are the things I guess that, I don't know, that kind of tip the scales a little bit more, maybe that's not the right way of looking at it but you know....'

Rebecca's struggle to negotiate dominant mothering ideologies that frame stay-at-home motherhood as best for children and her own experiences as a black immigrant woman is obvious. She sought to distance herself from this kind of good mothering, without belittling it, while actively asserting her own version that attends to the realities of raising a child of colour in a white-dominated society. In some previous studies of black motherhood, this tension between work and mothering has been framed as a white, middle-class concern (Forna, 2000). That black women have been constructed primarily as workers, regardless of their maternal responsibilities, is explained as a result of 'slavery, British colonialism in the Caribbean and economic migration of black women ... from the Caribbean during the post-war era' (Reynolds, 2001, p. 1049), during which black women's capacity to be economically productive came to define their status.

False consciousness? Or alternative futures?

It is through this construction of black women as workers that their mothering has been devalued and dismissed (Glenn, 1992). However, this argument is sometimes accompanied by the claim that, because the vast majority of black women experience paid work and mothering as 'interlocking and interdependent functions' (Reynolds, 2001, p. 1054), those black women who value full-time mothering over paid work are victims of false consciousness, 'trapped by a dominant, intransigent maternal ideal' (Forna, 2000, p. 370). However, I argue that Olive's decision to stay at home with her children, regardless of the financial or career development costs, cannot be reduced to the entrapment Forna suggests. Olive's parenting choices were carefully articulated and formed part of a broader commitment to leading a more 'natural' lifestyle, specifically rooted in "black culture" and "rebellion [against] the standards of society".

Neither can Rebecca's account be viewed as valuing economic productivity, and the access to good citizenship it may generate, over her daughter's wellbeing. Although she chose work, this choice was accomplished by overcoming a series of barriers, acknowledging both the forcefulness of the injunction to mothers to stay at home and the specific contradictions such an injunction creates for black mothers. By framing her decision to work as ultimately benefitting her daughter, Rebecca responded to these forces and used their contradictory logic to sustain her specific maternal practice. In concentrating on both Rebecca and Olive's stories, I highlight the different paths black mothers choose in their attempts to raise their children in a racist society and claim an oppositional good motherhood. Whether they mother or work full-time, black mothers negotiate with constructions of their motherhood and citizenship that frame them as failures. That Rebecca and Olive in different ways confronted such discourses with maternal practice that centres not only their children's wellbeing but also their own, racially derived subjectivity is evidence of the variety of self-definitions black feminist theory identifies as characteristic of black womanhood and provides a glimpse of what alternative practices could be possible in viewing motherhood through the lens of black mothers' experiences.

What these insights show is the nuance required when developing a critique of the broader social context that holds women primarily responsible for childrearing. This involves, for example, confronting the cultural pressures that good mothering ideologies impose on women, while acknowledging and respecting women's investment in the wellbeing of their children. That many women accept the central tenets of intensive mothering cannot be dismissed as merely an indication of their 'false consciousness' but might be understood as a commitment to the relational aspects of maternal relationships even in the face of neoliberal disavowal (Hays, 1996; Stephens, 2011; Tyler, 2011). This nuanced take on mothers' dedication to these ideologies is brought to bear by the accounts offered by the black women participants of this study. I read their commitment to the health and success of their children not merely as submission to neoliberal modes of good parenting and good citizenship but as opposition to racial discourses that construct their children as disposable. That their choice of parenting technique might express both these notions (both submission and opposition) is testimony to the complexity of all mothers' engagements with dominant ideologies and evidence of the need for structural changes to achieve a more equitable division of childrearing labour.

Conclusion

Both Rebecca and Olive valued AP for the room it provided them to bond with and respond to their children. For both women, AP offered an opportunity not available to their own parents. It is through recognition of the importance of a child's emotional development and the crucial role played by a primary (maternal) caregiver in those early months that justifies lengthy maternity leave policies in the first place. But not all mothers are eligible for paid parental leave and for those who are, leave comes to an end, and Olive and Rebecca deploy AP to respond to the dilemmas raised by the conclusion or absence of leave. For Olive, AP extended the amount of time she was 'needed' by her children; for Rebecca, AP was concentrated in those first few months but was now eclipsed by another need she had to fulfil for her daughter, that of countering the overwhelmingly white images of success her daughter would see in her community.

The stories told by the black mothers in this chapter, and in this book, offer expansion and critique of these new parenting citizens, suggesting myriad approaches to expressing maternal subjectivity that variably undermine and reinforce dominant ideas about good childrearing. In the identification of both working and staying at home as expressions of good black motherhood, my aim is not to offer a single pathway to 'revolutionary' maternal identity and experience but rather to illustrate the different ways black mothers, as individuals and as a group, organize their lives to best prepare their children for the futures that neoliberal racial ideologies attempt to deny them.

PART IV

Constructing an Oppositional
Model of Good Motherhood

9

Reclaiming AP

Welfare queen. Baby mother. Angry black woman. These are the representations of black womanhood that dominate popular culture and frame public policy making (Jordan-Zachery, 2009). Black feminist sociologist Patricia Hill Collins calls them controlling images, stereotypical representations of black womanhood that play a central role in the ideological justification of the 'intersecting oppressions of race, class, gender, and sexuality' (2000, p. 69). These images work to explain and perpetuate black women's inferiority and pathology, specifically linked to black women's failures as mothers. From the racial exclusions that underlined both the creation of welfare and its reform (Roberts, 1993; Davis, 2007; Kandaswamy, 2008) to the initiation of drug-testing programmes that criminalize poor black mothers (Roberts, 1991, 1997a, 1997b) to recent attempts to profit from low breastfeeding rates in African-American communities (Morrissey and Kimball, 2017), prevailing images of black motherhood have depicted black women as inferior, incapable and undeserving. Most pressingly, black motherhood has been understood as the source of social problems (Roberts, 1997a, p. 961), inspiring a multitude of controlling images and social policies (Jordan-Zachery, 2009) that in different ways regulate, discipline and criminalize black women's mothering.

The emergence and growing popularity of AP as one representation of 'good' mothering could work as yet another site for the disciplining of black mothers, particularly emphasizing the distance between the instinctively natural mothering of African women, as described by definitive AP experts William and Martha Sears, and their pathologically dependent counterparts in the Global North. However, black women do not merely accept such stereotypes. In response to prevailing cultural representations that frame black mothers as lesser, black women cultivate self-definitions that counter these dominant images and for the women this chapter discusses, AP plays a significant role in the development of a counter-hegemonic black motherhood. This chapter outlines the different ways that the black mothers I interviewed used AP to develop a critical mothering identity that challenged ideas of them as bad mothers and citizens, in ways, I argue, that both affirm and reject neoliberal values. The mothers developed this identity in different ways, working to reclaim AP from the Sears', offering critical views of 'home' that recall the fluidity and oscillation (Massaquoi, 2004; Reynolds, 2005) of British and Canadian blackness, using interest in AP as a strategy for belonging and the risks and rewards attached to that, and finally, deploying the philosophy for the purposes of building community and resisting racism, with varying success.

(Re)claiming AP

This chapter draws on a smaller subset of the larger study, focusing on the experiences of ten participants who either called themselves attachment parents or in other words described an affinity for the philosophy. Despite my collecting of these women into one category, their diverse experiences provide a small glimpse into the complex ways that they went about developing an AP-inspired view of good motherhood. This is evident, for example, in the array of different responses participants gave to the question, "Would you call yourself an attachment parent?" For many of the women I include in the category of 'attachment parents', the answer to this question was, if not an immediate "no", a reluctance to embrace the "label":

> 'I wouldn't because I don't like labels. But, um ... anyone who's ever been in my home or met me knows that I'm a very hands on parent.' (Lorde, 33, two sons aged four and two years respectively and expecting a third child, interviewed in Canada)

> 'I hate having labels, but I suppose if I was in any category I would say yeah.' (Harriet, 34, one son aged three years and one daughter aged one month, interviewed in the UK)

> 'Um, I would ... yeah, I guess I would say yeah, attachment parenting, gentle parenting, peaceful parenting, I think they're kind of all getting at the same idea.... I probably wouldn't use the word 'attachment parenting', don't know why. I think 'cause I don't feel like it, the phrase, explains a

lot. Whereas I think maybe gentle or peaceful parenting like, I dunno, just as a term sort of … resonates more with me.' (Barbara, 38, one daughter aged 12 months, interviewed in the UK)

The women's dislike of the "label" attachment parenting was not only rooted in a preference for more accurate terms to describe their parenting but also reflected their belief that this style of childrearing was more "natural" and familial:

> 'I did read Dr Sears' attachment parenting book and, um, I was attracted to that. I do have a background in early childhood education so that did seem *natural* for me. Um, a lot of it is also what I've seen my parents, well, what my mother did … especially when it comes to speaking to her and stuff like that. *Does it have a name? I would say it is attachment parenting mixed with a lot of like African influences.'* (Tracey, 31, one daughter aged five months, interviewed in Canada; emphasis added)

In this way, Tracey and others like her echoed 'the rhetoric of the natural' identified by parenting culture studies scholar Charlotte Faircloth in her study of (white) British and French AP mothers (2013, p. 120). Faircloth describes the mothers' 'elastic' (p. 122) use of nature, which seemed to discount the less alluring 'natural' behaviours of 'primates and primitives' (p. 125) and ignored the inevitable cultural, social and environmental context that informed particular parenting practices. For example, extended breastfeeding in such 'primitive' cultures is often a response to a shortage of weaning foods. As Faircloth explains, relying on 'nature' as an 'accountability strategy' (p. 120) is uniquely powerful, given wider cultural shifts towards nature's explanatory value in other areas of life such as eating and working. Such a strategy relies on evidence drawn the behaviours of extant 'primitive' societies who act as 'stand-ins' (p. 128) for the pure nature AP mothers in Britain and Canada are trying to emulate.

The women I interviewed, too, wished to use evidence from AP-favouring communities but did so in a way that required a more nuanced understanding of the context Faircloth argues is often dismissed in Western appraisals of the 'natural' superiority of AP. When they declared that their style of parenting is "natural" or follows the practices of their African families, these mothers' narratives accede to claims made by the Sears' about the naturally capable African mother, who parents in an attached manner because of 'tradition' rather than critical contemplation. But in doing so, it also challenges the Sears' (and other white, Western experts') ownership of the philosophy. By locating AP in her (African) family's long-established practices, Tracey implied that the philosophy predates the Sears' naming and claiming of it. This long-standing, African claim on AP was repeated by Eleanor:

> 'I feel like a lot of the information about attachment parenting is obviously there but because we don't see ourselves in it ... we don't necessarily take it on and we assume that it's a white thing not realizing that these people have seen this in our cultures back home.' (Eleanor, 33, two daughters aged 12 and six years respectively and one son aged four years, interviewed in the UK)

Eleanor's claim that AP comes from "back home" was complicated by her West Indian heritage. The "back home" she identified as the ancestral origin of AP was *not* the Caribbean nation from which her parents hailed. Nor could it be, according to Eleanor; the Caribbean had been "indoctrinated" by slavery, resulting in the loss of cultural practices. The "home" that spurred AP was Africa, with which Eleanor felt a deep spiritual connection. This reclamation of AP as an *African* parenting philosophy was one tool in these mothers' development of a counter-hegemonic image of black motherhood. Exploiting the Sears' stereotypical rendering of African motherhood shaped not by books but by tradition, the women claim a long history of good black mothering. For Eleanor, acknowledging that AP does indeed belong to black people is the first step towards raising awareness about the philosophy (and its African origins) among black communities in the diaspora. Such a project works to counter negative controlling images of black motherhood *and* provides material support to the optimal development of black children.

When 'home' is backwards

Unsurprisingly, Eleanor's reverence for Africa as "home" was not the only way participants in this study talked about 'home'; indeed, others described a rather different vision of home and in it, another vision of good black motherhood. Although only eight of the women I interviewed were born in a country other than Britain or Canada, all 19 women articulated a connection to or affiliation with a third country or region. For a few, this connection was tangential (such as Kimberlé's fleeting reference to her experiences in France) or distant (like Gloria's description of her family as being of "Caribbean descent") but a number of the participants made substantial links to this third place, exploring how this was an important aspect of their identity and informed their approach to parenting.

The word 'home' appeared as a way to describe this other location and its associated parenting practices, an association that was not always positive. Patricia and Stella, both Canadian-born, each used the phrase "back home" when discussing the differences between their approach to parenting and that of their parents or community, even as each woman had very different ideas about what good parenting ought to look like, with Stella favouring AP-style childrearing and Patricia seemingly enthusiastic about AP (insofar as it is seen as good parenting) but rejecting some of its fundamental practices. Regardless of this difference, for both women, "back home" possessed an ideological backwardness, something they had to leave behind in order to offer their children better:

> 'Back home, you know, babies slept on their tummies … I guess being back home … you did what they did and they did what they did … and there was no learning curve.' (Patricia, 41, two daughters aged six and three years respectively, interviewed in Canada)

Patricia prided herself on taking parenting classes and doing research, expressing a thirst for knowledge and betterment that she felt was lacking in the black community both in Canada and "back home" in the Caribbean. The practice of 'doing what you're doing' because that's the way it has always been done is precisely the kind of ancestral knowledge espoused by the Sears' but for Patricia, it indicated a failure to take the responsibilities of parenting seriously by engaging in the work of assessing and evaluating childrearing expertise, a crucial indicator of good mothering.

Similarly, for Stella, "back home" described a place where people fail to parent appropriately. After proclaiming that her mother has been a better grandmother than she was a mother I asked her to explain why. She answered:

> 'I think it's just a different time, you know, and … she wasn't back home, she's here and seeing a baby maybe once.… Maybe it's, you know, her getting to do things that she didn't

have the opportunity to do.' (Stella, 37, one daughter aged four years, interviewed in Canada)

Because Stella's mother was *not* "back home", she was able to access a different and, for Stella, better approach to childrearing. Stella also noted that her mother raised her children in a "different time" when expectations of parents were different and, implicitly, not as competent. Both Stella and Patricia described a desire to be a different, better mother to their children than their own mothers had been to them. Thus, they understood the path to better mothering as distinct from the mothering practices they associated with "back home". However, despite the critique of its practices, this other place remained "home" in the mothers' accounts, while Canada was described as a blank slate upon which they could enact 'new' (although, of course, for Eleanor and others, AP is *not* new) approaches to parenting, a place where this kind of parenting would be "accommodated" (Patricia). In this act, the naming of another place as "home" while also implicitly citing Canada, in this case, as a superior location in which to raise children, Stella and Patricia both affirm and challenge the dominant narrative of Canadian citizenship and the role motherhood ought to play in assuring that citizenship. On the one hand, their narratives reify the belief that blackness belongs elsewhere, "back home" is not in Canada. On the other, by claiming Canada as a space in which good parenting, and therefore good citizenship, can be performed, they root themselves in the Canadian landscape, directly challenging racial narratives that position blackness outside the Canadian nation.

The practice of good parenting to frame oneself as a good citizen in racially hostile contexts is part of a wider sense the mothers reported of having to be "twice as good ... to get half of what they have", as Lorde described:

> '[W]hen it comes to parenting and I think most black people have always heard the same, you know, you have to be twice as good ... to get half of what they have ... it affects my parenting, whether I want it to or not. I think that's why ... the things that I teach my son beyond what he learns in books and what he learns at school, it has no choice but whether I want it to, it is second nature to teach these things to my son.' (Lorde, 33, two sons aged four and two years respectively and expecting a third, interviewed in Canada)

As Lorde (and others) recalled, the 'twice as good' message is a crucial influence that begins in childhood, focused on things such as performance at school and appearance in public, and continues into adulthood, shaping the experience of mothering. In a parenting culture where childrearing choices are invested with great significance and subject to intense scrutiny, twice as good adds an additional, racially specific pressure that shapes both the mothers' sense of themselves as (twice as) good parents and the responsibilities of raising children of colour who must also be twice as good.

For those mothers who favoured AP, childrearing becomes another arena in which they may prove that they are twice as good. The "all-consuming" nature of AP requires almost constant childrearing labour and the commitment it necessitates can be a source of conflict with partners (as Rebecca's narrative shows in earlier chapters) and wider family. The innate capacity to 'do it all' carries particular risks for black mothers (Collins, 2000; Hill, 2004), although its attraction is understandable given dominant images of neglectful black motherhood. AP, especially if it is African, offers a way through this dilemma, demanding a great deal of individual work while also attempting to bring communities of mothers and parents together.

AP to belong (and stand out)

Reclaiming AP as a "natural", familial African parenting philosophy that can work towards both 'preparing their children for success in a white-dominated society' *and* 'maintaining their links to Black communities, cultures and histories' (Vincent et al, 2012, p. 432), suggests another purpose that this philosophy might fulfil: belonging. Interest in the philosophy can inspire a coming together of black communities potentially fractured by class polarization and geographical distance. However, as suggested by these same mothers' reluctance to share childcare with their family members, there are limits to the kinds of belonging AP can develop. For some of the mothers I interviewed, interest in AP at once enabled them to belong to an imagined community of (black) attachment parents and to stand out and apart from that community.

Tracey's narrative offered an illustrative example. Tracey, her husband and her young daughter lived in another city, some distance from her family, whom she identified as the source of her parenting cultural heritage. As our interview continued, however, it became clear that this sense of familial and cultural commitment to AP was unstable. Born in an East African country and raised in Canada, Tracey described AP as "just parenting", a common reframing of expertise among the more enthusiastic supporters of AP. For Tracey, while AP was the kind of childrearing that she had grown up with and witnessed in her family and community, when it came to her own practice of AP she found herself at odds with family members who were surprised by her desire for a homebirth and her persistent commitment to breastfeeding. On moving to a smaller, less racially diverse city than the one in which she was raised, AP became a source of a different kind of community. She cultivated a supportive (and racially diverse) network of mothers with whom she shared an almost political commitment to AP, including the freedom to breastfeed in public.

Moving to a new city away from her family also enabled Tracey to parent without judgement, particularly over those decisions where her family perceived her parenting choices as a step beyond the realms of appropriate AP, such as her preference for naturopathic medicine. Tracey speculated that the apprehension about her parenting choices was largely the result of its "all-consuming" nature, which serves as a particularly vivid contrast against the ineptitude and laziness commonly associated with black mothering (Roberts, 1991; Collins, 2000; Bezusko, 2013; Norwood, 2013). As Tracey explained:

> '[W]hen it comes to black mothers I think we want our voice to be heard about this, I think for a long time society kinda spoke for us and now that I think we're getting a little bit more educated in a lot of, just our own ... experiences, I think now we want people to know that "Hey, we do this too", right?' (Tracey, 31, one daughter aged five months, interviewed in Canada)

"We do this too" expresses two interrelated claims: first, it forcefully illustrates black women's performance of AP, especially against unspoken stereotypes about black women's failures as mothers. Second, in the desire for "people to know", Tracey suggested an equation between AP and good parenting. If black women "do this too", AP becomes a path for black women to assert themselves not only as good mothers but as good citizens, mothering being one of the few paths to good citizenship available to women. AP is a particularly effective device for the conspicuous performance of good parenting because it takes the norms of 'good' parenting as determined by public policy and expands the associated duties (Freeman, 2016). For example, if women are expected to breastfeed, AP suggests extended breastfeeding. Further, through practices such as babywearing, which the Sears' encourage mothers to do 'all the time … in the midst of their busy lives' (2001, pp. 65, 67), AP can be easily read on a mother's body.

The "all-consuming" nature that Tracey alluded to is additional evidence of black mothers' commitment to their children and therefore to good parenting. However, as Tracey's family's misgivings suggest, this "all-consuming" characteristic can be grounds to dismiss AP as 'extreme', thereby compromising black attachment parents' ability to access good parenting through their practice. Tracey was able to find an alternative community among her fellow attachment parents, which partly mitigated her family's distaste for her parenting style. She could maintain her claims to both her family and her AP community despite her family's apprehension. However, in Barbara's case, her family's racialized derision of AP practices intensified risks of alienation:

> 'I was at my parents' house and … I think I was washing up and I had [my daughter] on my back and [my mum] was in the next room and mum kind of said something like, "Oh, these two, my daughter and her husband, they're always carrying this child around, I don't know if it's back to Africa or, you know, what it is", you know, it kind of…. Yeah, so it's almost like she kind of found it humorous and a bit sort of like, maybe a bit baffling and there's a slight notion of 'the child has too much hand', like she's gonna be too used to being held.' (Barbara, 38, one daughter aged 12 months, interviewed in the UK)

For Barbara's mother, a return to Africa did not mark a turn towards good motherhood. Instead it suggested a temporal and cultural backwardness that engendered the adoption of outdated and potentially harmful parenting practices. These conflicting discursive constructions of AP and where it belongs in turn compromised Barbara's claims. If her good motherhood is defined through an African AP, it can succeed even when she frames her mothering style as unique. Mothers' belief that they are parenting against the norm can be part and parcel of their claim to be good mothers (Hoffman, 2013). However, the path to good motherhood via an African AP is less straightforward when Africa is dismissed as backward, especially when this dismissal originates in one's (black) family. AP cannot be enacted for the community if it is understood as a harmful, antiquated philosophy. Despite this critique of AP, Barbara maintained her critical claim on good motherhood by acknowledging the potentially African roots of AP but employing individualist language to justify her parenting choices: "I'm doing it for my reasons, I think that it works and, you know, that's all that matters ultimately." In the belief that AP works, in its production of an optimally developed, emotionally well-adjusted child, Barbara can prove the superiority of her parenting style, underlined by a covert reference to its non-Western origin.

AP for the community

As the narratives recounted in this chapter thus far suggest, AP has to balance several contradictions to remain a philosophy worth celebrating by the mothers I interviewed. That it 'works' or produces "brilliant, black child[ren]" is crucial, as is its ancestral origin in Africa. The origin story of AP told by the AP supporters in this study differs from the narrative created by the Sears'. In the mothers' story, AP *belongs* to black mothers and thus becomes a way for black mothers to belong in contexts where their mothering is framed as inadequate. The power of this story is challenged by fears that AP requires too much of mothers (as Tracey's family expressed) or that Africa is a site of backwardness (as Barbara's family suggested).

This section focuses on the challenge created by the apparent contradiction between the philosophy's emphasis on individual parents' responsibility to engage in particular parenting practices and the mothers' claim that AP can work for the community. In their reclaiming of AP, the mothers described deploying this individual responsibility in strategic ways in their efforts to share AP strategies with the wider black community. Eleanor, for example, revelled in her self-appointed role of AP trailblazer, leading by example and sharing her knowledge with the wider community. This role also fulfilled a second, related purpose for Eleanor:

> 'It's kind of funny because my appearance [chuckles] with black people they very, they ... have a hard time accepting me and the way I look. It's not until I talk and say and share what I know then they kind of relax about it.' (Eleanor, 33, two daughters aged 12 and six years respectively and one son aged four years, interviewed in the UK)

As a light-skinned black woman who could pass as "mixed race", Eleanor felt vulnerable to exclusion from the black community. Her embrace of 'African' AP practices served to counter this exclusion, shoring up her blackness and securing her a position in the community as a kind of elder. The practice of AP as a service to the black community was voiced by two other participants, Demita and Olive. When we met for the interview, Demita had only been living in the UK for a few months. She was an enthusiastic supporter of AP (though she preferred the term 'natural parenting') and like Eleanor, she claimed AP as a practice "very many black people" had been doing for generations, "naturally". She argued that the practice had recently become less popular in the black community and hoped to inspire more black women to engage in AP:

> 'I would love to see a lot more black women doing this also, you know. Not necessarily because it has a name but because ... and not necessarily because we're trying to set ourselves apart but I am thinking about the future and I'm thinking about the future of black youths and having ... good mothers, good examples to look up to.... I just want some company, like, I just want some other mother, black mothers' company that know that them youths can be turned into special things ... I just want company, I'm not trying to be the only one with a brilliant black child, you know? I'm not the only one that ... I need, like, hundreds of women, many thousands of women there with me.... The more we can get out there, the more info that people have and the more success stories also.' (Demita, 26, one son aged three years, interviewed in the UK)

For Demita, the practice of AP was a sure-fire path to the development of a "brilliant black child". Throughout the interview, she spoke earnestly about the confidence and independence that this style of parenting had afforded her son and the importance of cultivating these characteristics among black children given the damaging stereotypes that dominate British society. Her desire to spread the gospel, as it were, was motivated by a concern for the black community as a whole, even beyond the borders of the UK.

Similarly, Olive lamented the lack of interest in AP among the black community in Canada. Olive was born in the Caribbean but had lived most of her life in Canada. Her mother parented her in the "normal" way but, as Olive was pleased to report, she had recently shown interest in Olive's 'alternative' choices. Although Olive expressed some feelings of isolation and a sense of feeling misunderstood, she also expressed confidence in her parenting choices and described their potential long-term impacts:

> '[Attachment parenting is] just not common and I don't know why … maybe they don't know about it or maybe it's not the priority kind of thing, like I said [before]. I think just culturally or how we were brought up, the norm is just "Put them in school, da da da" … and maybe our parents not being into attachment parenting which they most of them weren't 'cause they're just coming to this country and just getting, living, working to pay the bills type of thing. So it wasn't really what we were raised around and that might've been the difference. Like maybe my son will think all this is normal, like "My wife needs to breastfeed my kids"'cause that's what he saw. So I think maybe, maybe future generations, even black kids will start seeing that as the norm and even just little things like breastfeeding even it's not all attachment parenting … hopefully at least a few things will become the norm for black people.' (Olive, 28, two sons aged three years and two months respectively, interviewed in Canada)

The tension between the need to work and earn money and the desire to parent in a more attached manner was a common theme in Olive's interview, and, in this extract, operated as an explanation for why first generation immigrant parents might choose a more 'scheduled' style of parenting. It captures a common tension black mothers experience, between the need for physical survival and the demands of good parenting, as well as demonstrating the classed dimensions of these struggles. As Olive suggested, AP requires a different set of financial priorities than that possessed by recently arrived migrants, specifically, delaying a return to full-time paid work and avoiding the use of institutionalized childcare. Such decisions are made possible by occupation of privileged positions in the economic structure. It is precisely these classed differences in access to good parenting practice that limit AP's ability to build community in the way that many of the women strive for. By attributing distinctly anti-AP priorities to the black community as a whole, Olive revealed the racialization of poverty that persists in a postracial context despite colour-blind claims to the contrary, but in such a claim also assumes the absence of a 'will to improve' among the black community.

Eleanor, Demita and Olive's hopes for AP as a racially specific childrearing practice is an expression of what Paul Kershaw calls 'motherwork' (2005, p. 107). Following the tradition identified by black feminist scholars Patricia Hill Collins and Dorothy Roberts, Kershaw describes the alternative visions of motherhood expressed by racialized women excluded from good motherhood. In his attempt to challenge and expand the dominant conceptualization of citizenship that assumes participation in the labour market as defining characteristics of citizenship and social inclusion, Kershaw argues that the care work carried out by racialized women serves not just the purpose of preparing children for future citizenship but performs the specific and 'political projects of resistance and cultural survival' (2005, p. 119).

These 'political projects' are evident in Olive, Demita and Eleanor's narratives as each woman articulated the broader purposes that AP serves to the black community. Eleanor for example, by claiming AP as specifically African, resists the narrative exclusions executed by the Sears' and other AP 'experts'. She draws on a cultural heritage to which she has no direct connection but nevertheless serves as a source of resistance to white retellings of the AP story. While it is important to note that the vision of Africa that Eleanor creates is largely an imaginary one (Gilroy, 1993, cited in Reynolds, 2005), punctuated by the same problematically narrow beliefs about Africa for which I criticise the Sears', it nevertheless serves as a protective mechanism against both broader patterns of black exclusion and dominant ideas about AP, and by extension, good mothering.

While Olive and Demita do not explicitly frame their versions of AP as African, they put the philosophy to work as a means of 'cultural survival' as they describe AP as having the potential to save their communities. The three women's narratives reflect the tradition Collins and Roberts identify in the African-American community: mothering that is more than the preparation of children for responsible citizenship but encompasses the politics of identity formation as well as protection from and resistance to racist exclusion.

A crucial component of this form of mothering is a rejection of the exclusivity of the mother–child bond promoted in mainstream ideologies of motherhood (Collins, 2000; Forna, 2000). As Forna (2000) puts it, the difference between the promotion of an exclusive mother–child bond and a more community-orientated, collectivist approach to childrearing is racial, with the former preferred by white mothers and the latter apparently favoured by black mothers. Forna argued that black mothers raise their children caught between 'two co-existing scripts for motherhood: the one they received through their own family and cultural heritage and the other which predominates everywhere else in society' (2000, p. 364).

However, for the black mothers I interviewed, a racialized distinction between the primacy of an exclusive mother–child bond and more community-orientated approaches does not accurately capture their experiences and beliefs about parenting. For those mothers who favoured AP, it was mainstream ideas about parenting that required *distance* between mother and child. For women like Demita and Eleanor, it was (African) 'cultural heritage' that allowed them to defend their commitment to close, maternal bonding. Instead of being caught between two apparently racially disparate ideas, these mothers produced a hybrid response, claiming an exclusive mother–child bond *through* a new, complex reading of community and collectivism.

Such a vision of collectivism inevitably involves rejection of existing models of managing racialized contradictions, such as 'othermothering'. Othermothers are 'women who assist bloodmothers by sharing mothering responsibilities' (Collins, 2000, p. 178), described by Collins among African Americans but also present in other diasporic communities. As Roberts (1995) argues, because 'the conception of motherhood confined to the home and opposed to wage labor never applied to black women' (p. 201), black women have rarely been afforded the opportunity to give up paid work altogether to dedicate themselves to full-time motherhood. The realities of balancing participation in the paid labour force with childrearing and other caregiving responsibilities have led to the creation of what Collins calls 'woman-centered networks' (2000, p. 178) in which women provide temporary and sometimes even long-term childcare for one another. Roberts (1995) traces this tradition to slavery where mothers had little guarantee that they would be able to stay with their children throughout their childhood. There are conflicting reports about whether othermothers remain a fixture of African-American communities (see Blum, 1999, Hill, 2004 and McDonald, 1997 for competing theories[1]), especially given recent patterns of class mobilisation and polarisation that disrupts black communities and their ability to support one another (McDonald, 1997).

In the British and Canadian contexts, these effects also shaped the experiences of the women in this study. However, I draw particular attention to how the individualist expectations of contemporary parenting culture and the women's choice of AP-influenced parenting style, in particular, have largely undermined the potential for traditional othermothering. This is evident in the fact that, for example, 15 of the 19 participants reported that their parents' approach to childrearing was different from their own, and, for a significant proportion of the participants, this resulted in a reluctance to rely on their parents or other family members for childcare. This was particularly true for those participants who named themselves as 'attachment parents'. For some, like Eleanor, the lack of family support did not present much of a problem. Eleanor preferred to spend as much time as possible with her children and enjoyed homeschooling for precisely this reason. For others, like Lorde, the problem was solved with limited use of paid childcare, provided by an individual who shared Lorde's parenting philosophy.

Regardless of how they addressed this problem, the attachment parents' commitment to this philosophy meant that, while they sought to promote it for the purposes of community building and development, it remained an individual practice. I do not intend to undermine the value of black mothers' stated commitment to uplifting the entire community but to draw attention to the ways that particular ideologies can shape people's expressions of resistance. The same can be said of othermothering. It emerges as a response to the expectation that black mothers ought to participate in paid work rather than as an organic expression of more 'effective' mothering. That black mothers have managed to find ways to continue raising their children despite the combined effects of poverty, racism and sexism that drive them into largely underpaid, little-appreciated work is not grounds to claim that 'such a system of mothering is in the best interests of the child' (Forna, 2000, p. 368). However, what othermothering *can* do is demonstrate that mothers require support in order to fulfil whatever kind of childrearing they deem appropriate. It also suggests that engagement in paid work does not preclude good mothering. The approach advanced by Demita, that of widespread but individualist adoption of AP as a salvo for the black community, need not necessarily undermine the political activism that Roberts and Collins argue is often an outgrowth of othermothering and woman-centred networks. Instead, it might inform a different kind of politics, perhaps more suited to the current sociopolitical climate in which rights are won on the basis of individual claims rather than collectivist struggles (Duggan, 2003). That Demita (as well as Olive and Eleanor) advanced a simultaneously collectivist and individual argument might engender new approaches to social justice and activism.

Parenting to resist racism

A parenting philosophy that can combine individual responsibility with collectivist community building is especially well suited to a postracial context, where structures of racism are located in the past or reframed as interpersonal problems to be resolved privately. While black women's mothering has always involved an explicit attempt to protect their children from racism, AP offers a unique bundle of strategies that the mothers in this study in different ways took up to shield their children from the persistent indignities of neoliberal racism.

One of the strategies that women reported as a method of resisting racism and claiming good black motherhood was to value blackness, which dialogues with the self-valuation principles of black feminist thought. Margaret, for example, described her practice of buying black dolls and black-centred books that celebrated features commonly attributed to the black community including woolly hair and dark skin. Such a celebration also motivated her decision to avoid chemically straightening her daughter's hair. Margaret herself had recently decided to 'go natural' and viewed this choice as a recuperation of black people's 'natural' beauty. As with other mothers who framed AP as 'natural', so Margaret's interest in AP was contextualized by this wider interest in all things natural. Other women reported similar experiences:

> 'And it's not something that I thought about until one day I was out with my mother, my son really, really wanted this book. I'm flipping through the book and there is not a single, not one brown, the book was 200 and something pages, not one brown face. So I spent an entire Saturday colouring the faces brown in the book. By the end of the day I was really pissed off, like I'm clearly losing my mind, what the hell am I doing, it doesn't matter. When I read that book to my son that night my son was like, "It looks like me!" He was screaming, he was so happy, and he was, he'd just turned three, he was so happy. And I'm like, the fact that it actually matters and he notices that at the age of three, it makes a huge difference, it makes a really big difference.' (Lorde)

> '[M]y daughter's the only black child at her school. The *whole* school. That's a different pressure that I actually have to buy into. Because one day she told me she wanted to have white skin, because all of her friends have white skin

and I was shattered. Shattered. But none of her friends talk about it, you know. It's just an observation that she made at three. She's so aware at three.... [So] we have brown girl time where we spend time every night after bath time in the mirror, you know, so while she doesn't get to see any representation of herself during the day she gets to see it at night time.' (Stella)

By enacting these strategies, mothers countered the dominant narrative about blackness that they suggest their children had already begun to recognize and internalize. As Stella's narrative suggests, the work of countering stereotypes is inevitably informed by class. Such strategies are deployed in specific ways for children raised in predominantly middle-class, white contexts where exposure to representations of the black community, let alone positive ones, would be limited. Echoing the findings of Lareau's (2011) study of black and white families from the poor, working and middle classes, beyond their investment in the dominant childrearing ideology of concerted cultivation, middle-class black mothers go to special efforts to protect their children, particularly in educational settings. Lareau (2011) describes one such mother who monitors her child's experiences and activities to ensure first, that he is not the only black child present and second, that 'the whites with whom her son interacts [are] "cultured"' (p. 121).

Lorde, who confidently[2] named herself as "upper middle-class", reported similar goals and described her reasoning for choosing her sons' private school:

'So for school, the main focus for me was education, education and curriculum and diversity. I found *that* was the hardest thing for me, I never want my son to go to a place where he's the only black face he sees. That's very important for me. I don't want him to be ... amongst everyone all black either because that's not the world and that's, that's just not the world. So, I needed education to be number one and then diversity be number two.'

Lorde's interest in ensuring that her children receive a good education reflects broader cultural imperatives that require all parents to participate more actively in their children's education (Reynolds, 2005; Lareau, 2011; Gillies, 2012) but is clearly inflected with a deeper concern for the education of her *black* children. Even in the language she used to describe her priorities when looking for a school she could not help but entangle the need for a quality education with her desire for a diverse student body and curriculum. The preference for avoiding all-black spaces, on the other hand, was shared by Notisha and Harriet:

> '[W]here we live right now we like to live, we like living in a place where it's multicultural so it's not, you know, one culture. So, that's another thing that's kind of, where in terms of race playing a role. Like even in the church that we go, we wanted to make sure that it was, you know, that it was multicultural and it wasn't skewed, like an all-black church or, you know, or all-white or whatever but it was a nice good mix 'cause I think it's essential to understand other races and other cultures. Yeah, so I think in that regard that also, yeah, that also plays a part. Even their school, we chose a school that was multicultural, that had a good mix.' (Notisha, 34, two daughters aged three years and one year respectively, interviewed in Canada)

Harriet: '[T]he church we used to go to was very, like, traditional Caribbean Pentecostal church and we left for that reason. And that's a very, that's a good grounding for Caribbean children to grow up in because it is quite cultural and historic and that will give you a good sense of your roots but ... the church we go to now is not and it's very mixed and, yeah. Yeah, so that's kind of lost, I don't know.'

PH: 'What made you leave?'

Harriet: 'Um ... I think because it was kind of, it's more about tradition and, um, it was more, like, religious rather than the faith of, you know, what we believe in. So, decisions and actions were being made that were governed by culture which I didn't always think was a positive demonstration of what we believe. So, we just wanted to leave. And it's sad because you miss aspects of it and it's funny and you can snigger and you remember times as a kid and all that kind of stuff but ... it wasn't, um ... yeah. It wasn't what, we couldn't see ourselves growing there.' (Harriet, 34, one son aged four years and one daughter aged one month, interviewed in the UK)

The desire for a "multicultural" school, neighbourhood or church setting was not shared by any participants who identified as working-class. I suggest that such stated preferences are classed, especially when understood as a strategy for ensuring that children are best prepared to maximize their opportunities in "the world". The language used, particularly by Notisha and Lorde, echoes a kind of corporatized discourse about diversity and opportunity where familiarity with other cultures is a marker of mobility, career and financial success. The kind of good black motherhood they evoke places less emphasis on 'black people fostering links with other black people transnationally' (Reynolds, 2005, p. 88) and more on a cosmopolitan, Benneton-like vision, reflecting neoliberal models of race that favour 'individual multiculturalism' over collectivist, politically oriented racial identities (Rhee, 2013, p. 570). Such a take is understandable given these mothers' efforts to counteract a stereotype of blackness that emphasizes black people's poverty, laziness and dependence. To portray their children as ideal middle-class subjects, poised to employ their non-threatening blackness and knowledge of diversity in the world of work, is an attempt to protect their children from the actual, physical harm that could ensue from being read in a more stereotypical manner (Lawson, 2018). Such a perspective also demonstrates the limited and contradictory options available to black mothers as they try to prepare their children to succeed in a racist society while also providing those children with the tools to resist racial oppression (Reynolds, 2005, p. 74).

This is not to suggest that working-class parents do not share the same concerns with preparing their children for future success, but rather that they may advance different strategies that draw on the resources available to them. Eleanor offers a good example. Having already established AP as African (and *not* Caribbean), Eleanor claimed a 'transatlantic black consciousness' (Reynolds, 2005, p. 90) that informs her vision of black mothering. Eleanor's claim on an African AP unjustly but unsurprisingly appropriated by white parenting experts becomes a pathway through which she can assert a particular good black motherhood and tie herself to a diasporic black community whose members need reminding of their ancestral practices.

Eleanor's transnational consciousness was defined by celebrations of connections to Africa and elsewhere as well as rejections of a repressive Britain, where the culture requires stifling conformity, particularly from people of colour. Recognizing these limitations and their particular implications for her black children, Eleanor emphasized the importance of teaching 'business and economics' skills to her children:

> '… business and economics is something that from young I'm teaching them in a way so that they understand, 'cause that's what life is really, not life so much but being able to

eat is about.' (Eleanor, 33, two daughters aged 12 and six years respectively and one son aged four years, interviewed in the UK)

Her correction of herself, that economics is *not* what life is "really about" but is only a means to an end (the ability to eat), reflects Eleanor's broader value system that both rejects and confirms normative neoliberal visions of good motherhood and citizenship. At the same time, Eleanor clearly invested a great deal of importance in providing her children with the skills that will allow them to eat. She emphasized what seems like a basic, taken-for-granted aspect of lived experience, reflecting the extra work entailed in black motherhood of ensuring children's survival. Still, in distinguishing between "life" and "being able to eat", Eleanor prioritized her children's happiness[3] above all else and has chosen to homeschool, for example, to ensure that her children's needs are met and to protect them from racialized practices of exclusion. In this decision, her children's capacity for economic productivity, the central marker of good neoliberal citizenship, is subordinated to the more important, in Eleanor's eyes, goal of personal fulfilment.

The subordination of economic productivity sits alongside Eleanor's recognition that while "business and economics" skills might serve as methods of enhancement and optimization for white, middle-class children, such skills are essential to her black children's very survival. The tension in Eleanor's maternal practice shows the complexities of contemporary black motherhood, negotiating the fundamental of duties of black mothering (survival) and broader childrearing strategies. In her recognition of racism as an ongoing threat to her children's happiness and survival and her naming of a longer history of racist practices in which she names Britain as specifically complicit, Eleanor also rejected the postracial characteristic of neoliberal Britain. At the same time, her decision to focus on individual strategies such as homeschooling suggests an affirmation of neoliberal values, particularly those that encourage 'self-managing and self-enterprising' (Erel, 2011, p. 705). She also failed to challenge the construction of mothering as a practice through which moral worth is measured (Erel, 2011). Her transnational subjectivity is less a celebration of the occupation of both "home" and Britain than an expression of the awkwardness and discomfort that can accompany existing in these two places, an awkwardness only intensified by her attempts to marry "business and economic" skills with a reverence for Africa and African AP.

Conclusion

The complexities of using AP to build community and stake a claim to good motherhood reflect the larger contradiction that encompasses black mothering in a racially stratified and unequal society. In this chapter, I have focused mainly on those participants who embraced or drew from AP to discuss how the philosophy has facilitated the construction of a critical mothering identity challenging dominant narratives about black womanhood that preclude good mothering and good citizenship. The strategies employed to reclaim AP and repurpose it in service of a wider black community have limitations. However, I argue that they draw attention to black mothers' tradition of resistance and critique in a context in which race-attentive analyses are increasingly discouraged.

The thread that connects all the women's narratives in this chapter is an articulation of good black motherhood that does not conform to rules of ideal citizenship and motherhood conceived in the west for the benefit of white people but is instead situated in a rooted rootlessness (McKittrick, 2002) that celebrates and draws strength from the black diaspora's connections to other parts of the world (Gilroy, 1987). The claim that black people belong elsewhere is intended to disarm black subjectivities in Britain and Canada, and yet, the women in this study use that 'elsewhere' (through a claim on AP as also emerging from 'elsewhere') to claim good (black) motherhood. This version of good black motherhood revels in its transnationality, suggesting a vision that draws from Africa, the Caribbean, Europe and North America. Such a vision is not monolithic and is differently articulated by women in different social classes, with different views on the usefulness of AP and in different national contexts. Nor is this vision shared by all the participants in this study. Gloria, for example, argued that black mothering was no different from white or Asian mothering, while Florynce derisively dismissed her husband's objections to European "teefing" of African and Caribbean practices. Nevertheless, I argue that in their reclaiming of AP as African and 'theirs', their claims on AP as a tool of black community uplift and belonging, their claims about the value of "home" and their resistance against racism, the mothers in this study construct a counter discourse, what Collins might call a 'self-definition' (2000, p. 97), that rejects the standards of black motherhood set by dominant pathologizing discourses and instead celebrates black mothering.

10

Conclusion

At the beginning of their 2001 guide to attachment parenting, William and Martha Sears define AP as an 'approach' to parenting that, rather than requiring specific childrearing activities such as breastfeeding or refusing the use of a dummy, emphasizes the importance of responding to babies' need instinctively (p. 2). AP is not a 'strict set of rules' but a philosophy that calls on parents to open their 'minds and heart to the individual needs' of their babies (Sears and Sears, 2001, p. 2). Despite these claims, the very next page and the remainder of the 182-page childrearing manual is dedicated to delineating the superiority of the seven attachment tools. Although parents can 'choose' which of these tools to follow and which to abandon, they are described by the Sears as making the 'job' of parenting easier and 'better' (2001, p. 3).

Of these seven tools, this book has examined the three that emerged as especially significant in my conversations with black mothers about AP: breastfeeding, bedsharing and babywearing. And in many ways, these three are emblematic of the position AP has come to hold in the contemporary moment. Like the ideology of intensive mothering that facilitates its emergence, AP assumes women's biological responsibility for raising children and identifies women's bodies, in particular, as best suited to securing attachment, bonding and raising the well-disciplined adults that AP promises. But more than gendering the work of childrearing, AP rests on racial narratives about the practices of 'traditional' and African peoples as well as classed assumptions about what appropriate childrearing looks like. Any examination of AP, therefore, demands an intersectional analysis that attends to the intersection of race, gender and class ideologies that facilitate the philosophy's growing popularity. This book presents such an analysis, considering AP through the experiences of black mothers who use, refuse and alter it for their own ends.

Baby Bs, divisions of parenting labour and reclaiming AP

Breastfeeding, bedsharing and babywearing each show the limits of the kind of expertise espoused by the Sears' and public health bodies that represent contemporary parenting culture: even when the women adhere to the advice, as with breastfeeding, their compliance does not always guarantee attainment of good motherhood whether that is because they breastfeed for too long and cannot work or because they do not breastfeed enough. When they reject the advice, as demonstrated in the extensive practice of bedsharing among the sample, despite warnings against it, the mothers resort to complex tactics and negotiations to justify what the Sears' and wider contemporary parenting culture tells them they are: experts of their own babies. Even the mothers' experiences of babywearing, perhaps the most mainstream and inoffensive of the three Bs, has its harms. Poor design and usage of this allegedly instinctive practice poses a danger to babies, and for some black mothers risks an association with Africa that is demeaning rather than inspiring. Babywearing especially shows the particular limits of contemporary parenting expertise for black mothers: the gap between their assumed African heritage and the access to instinctive parenting, and especially babywearing expertise that it supposedly confers, and the realities of the imagined Africa on which both the Sears' and some of the participants rest their superior childrearing knowledge. Barbara, for example, must turn to (white, middle-class) sling libraries, not a knowledgeable 'auntie' (or collective memory) for babywearing advice, while her mother expresses disdain for parenting practices that appear to be going 'back to Africa'.

The baby Bs of AP lay the groundwork for an explicitly gendered construction of ideal parenting, despite indications to the contrary. Even as there is renewed interest in the role of fathers (Gatrell and Dermott, 2018) and calls for their intensive involvement in the work of childrearing, gendered ideas endure about who is responsible for and best suited to parent young babies in particular. The assumption, for example, that only cis women are capable of breastfeeding informs public health advice about the practice (Lee, 2018) and the division of parenting labour described by the women interviewed. As Tracey humorously explained, her male partner "does not have a boob" so is not entitled to the initial months of parental leave. Even if Tracey and her husband had opted to share parental leave in the early months of their daughter's life, Tracey's choices would still be subject to scrutiny. After all, these early months of leave are gendered in specific ways, whether that means they ought to be spent performing other 'wifely' duties in addition to infant care, as Gloria described, or in serving as a buffer against the compromises of paid work, enabling a claim to good mothering even if the mother returns to work at the end of her leave (Christopher, 2015) as Rebecca reported. The women's accounts of bedsharing too involve a specifically maternal expertise that excludes male partners, constructed as incapable of sleeping attentively enough to safely bedshare. That practices of bedsharing and breastfeeding reinforce each other (Tomori, 2014) only entrenches this gendered division of labour that cannot be recovered by fathers engaging in babywearing, one of the few tools where maternal bodies do not appear to be centred. And yet, as the responses to actor Daniel Craig's babywearing suggest, even this practice cannot escape these persistent notions.

Even as leave policy appears to turn towards a more equitable division of labour, at least rhetorically, mothers maintain an ideological and moral claim on leave, an appeal especially attractive to black mothers who have historically been excluded from policy instruments meant to facilitate good motherhood (Kandaswamy, 2008). It is precisely through policies that are apparently gender- and race-neutral that a third of Canadian parents' lack of access to parental leave benefits (McKay and Doucet, 2010) are eclipsed by talk of the state's generosity, especially when contrasted with the US, which both participants and the general public alike are wont to do. There are limits to this generosity, felt by women like Olive, whose commitment to AP has financial implications but who nevertheless believes in the superiority of its tenets. The overburdening that might result from such a division of labour is a fair price to pay, for many of these mothers, even among those who resist the appeal of AP.

Self-definitions and attempts to reclaim AP

However, the story of AP is incomplete if it is only described as a mechanism of upholding oppressive ideologies. Olive presents an interesting case study of mothers' efforts to challenge and navigate such ideologies, crafting a self-definition (Taylor, 1998; Alinia, 2015) especially in response to the particular constraints of a neoliberalized parenting culture. She accepted the discourse of the early years (Gillies et al, 2017) and bent it to her will: directing her doctor to treat her newborn son's tongue tie to ensure continued breastfeeding, bedsharing for as long as her young children need it, even as the presence of both a newborn and a three year old in the family bed raises safety concerns, and foregoing a career in favour of investing her time in this stage of her children's life when they "need [her] the most". This is the legacy she wishes to leave for her sons, that their wives (and in this, Olive acceded to a gendered, heteronormative ideal of family) might breastfeed and bedshare and babywear too.

As captured in the same chapter, Rebecca's legacy, on the other hand, is to challenge the dominant image of blackness her child will see growing up in a predominantly white neighbourhood and for her, that means working, living up to classed aspirations and putting her hard-earned Master's degree to use. This does not require giving up AP, however. Rebecca remained just as committed to breastfeeding, bedsharing and to a lesser extent, babywearing, even against resistance from her partner and his family. Although she questioned whether she had made things too "baby-centric", giving up the 'balance' the Sears' include among their seven tools (but do not invest with as nearly as much significance as the embodied responsibilities), Rebecca continued to parent in an attached manner, even when she found work and society at large incapable of properly accommodating it.

Rebecca and Olive's stories provide a glimpse of the wider sample's attempts to refashion AP, to reclaim it from the Sears' and return it to where it 'rightly' belongs. AP is a mechanism for asserting a particular vision of good black motherhood that rests on an imagined Africa and a "boldness" (Stella) forged in response to societies that have repeatedly and in different ways framed blackness as a source of failure (Tyler, 2010) and poor citizenship. AP enables a direct response to such a framing, showing that not only do black women do it "too", it belongs to them. There are, of course, limits to the philosophy's powers especially given its emergence in this particular sociohistorical moment, context that it is necessary to unpack to understand more comprehensively black mothers' engagements with AP.

Neoliberal contexts

The mothers' negotiation of AP as one example of what good mothering might look like is fundamentally shaped and made possible by the contemporary socioeconomic context of neoliberalism. Looking at AP's appearance in contemporary policy and state-produced parenting advice reveals the ways that the philosophy both upholds and undermines neoliberal ideology. In their varying interactions with AP, black mothers similarly conform to the norms and standards set by neoliberal rationality and upend them, articulating a model of good black motherhood that centres black children's value.

The experiences of the black mothers narrated here reveal AP's congruence with neoliberal frameworks of good parenting that seek to attribute both society's ills and their solutions to the work of childrearing. Contrary to their postracial façade, these frameworks operate on a raced, gendered and classed basis, constructing appropriate childrearing techniques that reflect white, middle-class norms (Hoffmann, 2010; Lareau, 2011) and deploying these techniques in ways that perpetuate existing, but now increasingly overlooked or disguised, inequities. AP seen from the perspective of black mothers draws attention to both the material effects of race and racism (in charting the different ways that black mothers develop their parenting) and its discursive capacities and its ability to highlight 'the processes by which meaning is constructed' (Lewis, 2000, p. 16). In other words, race provides an essential entry point to the analysis of how ideal parenting subjects, and therefore ideal citizens, are produced.

Thus, to examine AP, not from the perspective of those often represented as exemplars of its practice (that is, white middle-class mothers in the West), but through the experiences of women categorically excluded from dominant notions of good motherhood, reveals the complex relationship between individual parenting style choices and the structures that govern appropriate childrearing and ideal citizenship. To choose to parent in an attached manner is to echo the prevailing ideologies that construct children as sacred, an especially fraught endeavour for the mothers of children whose sacredness is not assured but one that, nonetheless, asserts a right to ideal citizenship routinely denied to people of colour. Black mothers' engagements with the philosophy reveal both the persistence of racial and gender ideologies in constructions of good parenting, especially as such constructions operate in policy and parenting recommendations, as well as mothers' capacity to resist these notions and offer alternative maternal subjectivities that alternately reject and appropriate dominant ideas.

The women's diverse engagements with AP reveal a particular, culturally specific image of black mothering produced in a neoliberal context. This image responds to and expands previous scholarship on black motherhood, most iconically captured in the work of Patricia Hill Collins. In her influential *Black feminist thought*, Collins (2000) described the 'five enduring themes' that capture black women's standpoint on motherhood: 'bloodmothers, othermothers and woman-centered networks; mothers, daughters, and socialization for survival; community othermothers and political activism; motherhood as a symbol of power; and the personal meaning of mothering' (pp. 178–95). Collins argued that these themes are particularly visible during the 'pre-World War II era' and that her discussion of the themes is rooted in the particular context of 'slavery, Southern rural life, and class-stratified, racially segregated neighborhoods of earlier periods of urban Black migration' (2000, p. 177). Such themes are dynamic and emerge in response to and negotiation with social practices that inevitably change over time. As social conditions change, new 'resilient lifelines' (Collins, 2000, p. 177) may develop.

The rise of AP and broader discourses of intensive mothering facilitate the forging of new 'lifelines', particularly in response to and directly influenced by our neoliberal, purportedly postracial context. It is black mothers' response to neoliberalism, both in accepting and questioning its central tenets, that informs the development of their maternal practice, practice that is inseparable from their engagements with AP. In particular, such practice is shaped by the ubiquity and influence of neoliberal values and its specific effects on intra-racial relations (Spence, 2012), which have de-emphasized community-orientated living and organizing in favour of the clarion call of individual achievement and consumption, and disguised the effects and explanatory value of social class (Tyler, 2008).

Neoliberal politics of class categorization

The absence and hiding of class that characterizes contemporary society (Tyler, 2013) is linked to transformations and disruptions in the politics of community ushered in by neoliberal emphasis on individual achievement. The assumption that black people (and their experiences) can be collected under the 'seeming unity' (Collins, 2010, p. 11) of the category 'black community' requires overlooking the ways gender, ethnicity, sexuality, dis/ability and, especially social class, can intersect with blackness to produce varied experiences. Contemporary forms of respectability politics intensify this obscuring of class, advocating individual measures of overcoming racism and thus obscuring the role class plays in determining both how social problems are framed and the solutions proposed to address them (Spence, 2012). This is not to discount the class-effacing effects of neoliberal postracism or to suggest that social class ought to supersede race in explanations of how neoliberal society functions, but rather to propose a genuinely intersectional analysis of black motherhood that attends to both similarities and differences across black mothers' experiences, especially as they are played out through class.

Class is central in the emergence and exercise of AP and especially significant for the black mothers I interviewed, shaping the way they negotiate the three Bs of AP expertise and state guidance, in the decisions they make about whether and how to stay at home and in their complex and sometimes contradictory attempts to reclaim AP. Social class inevitably informs their mothering, evident, for example, in some of the middle-class black mothers' specifically racialized attempts to instil their children with skills and experiences that would make them competitive on the job market and distinguishable from the stereotyped blackness that could cause them physical harm (Lawson, 2018). The preference for 'multicultural' experiences expressed by Lorde, Notisha and Harriet are noteworthy because while these mothers are understandably (and reflecting wider norms of good mothering) invested in maximizing their children's potential and opportunities, such strategies deftly reveal the raced *and* classed complexities of black mothers' parenting expertise and their consequent choices. Paying intersectional attention to the ways that social class (and other issues) inform expertise, even within marginalized groups, is a crucial step in the construction of a more complex, complete and therefore relevant image of contemporary motherhood.

The interaction between social class and race functions in complex and contradictory ways in a neoliberal, postracial context. Although class has fallen out of favour both analytically and in popular culture (Tyler, 2008, 2013), it continues to shape and determine access to housing, education, healthcare and, significantly for our purposes, policy makers' and the broader public's conception of good parenting. It is middle-class norms that determine the ideals of parenting (Hays, 1996; Gillies, 2005; Fox, 2006; Lareau, 2011) and because the production of future citizens is one of the duties of good parenting, it follows that ideals of neoliberal citizenship are similarly rooted in middle-class values. For black middle-class parents, efforts to adopt middle-class strategies of investing in and preparing for their children's success are always inflected with race, whether in the form of acknowledging the kind of danger their children face, regardless of their class position, or in others' perception of them. As work by Blum (2011) and Maylor and Williams (2011) shows, racist narratives are often classed, with black people's 'badness', explained as a consequence of their 'lower class', 'deeply dysfunctional' families (Blum, 2011, p. 959) and a pervasive construction of black people as lacking any distinguishable class identity or indicator (Maylor and Williams, 2011).

Thus, while black mothers' attempts to achieve such goals of good parenting and citizenship are hindered by simultaneously raced and classed constructions of black motherhood, regardless of their actual class position, nevertheless social class informs the strategies they adopt to counter and resist oppressive constructions. This is evident in the diversity favoured by Lorde, Notisha and Harriet, who each identified as middle-class and each rejected all-black environments as ill equipped to adequately prepare their children for future success. Such an approach is contrasted by Eleanor, who identified as working-class and in her decision to homeschool her children, arguably restricted their racial environment. While all four women were clearly concerned with their children's survival and reflect Blum (2011) and Lareau's (2011) findings that, despite the protection offered by their financial privilege, black middle-class mothers must do more to protect their children, there are still distinctions to be drawn between the experiences of working- and middle-class black mothers and in such distinctions *insight* about both the specifically classed (and gendered) way racism operates and the multitude of resistances black mothers produce to challenge their oppression.

The classed distinctions between mothers' experiences is evident even in how they named themselves as belonging to a particular social class. During data collection, the most common experience across interviews in both Canada and the UK was the confusion and debate generated by one of the questions listed on the demographic form I asked participants to complete: 'How would you identify your class?' Most strikingly, it was the women who eventually identified themselves as 'working-class' that struggled most vividly with the question, while the only participant to name herself as 'upper-middle-class' did so without hesitation. The difficulties the women had in expressing their class position not only reflects the depletion of meaning that 'class' has suffered in recent years, just at the historical moment when economic inequality has deepened (Tyler, 2008, 2013) but also communicates a significant complexity in intersectional analyses of black experience. For some black communities, class distinctions are viewed as a divisive tactic, designed to draw attention away from the 'shared history of domination, subordination and collective struggles owing to slavery, colonialism and migration' (Maylor and Williams, 2011, p. 350). This view of shared black identity also upholds continued belief in the widespread practice of community or othermothering, despite evidence to the contrary (McDonald, 1997). As Collins suggests, othermothering is produced out of specific social conditions, particularly racial segregation and the 'strong, cross-class maternal support' (McDonald, 1997, p. 774) enabled by the geographical concentration of black communities. To insist on its applicability to the contemporary context is to obscure the effects of class polarization, migration patterns and the changed lived experiences of families, as Angela described:

> 'I think mothering and I suppose parenting has changed in the fact that we don't live, well, we don't live close to my family and my husband's family live in [another city], so that's about almost an hour away from here. And I know a lot of my friends, their families don't live close by whereas you know, years ago, you'd have quite close-knit families where they were all together.' (Angela, 35, one daughter aged two years, interviewed in the UK)

The narratives in this book show that in the context of border crossing, class stratification and, I would argue, most significantly, the domination of neoliberal ideology, black mothers have constructed different views of motherhood that direct them away from practices of othermothering and towards philosophies such as AP, especially as it is understood as 'African', to solve the question of how to balance the need to work and the care of children as well as the broader question of how to 'ensure collective survival' (Collins, 2000, p. 177; Mullings, 2000). Social class plays a significant role in this shift, offering working- and middle-class black mothers different routes to claiming good black motherhood and ensuring the survival, protection and success of their children. This is expressed, for example, in the two approaches adopted by Rebecca and Olive, whose opposing decision to work and mother full-time respectively, are informed by their class position. Olive's rejection of work is made possible by the absence of a particularly fulfilling career, one key marker of working-class status in a contemporary neoliberal context (Fox, 2006; Christopher, 2015), while Rebecca's decision to work is bolstered by the decision to continue a middle-class trajectory that is marked by progressive milestones such as an international Master's degree and a well-paying job. This is not to reduce either woman's decision to merely the product of social class pressures but to demonstrate the intersection of classed, raced and gendered ideologies in shaping black mothers' decision making and in the kind of resistive self-definitions they create.

These self-definitions suggest new themes of black motherhood that emerge from the contemporary moment, where social class has seemingly disappeared as a 'central site of analysis' (Tyler, 2008, p. 20) and community has taken on new, expanded meaning. In their unique engagements with AP, the black mothers interviewed for this project suggested a new form of politics that both accepts the premise of individual responsibility and attempts to extend its benefits to a wider black community. Their complex negotiation of social class is evidence of the tensions and difficulties that this form of politics generates and also calls attention to the dangers of neoliberal co-optation. In implicitly identifying their AP-inspired maternal practice as political, the mothers I interviewed resist co-optation and perhaps offer new models of motherhood and glimpses of alternative futures (McKittrick, 2013) for mothering.

AP may be especially well suited to resisting co-optation because of the attention it brings to the work of childrearing. AP is often practised on and through the body, with breastfeeding, babywearing and bedsharing each requiring physical and often public displays of maternal practice. This visibility can operate as a site of resistance (Tyler, 2011), where the work of raising children is plainly revealed on mothers' bodies and, for black women, is a particularly effective visual rebounder to stereotypes about black mothers' purported negligence. This style of childrearing marks parenting as work and crystallizes the contradiction of insisting on economic productivity while demanding maternal devotion. Visibly displaying the work of mothering also draws attention to the relational aspects of mothering, aspects that sociologist Imogen Tyler argues 'troubles neoliberalism' (2011, p. 31). To focus on mothering as a relationship between mother and child is to emphasize the essential dependency that this relationship is founded on, a dependency that exposes the fantasy of self-sufficiency at the heart of neoliberal capitalism (Stephens, 2011). This mother–child relationship does not need to exclude others, as some critics suggest (Forna, 2000), but in fact, in the institution of black motherhood, this relationship forms the basis of connection to others, including the larger community (Collins, 2000). The mothers I interviewed use AP in precisely this fashion, centring their individual relationships with their children while attempting to sustain links with a broader black diaspora. Whether their efforts are successful, either at reaching and ensuring change for the wider community or at troubling neoliberalism, is less critical than the insight their narratives offer about the intersectional politics of contemporary motherhood.

Neoliberal openings

One of the most significant differences between black feminist scholars such as Collins' (2000) and Forna's (2000) articulations of black motherhood and the experiences examined in this book is precisely this rejection of a more community-orientated form of mothering, a form that is often described as quintessentially black or African (Forna, 2000). While some of the women I interviewed referred to church, friendship groups and family members as playing important roles in their wider lives, for most, even those less enthusiastic about AP, their choice of parenting practices largely excluded other people's involvement in raising their children. From the kind of maternal expertise they asserted, often distinguished from and framed as superior to that of their mothers, aunts and sisters, to their approaches to the division of labour in their households in which their partners' involvement was subordinated to mothers' superior abilities, many of the mothers favoured individualistic childrearing techniques and affirmed an exclusive bond between mother and child.

The elasticity of community (Collins, 2010) is evident further in the women's revision and reclaiming of AP, which almost seamlessly drew on local, national and global constructions of blackness. Mothers articulated new visions of community where work for the community translated into promoting AP, as Demita, Eleanor and Lorde wished to do, rather than raising fictive kin, as Collins (2000) and hooks (2007) describe. Such women's connection to the black community was of a more ephemeral, philosophical nature, involving, in many cases, attachment to an imagined Africa, where such parenting practices as babywearing and extended breastfeeding were apparently 'normal'. Such a view of community is inevitably shaped by the neoliberal context in which such community connections are forged. Constructions of community that centre individuals are particularly relevant in neoliberal, postracial times as the explanation and solution for persistent inequalities is reduced to individual behaviour (Spence, 2012). Class segregation (attachment parents are disproportionately middle-class, as is my sample), geographic mobility and neoliberal ideology combine to disrupt traditional modes of community organizing (McDonald, 1997; Mullings, 2000), creating the conditions under which AP may appear as a worthwhile, all-encompassing solution to the problems of racialized poverty, discrimination and oppression. The question then shifts from whether breastfeeding may be compatible with shared mothering (as historical evidence from the antebellum South suggests it was [West with Knight, 2017]) to how the promotion of breastfeeding might both reinforce individualistic, responsibilizing regimes and provide an avenue for black mothers to claim good motherhood.

Shifting the question in this manner prompts a more complex consideration of the effects of neoliberal political rationalities, particularly that which rereads individuals' negotiation of neoliberal ideas and frames them as neither 'cultural dupes' nor 'revolutionary characters' (Davids and Willemse, 2014, p. 2; see also Sa'ar, 2005). It inspires an analytic that does more than frame participation in seemingly oppressive activities as the result of false consciousness and instead attends to the 'enabling of new skills and capacities' (Heyes, 2006, p. 128) that discourses produce. It is in these new skills and capacities, and the knowledge they produce, that there may be 'new strategies of power that are yet harder to identify' (Heyes, 2006, p. 132).

The enabling of new skills and capacities has 'a resonance and potential that could exceed the regime of normalization that has generated them' (Heyes, 2006, p. 138) and it is precisely this potential that draws my attention. AP offers an opportunity to black mothers to focus attention on children that a postracial society has constructed as disposable and beyond redemption. To dismiss their investment in such practices as false consciousness is to miss the potential for resistance and/or alternative modes of mothering contained in their childrearing practice. That is not to suggest that it is not important to identify the ways in which AP contributes to self-responsibility and shores up the state's withdrawal of supportive services for parents but to expand this critique by also attending to the avenues AP opens for black mothers and black communities at the height of neoliberal individualism and class polarization.

Possible futures

One of the primary goals of this research has been an examination of AP as it emerges at this particular sociohistorical moment. How can the rise of AP be read as one of many variably successful attempts to resolve the fundamental contradictions of a neoliberal age? What answers does the philosophy offer to manage the competing demands of ensuring a vision of optimal child development tied to good mothering and the economic activation of female citizens? How does it contribute to the requisite erasure of persistent racial, gendered and class inequities? Living at the intersection of race, gender and social class, black mothers' engagement with AP reveals and complicates the socially constructed 'nature' on which the philosophy relies and illustrates the individualizing and responsibilizing work AP performs in its appearances in policy, media and individual mothers' experiences. Their rejections, alterations and embraces of AP offer a complex vision of mothering in the neoliberal states of Britain and Canada. In these states, individual responsibility for economic wellbeing is heightened for racialized, working-class and other marginalized groups. However, such emphasis on the deterministic power of parenting also opens space for black mothers to forge maternal subjectivities that are at once conformist and oppositional. In using (or avoiding) AP, the mothers whose stories are captured in this book have carved out room for valuing their black children even as doing so involves, at times, conforming to neoliberal models of postracial, responsibilizing citizenship. This tension is captured in Collins' (2000) identification of the negotiation between physical survival and emotional wellbeing as one of the central tensions characterizing black motherhood. As Collins explains, black mothers balance the often contradictory tasks of teaching their children to navigate institutions that dehumanize them and imbuing their children with oppositional definitions of self that resist this dehumanization (p. 184). Although we cannot pretend that these participants' individual decisions and strategies alone can upset the patriarchal, white supremacist, neoliberal order, through attending to their insights the possibilities for alternative futures (McKittrick, 2013) are laid bare.

The story of AP's emergence and its particular relevance for black motherhood rests on histories of oppression and captures how historical legacies appear, transformed and renegotiated, in the present (Fassin, 2011). But more than just documenting these enduring threads, this book serves to draw links between these histories and contemporary experiences of blackness that offer an anticipation of black life (McKittrick, 2013). The mothers' claims of good mothering are in diverse ways underlined with long histories of racial oppression, sharpened by the cultural forgetting that neoliberal postracial ideology demands. These narratives of maternal experience, however, also offer evidence of resistance and signal future possibilities. And my analysis is situated in the tension between these two accounts of black mothering, oppositional and oppressed.

This book might be described as an exercise in situating women's maternal decision making, practices and experiences within a broader social and political context, a key theme of intersectional analysis (Collins and Bilge, 2016). In each of the chapters that have preceded this one, dominant narratives (of appropriate expertise, of acceptable divisions of labour, of proper ownership of AP) are disrupted by black mothers' articulations of their experiences of and approaches to mothering. The accepted narrative about maternal expertise, particularly as it relates to the three Bs of AP and related state-produced parenting advice, as well as the feminist critique that has focused on social class to the exclusion of race, are both challenged by participants' experiences. The narrative of state-funded and endorsed gender equality through parental leave, as well as the narrative of work–family balance (a fiction invented to disguise the dominance of work and the preservation of family for only a selected few), is confronted by attending to these women's experiences, which highlight the limitations of a tacitly maternalist parental leave regime and the economically orientated imbalance on which the construction of work–life balance is predicated. The dominant narrative about the origin of AP that identifies Africa as its source but strips African mothers of expert ownership of the philosophy is disrupted by women reclaiming AP and, therefore, good motherhood. These disruptions reveal not just challenges to accepted explanations of contemporary mothering but suggestions of alternative visions of motherhood, not utopian but signaling a future that holds the realities of racial, gendered and classed oppression in tension with the creative oppositional resistance that the experience of oppression produces. This tension is quintessentially encapsulated in Tracey's assertion that "black mothers do this too". In this "too" there is recognition (but not acceptance) of the stereotypes that purport to describe black mothering in order to refute and resist them. The "too" demands black women's inclusion in a construction of good motherhood that has long excluded them and in such an inclusion, good motherhood is transformed, its boundaries are expanded and its foundational principles rocked. And it is in this destabilization (O'Reilly, 2004) that there is the possibility of something more, a glimpse or anticipation of a different vision of mothering.

Alternative futures

While this book has articulated the numerous strategies that black mothers employ to ensure their children's survival, to focus only on such strategies would not tell the complete story of black women's maternal practice. The constructions of black children as disposable and of their mothers as failures are 'neither uncontested nor completely efficient' (Gilroy, 1987, p. 153). Black mothers resist these and other oppressive representations of their lives by claiming superior maternal expertise, by anchoring their mothering in a 'distinct cultural heritage' (Taylor, 1998, p. 234), by highlighting the transformative capacity of their maternal bodies, by staying home when policy and dominant discourses demand that they work and by working when dominant stereotypes depict them as lazy. More than raising children who survive, which is, in itself, a radical act, black mothers strive to strike a balance between physical survival and emotional strength (Collins, 2000) and, in doing so, alter the norms and discourses that determine the racial and classed (and gendered) boundaries of neoliberal success.

Black mothers do more than just prepare their children to survive the status quo; their resistive efforts challenge it, opening space for another way. The underlying message many black mothers deliver is not just that black children can succeed 'no matter what'; it also teaches children that the boundaries of success are warped (as noted by Florynce) and that the institutions society has allegedly created to help all citizens discriminate on racial grounds (as Lorde reported). In their recognition of and challenge to these realities, black mothers gesture towards alternative futures built from these tensions, between freedom from racial oppression and recognition that one's subjectivity is, in part, borne of resistance to this oppression, what Afrofuturism scholar Katherine McKittrick (2013) describes as:

> ... a conception ... imbued with a narrative of black history that is neither celebratory nor dissident but rooted in an articulation of ... life that accepts that relations of violence and domination have made our existence and presence in the Americas possible as it recasts this knowledge to envision an alternative future. (p. 14)

McKittrick draws attention to the continuities between the plantation and contemporary articulations of 'antiblack violence and death' and, crucially, suggests the possibility of something more, the scope to 'notice' spaces of resistance, survival and the potential for black life (pp. 2–3). In her conceptualization of the plantation as representing both the site of black death and the anticipation of black life, McKittrick provides the theoretical room for an analysis of black motherhood that is more than just a catalogue of the oppressions visited upon black women's bodies. The anticipation McKittrick identifies is evident in black mothers' various modes of resistance, especially as they attempt to articulate a resistive vision of good mothering and suggest an 'alternative future'. This future (or futures, as I suggest) does not offer a single view of what a transformation in discrimination and oppression might look like but instead alludes to a multiplicity of maternal subjectivities and embodiments of mothering that emerges from these tensions of the in between. While these futures may not be fully articulated, they ask critical questions about taken-for-granted aspects of contemporary mothering ideology. They uncover and begin to unpick the tangle of contradictions at the heart of much of the current policy guidance about appropriate childrearing, especially the work such guidance performs to uphold existing gender, race and class hierarchies. The questions explored here about parenting practices, work and dividing parenting labour, all crucial components in the larger construct of good mothering, are contemplated and complicated through black mothers' experiences and it is through the lens of their perspectives that the breaches in this construction are exposed. In their narratives, I have highlighted small, limited but potentially significant opportunities for disruption and resistance and it is in these instances that I identify the possibility of alternative ways of organizing, both in terms of childrearing policies and in the lived experience of motherhood.

Notes

Chapter 1

[1]   This notion of 'low' is of course informed by efforts to capitalize on breastfeeding's reported health and financial benefits (Renfrew et al, 2012; UNICEF, 2017). While the World Health Organization's Global Breastfeeding Scorecard 2018 reports that only 42 per cent of babies are breastfed within an hour of birth (UNICEF and WHO, 2018), the women in the two countries this study examines are reportedly much more successful. The last infant feeding survey in Britain, held in 2010, found that 81 per cent of women initiated breastfeeding (McAndrew et al, 2012) and Canadian data from 2011 to 2012 recorded that 89 per cent of women breastfed their babies shortly after birth (Gionet, 2013). Much breastfeeding promotion is concerned not only with increasing initiation rates but also the duration of breastfeeding, aiming for women to reach six months of breastfeeding, preferably exclusively. When measured against this standard, Canadian and British mothers are less successful, reporting 53.9 per cent and 34 per cent respectively. By this measure, breastfeeding rates in the UK and Canada are 'low' but also suggest that the reasons why breastfeeding rates drop to this extent are complex.

Chapter 3

[1]   Increasingly, childrearing advice is directed to 'parents', obscuring the ongoing gendered division of parenting labour. This phenomenon is clearly at play in the promotion of attachment *parenting*, which, as this book captures, is overwhelmingly directed at mothers.

Chapter 4

[1]   Prior to 2018 and during data collection (2015–16), NHS advice was offered under the NHS Choices initiative, a service created in 2007 as a 'one-stop shop' for health-related information and advice as well as offering patients access to a review system of NHS services where they could read and report on their satisfaction with institutions and health professionals (NHS Choices, 2009). Research suggests that such websites are an effective means of reducing the burden on an overstrained healthcare system by encouraging patients to manage their own ailments before turning to NHS services (Murray et al, 2011).

Chapter 5

[1] Although 'co-sleeping' appears to be the preferred phrase among the sample, for the sake of clarity, I use the term 'bedsharing'. According to some attachment parenting experts, co-sleeping is an umbrella term that includes both sharing a bed and sharing a room (where baby sleeps in a cot or crib) (Kellymom, 2019). While the Sears' prefer the term 'sleep sharing' (2001, p. 91), I find bedsharing the most accurate phrase to distinguish it from the more sanctioned forms of infant sleep practice advised by public health bodies.

[2] A technique created by contemporary parenting expert Dr Richard Ferber that advises controlled crying as a method of teaching infants to sleep through the night. This method is associated with more scheduled approaches to parenting.

Chapter 7

[1] Manuel and Zambrana suggest that this finding may be explained by the higher likelihood that such women are the sole or majority earners in their households and thus are unable to afford the reduction in income required by taking maternity leave. This explanation likely does not apply to the women I interviewed; 16 out of 19 participants reported that they were married or in long-term relationships and only one, Claudia, identified herself as the majority earner. Nevertheless, Claudia took a lengthy period of leave.

[2] Since March 2017, there have been two significant changes to the parental leave policy landscape in Canada: the introduction of an extended leave (up to 18 months) that is paid at a lower rate (33 per cent rather than 55 per cent) and, echoing Quebecois policy, a new Parental Sharing Benefit, which provides an additional five weeks only available to the second or 'non-birthing' parent.

[3] Between her and her husband Notisha stated that she was the parent more likely to be "silly [and] fun". According to Notisha, it was her husband's subdued emotional expressiveness that explained why he was not suited to taking parental leave.

[4] The breastfeeding-promotion efforts of movements such as Black Women Do Breastfeed and activists such as Kimberly Seals Allers suggest that breastfeeding is a powerful tool for black communities to alleviate racialized health disparities, including infant mortality rates (Bayne, 2015; Allers, 2016).

Chapter 9

[1] Blum (1999) identifies a tradition of othermothering in her examination of working-class African-American women's attitudes towards breastfeeding. She argues that African-American women's decision to reject breastfeeding can be partly explained by the fact that the practice is incompatible with informal shared childcare arrangements. Hill (2004) and McDonald (1997), on the other hand, suggest that class stratification and the prison industrial complex have irrevocably altered what patterns of othermothering existed, isolating upwardly mobile African Americans in white-dominated, middle-class neighbourhoods and depriving working-class African Americans of the support they may have relied on in earlier contexts.

2   This confidence was not shared by other participants, many of whom struggled with this question. Indeed, it was particularly those women who eventually called themselves 'working-class' who struggled to identify their class position.

3   However, some critics have suggested that a focus on emotional wellbeing can mask the prioritization of economic productivity (Hoffman, 2010), in other words, happiness is only important in so far as it facilitates consumption and competitive involvement in the labour market.

References

Abdi, A.A. (2005) 'Reflections on the long struggle for inclusion: The experiences of people of African origin', in W.J. Tettey and K.P. Puplampu (eds) *The African diaspora in Canada: Negotiating identity and belonging*, Calgary, AB: University of Calgary Press, pp. 49–60.

Alinia, M. (2015) 'On black feminist thought: Thinking oppression and resistance through intersectional paradigm', *Ethnic and Racial Studies*, 38(13): 2334–40.

Allen, G. and Duncan Smith, I. (2008) *Early intervention: Good parents, great kids, better citizens*, London: Centre for Social Justice and Adam Smith Institute.

Allers, K.S. (2016) 'More than just talking equity: Why Black Breastfeeding Week is central to achieving equity #BlackBFJoy', *MomsRising*, [Blog] 31 August, Available from: www.momsrising.org/blog/more-than-just-talking-equity-why-black-breastfeeding-week-is-central-to-achieving-equity-blackbfjoy [Accessed 22 October 2019].

Anim-Addo, J. (2014) 'Activist-mothers maybe, sisters surely? Black British feminism, absence and transformation', *Feminist Review*, 108: 44–60.

Apple, R. (1995) 'Constructing mothers: Scientific motherhood in the nineteenth and twentieth centuries', *Social History of Medicine*, 8(20): 161–78.

Apple, R. (2006) *Perfect motherhood: Science and childrearing in America*, New Brunswick, NJ: Rutgers University Press.

Arnup, K. (1990) 'Educating mothers: Government advice for women in the inter-war years', in K. Arnup, A. Levesque and R.R. Pierson (eds) *Delivering motherhood: Maternal ideologies and practices in the 19th and 20th centuries*, London: Routledge, pp. 190–210.

Associated Press (2014) 'Arizona mother loses "deal of a lifetime" offered after she left sons in hot car', *The Guardian*, [online] 7 November, Available from: https://www.theguardian.com/us-news/2014/nov/07/shanesha-taylor-children-money-trust-fund-car [Accessed 22 October 2019].

Ayo, N. (2012) 'Understanding health promotion in a neoliberal climate and the making of health conscious citizens', *Critical Public Health*, 22(1): 99–105.

Baby Carrier Industry Alliance (2019) 'About us', *Baby Carrier Industry Alliance*, [Industry association website], Available from: www.babycarrierindustryalliance.org/about-us [Accessed 18 October 2019].

Baillargeon, D. (2009) *Babies for the nation: The medicalization of motherhood in Quebec 1910–1970* (W.D. Wilson, Translator), Waterloo: Wilfrid Laurier University Press.

Baird, M. and Cutcher, L. (2005) ' "One for the father, one for the mother and one for the country": An examination of the construction of motherhood through the prism of paid maternity leave', *Hecate*, 31(2): 103–13.

Baird, M. and O'Brien, M. (2015) 'Dynamics of parental leave in Anglophone countries: The paradox of state expansion in the liberal welfare regime', *Community, Work & Family*, 18(2): 198–217.

Baker, J. (2010) 'Natural childbirth is for the birds', in S. Lintott (ed) *Motherhood philosophy is for everyone: The birth of wisdom*, Chichester, MA: Wiley-Blackwell, pp. 154–66.

Banet-Weiser, S. and Mukherjee, R. (2012) 'Introduction: Commodity activism in neoliberal times', in S. Banet-Weiser and R. Mukherjee (eds) *Commodity Activism: Cultural resistance in neoliberal times*, New York, NY and London: New York University Press, pp. 1–21.

Bannerji, H. (2000) *The dark side of the nation: Essays on multiculturalism, nationalism and gender*, Toronto, ON: Canadian Scholars Press.

Bashi, V. (2004) 'Globalized anti-blackness: Transnationalizing Western immigration law, policy, and practice', *Ethnic and Racial Studies*, 27(4): 584–606.

Bayne, E. (2015) 'Chocolate milk: The documentary promo #1', [Video file] 26 August, Available from: www.youtube.com/watch?v=DKh49uUr1Tk [Accessed 22 October 2019].

Berry, J.L. (2010) 'Childhood decides: Towards an understanding of attachment parenting mothers', Master's dissertation, University of Arkansas.

Bezusko, A. (2013) 'Criminalizing black motherhood: How the war on welfare was won', *Souls*, 15(1–2): 39–55.

Bieri, K. (2014) 'Shanesha Taylor explains decision not to fund trusts', *AZ Central*, [online] 6 November, Available from: www.azcentral.com/story/news/local/scottsdale/2014/11/06/shanesha-taylor-misses-deadline-abrk/18585269 [Accessed 22 October 2019].

Bloch, K. and Taylor, T. (2014) 'Welfare queens and anchor babies: A comparative study of stigmatized mothers in the United States', in M. Vandenbeld Giles (ed) *Mothering in the age of neoliberalism*, Bradford, ON: Demeter Press, pp. 199–210.

Blum, L.M. (1999) *At the breast: Ideology of breastfeeding and motherhood in the contemporary United States*, Boston, MA: Beacon Press.

Blum, L.M. (2011) '"Not this big, huge, racial-type thing but…": Mothering children of color with invisible disabilities in the age of neuroscience', *Signs*, 36(4): 941–67.

Bobel, C. (2002) *The paradox of natural mothering*, Philadelphia, PA: Temple University Press.

Bobel, C. (2008) 'Resisting, but not too much: Interrogating the paradox of natural mothering', in J. Nathanson and L.C. Tuley (eds) *Mother knows best: Talking back to the "experts"*, Toronto, ON: Demeter Press, pp. 113–23.

Boseley, S. (2015) 'The longer babies breastfeed, the more they achieve in life – major study', *The Guardian*, [online] 18 March, Available from: www.theguardian.com/lifeandstyle/2015/mar/18/brazil-longer-babies-breastfed-more-achieve-in-life-major-study [Accessed 13 May 2020].

Bowleg, L. (2008) 'When black + lesbian + woman ≠ black lesbian woman: The methodological challenges of qualitative and quantitative intersectionality research', *Sex Roles*, 59: 312–25.

Boyer, K. (2011) '"The way to break the taboo is to do the taboo thing" breastfeeding in public and citizen-activism in the UK', *Health & Place*, 17: 430–7.

Boyer, K. (2014) '"Neoliberal motherhood": Workplace lactation and changing conceptions of working motherhood in the contemporary US', *Feminist Theory*, 15(3): 269–88.

Brah, A. and Phoenix, A. (2004) 'Ain't I a woman? Revisiting intersectionality', *Journal of International Women's Studies*, 5(3): 75–86.

Bretherton, I. (1992) 'The origins of attachment theory: John Bowlby and Mary Ainsworth', *Developmental Psychology*, 28(5): 759–75.

Brewer, R.M. (1993) 'Theorizing race, class and gender: The new scholarship of black feminist intellectuals and black women's labor', in S.M. James and P.A. Busia (eds) *Theorizing black feminisms: The visionary pragmatism of black women*, London: Routledge, pp. 13–30.

Bridges, K.M. (2011) *Reproducing race: An ethnography of pregnancy as a site of racialization*, Berkeley, CA: University of California Press.

Brown, W. (2006) 'American nightmare: Neoliberalism, neoconservatism, and de-democratization', *Political Theory*, 34(6): 690–714.

Brown, W. (2015) *Undoing the demos: Neoliberalism's stealth revolution*, Brooklyn, NY: Zone Books.

Burke, S. (2007) 'Women of Newfangle: Co-education, racial discourse and women's rights in Victorian Ontario', *Historical Studies in Education*, 19: 111–33.

Cameron, D. (2016a) 'Prime Minister's speech on life chances', [online] 11 January, Available from: www.gov.uk/government/speeches/prime-ministers-speech-on-life-chances [Accessed 22 October 2019].

Cameron, D. (2016b) 'Watch out, universities; I'm bringing the fight for equality in Britain to you', [online] 1 February, Available from: www.gov.uk/government/speeches/watch-out-universities-im-bringing-the-fight-for-equality-in-britain-to-you-article-by-david-cameron [Accessed 22 October 2019].

Campbell, M. (2008) 'Labour's policy on money for parents: Combining care with paid work', *Social Policy & Society*, 7(4): 457–470.

Carter, P. (1995) *Feminism, breasts and breast-feeding*, Basingstoke: Palgrave Macmillan.

Carter, S.K. and Anthony, A.K. (2015) 'Good, bad, and extraordinary mothers: Infant feeding and mothering in African American mothers' breastfeeding narratives', *Sociology of Race and Ethnicity*, 1(4): 517–31.

Chanfreau, J., Gowland, S., Lancaster, Z., Poole, E., Tipping, S. and Toomse, M. (2011) *Maternity and paternity rights and women returners survey 2009/10*, Research Report No. 777, Department for Work and Pensions and the Department for Business Innovation and Skills, London.

Cheek, J. (2008) 'Healthism: A new conservatism?', *Qualitative Health Research*, 18(7): 974–82.

Cho, S. (2009) 'Post-racialism', *Iowa Law Review*, 94: 1589–649.

Christopher, K. (2015) 'Paid leave as buffer zones: Social policies and work-life balance among Canadian mothers', *Journal of Research on Women and Gender*, 6: 24–39.

Collins, P.H. (1989) 'The social construction of black feminist thought', *Signs*, 14(4): 745–73.

Collins, P.H. (2000) *Black feminist thought: Knowledge, consciousness and the politics of empowerment*, New York, NY: Routledge.

Collins, P.H. (2009) 'Foreword: Emerging intersections – building knowledge and transforming institutions', in B.T. Dill and R.E. Zambrana (eds) *Emerging intersections: Race, class, and gender in theory, policy, and practice*, New Brunswick, NJ: Rutgers University Press, pp. vii–xiii.

Collins, P.H. (2010) 'The new politics of community', *American Sociological Review*, 75(1): 7–30.

Collins, P.H. and Bilge, S. (2016) *Intersectionality*, Cambridge: Polity Press.

Combahee River Collective (1977) 'The Combahee River Collective statement', [Blog], Available from: http://circuitous.org/scraps/combahee.html [Accessed 25 October 2019].

Contratto, S. (2002) 'A feminist critique of attachment theory and evolutionary psychology', in M. Ballou and L. S. Brown (eds) *Rethinking mental health and disorder: Feminist perspectives*, New York, NY: The Guilford Press, pp. 29–47.

Cooper, C.W. (2010) 'Racially conscious mothering in the "colorblind" century: Implications for African-American motherwork', in A. O'Reilly (ed) *Twenty-first-century motherhood: Experience, identity, policy, agency*, New York, NY: Columbia University Press, pp. 338–51.

Cox, S.M. (2006) 'Bridging attachment theory and attachment parenting with feminist modes of inquiry', *Journal of the Association for Research on Mothering*, 8(1–2): 83–95.

Craven, C. (2007) 'A 'consumer's right' to choose a midwife: Shifting meanings for reproductive rights under neoliberalism', *American Anthropologist*, 109(4): 701–12.

Crenshaw, K.W. (1989) 'Demarginalizing the intersection of race and sex: A black feminist critique of antidiscrimination doctrine, feminist theory and antiracist politics', *University of Chicago Legal Forum*, 139–67.

Daminger, A. (2019) 'The cognitive dimension of household labor', *American Sociological Review*, 84(4): 609–33.

Davids, T. and Willemse, K. (2014) 'Embodied engagements: Feminist ethnography at the crossing of knowledge production and representation – An introduction', *Women's Studies International Forum*, 43: 1–4.

Davis, D.A. (2007) 'Narrating the mute: Racializing and racism in a neoliberal moment', *Souls*, 9(4): 346–60.

Dear-Healey, S. (2011) 'Attachment parenting international: Nurturing generations of mothers, children and families', in A. O'Reilly (ed) *The 21st century motherhood movement: Mothers speak out on why we need to change the world and how to do it*, Bradford, ON: Demeter Press, pp. 383–93.

DeVault, M.L. (1991) *Feeding the family: The social organization of caring as gendered work*, Chicago, IL: The University of Chicago Press.

Dill, B.T. and Zambrana, R.E. (2009) 'Critical thinking about inequality: An emerging lens', in B.T. Dill and R.E. Zambrana (eds) *Emerging intersections: Race, class, and gender in theory, policy, and practice*, New Brunswick, NJ: Rutgers University Press, pp. 1–21.

Dillaway, H. and Paré, E. (2008) 'Locating mothers: How cultural debates about stay-at-home versus working mothers define women and home', *Journal of Family Issues*, 28(4): 437–64.

Dillon, S. (2012) 'Possessed by death: The neoliberal carceral state, black feminism, and the afterlife of slavery', *Radical History Review*, 112: 113–25.

Doucet, A. (2009) 'Dad and baby in the first year: Gendered responsibilities and embodiment', *The Annals of the American Academy*, 624: 78–98.

Douglas, S.J. and Michaels, M.W. (2004) *The mommy myth: The idealization of motherhood and how it has undermined women*, New York, NY: Free Press.

Duggan, L. (2003) *The twilight of equality? Neoliberalism, cultural politics, and the attack on democracy*, Boston, MA: Beacon Press.

Dunn, T.R. (2016) 'Playing neoliberal politics: Post-racial and post-racist strategies in "Same Love"', *Communication and Critical/Cultural Studies*, 13(3): 269–89.

Edwards, R. and Gillies, V. (2011) 'Clients or consumers, commonplace or pioneers? Navigating the contemporary class politics of family, parenting skills and education', *Ethics and Education*, 6(2): 141–54.

Edwards, R., Gillies, V. and Horsley, N. (2016) 'Early intervention and evidence-based policy and practice: Framing and taming', *Social Policy & Society*, 15(1): 1–10.

Elliott, S., Powell, R. and Brenton, J. (2013) 'Being a good mom: Low-income, black, single mothers negotiate intensive mothering', *Journal of Family Issues*, 36(3): 351–70.

Ennis, L.R. (2014) 'Intensive mothering: Revisiting the issue today', in L.R. Ennis (ed) *Intensive mothering: The cultural contradictions of modern motherhood*, Bradford, ON: Demeter Press, pp. 1–23.

Erel, U. (2011) 'Reframing migrant mothers as citizens', *Citizenship Studies*, 15(6–7): 695–709.

Evans, P.M. (2007) 'Comparative perspectives on changes to Canada's paid parental leave: Implications for class and gender', *International Journal of Social Welfare*, 16: 119–28.

Eyer, D.E. (1992) *Mother-infant bonding: A scientific fiction*, New Haven, CT: Yale University Press.

Faircloth, C. (2013) *Militant lactivism? Attachment parenting and intensive motherhood in the UK and France*, New York, NY: Berghahn Books.

Faircloth, C. (2014a) 'Intensive parenting and the expansion of parenting', in E. Lee, J. Bristow, C. Faircloth and J. Macvarish (eds) *Parenting Culture Studies*, Basingstoke: Palgrave Macmillan, pp. 22–50.

Faircloth, C. (2014b) 'Is attachment mothering intensive mothering?', in L.R. Ennis (ed) *Intensive mothering: The cultural contradictions of modern motherhood*, Bradford, ON: Demeter Press, pp. 180–93.

Fassin, D. (2011) 'The trace: Violence, truth, and the politics of the body', *Social Research*, 78(2): 281–98.

Field, F. (2010) *The foundation years: Preventing poor children becoming poor adults*, Report of the Independent Review on Poverty and Life Chances, London: Cabinet Office, Available from: www. poverty.ac.uk/report-poverty-measurement-life-chances-children-parenting-uk-government-policy/field-review [Accessed 22 October 2019].

Findlay, L. and Kohen, D.E. (2012) 'Leave practices of parents after the birth or adoption of young children', *Canadian Social Trends*, July 2012: 3–12.

Firth, J. (2012) 'Healthy choices and heavy burden: Race, citizenship and gender in the "obesity epidemic"', *Journal of International Women's Studies*, 13(2): 33–50.

Fisher, T. (2012) *What's left of blackness: Feminisms, transracial solidarities, and the politics of belonging in Britain*, New York, NY: Palgrave Macmillan.

Forna, A. (2000) 'Mothers of Africa and the diaspora: Shared maternal values among black women', in K. Owusu (ed) *Black British culture and society*, London: Routledge, pp. 358–72.

Fox, B. (2006) 'Motherhood as a class act: The many ways in which "intensive mothering" is entangled with social class', in K. Bezanson and M. Luxton (eds) *Social reproduction: Feminist political economy*, Montreal, QC and Kingston, ON: McGill-Queen's University Press, pp. 231–62.

Fox, B. (2009) *When couples become parents: The creation of gender in the transition to parenthood*, Toronto, ON: University of Toronto Press.

Freeman, H. (2016) 'Attachment parenting: The best way to raise a child – or maternal masochism?', *The Guardian*, [online] 30 July, Available from: www.theguardian.com/lifeandstyle/2016/jul/30/ attachment-parenting-best-way-raise-child-or-maternal-masochism [Accessed 22 October 2019].

Gallagher, J. (2016) 'UK "world's worst" at breastfeeding', *BBC News*, [online] 29 January, Available from: www.bbc.com/news/health-35438049 [Accessed 23 October 2019].

Galtry, J. and Callister, P. (2005) 'Assessing the optimal length of parental leave for child and parental well-being: How can research inform policy?', *Journal of Family Issues*, 26(2): 219–46.

Gatrell, C. and Dermott, E. (2018) 'Introduction', in E. Dermott and C. Gatrell (eds) *Fathers, families and relationships: Researching everyday lives*, Bristol: Policy Press, pp. 1–9.

Gillies, V. (2005) 'Raising the "meritocracy": Parenting and the individualization of social class', *Sociology*, 39(5): 835–53.

Gillies, V. (2012) 'Personalising poverty: Parental determinism and the "Big Society" agenda', in W. Atkinson, S. Roberts and M. Savage (eds) *Class inequality in austerity Britain: Power, difference and suffering*, Basingstoke: Palgrave Macmillan, pp. 90–110.

Gillies, V., Edwards, R. and Horsley, N. (2017) *Challenging the politics of early intervention: Who's 'saving' children and why*, Bristol: Policy Press.

Gilroy, P. (1987) *'There ain't no black in the Union Jack': The cultural politics of race and nation*, London: Hutchinson.

Gionet, L. (2013) 'Breastfeeding trends in Canada', *Statistics Canada*, [online], Available from: www.statcan.gc.ca/pub/82-624-x/2013001/article/11879-eng.htm [Accessed 22 October 2019].

Giroux, H.A. (2006) 'Reading Hurricane Katrina: Race, class, and the biopolitics of disposability', *College Literature*, 33(3): 171–96.

Giroux, H.A. (2008) *Against the terror of neoliberalism: Politics beyond the age of greed*, Boulder, CO: Paradigm Publishers.

Glenn, E.N. (1992) 'From servitude to service work: Historical continuities in the racial division of paid reproductive labor', *Signs*, 18(1): 1–43.

Gornick, J.C. and Meyers, M.K. (2009) 'Institutions that support gender equality in parenthood and employment', in J.C. Gornick and M.K. Meyers (eds) *Gender equality: Transforming family divisions of labor*, New York, NY: Verso Press, pp. 3–64.

Gray, A. (2006) 'The time economy of parenting', *Sociological Research Online*, 11(3), Available from: www.socresonline.org.uk/11/3/gray.html [Accessed 22 October 2019].

Green, K.E. and Groves, M.M. (2008) 'Attachment parenting: An exploration of demographics and practices', *Early Child Development and Care*, 178(5): 513–25.

Guerrero, L. (2011) '(M)other-in-chief: Michelle Obama and the ideal of republican womanhood', in R. Gill and C. Scharff (eds) *New femininities: Postfeminism, neoliberalism and subjectivity*, Basingstoke: Palgrave Macmillan, pp. 68–82.

Hamilton, P. (2016) 'The "good" attached mother: An analysis of postmaternal and postracial thinking in birth and breastfeeding policy in neoliberal Britain', *Australian Feminist Studies*, 31(90): 410–31.

Hamilton, P. (2019) '"Now that I know what you're about": black feminist reflections on power in the research relationship', *Qualitative Research* [Online First].

Hardyment, C. (1983) *Dream babies: Child care from Locke to Spock*, London: Jonathan Cape.

Harris, A. (2004) *Future girl: Young women in the twenty-first century*, New York, NY: Routledge.

Hausman, B. (2003) *Mother's milk: Breastfeeding controversies in American culture*, New York, NY: Routledge.

Hawkins, S.S., Griffiths, L.J., Dezateux, C., Law, C. and the Millennium Cohort Study Child Health Group (2007) 'The impact of maternal employment on breast-feeding duration in the UK Millennium Cohort Study', *Public Health Nutrition*, 10(9): 891–6.

Hays, S. (1996) *The cultural contradictions of motherhood*, New Haven, CT: Yale University Press.

Health Canada (2014) 'Baby sling and carrier safety', Health Canada, [online], Available from: www.canada.ca/en/health-canada/services/infant-care/baby-slings-carriers.html [Accessed 25 October 2019].

Henry, F. (1968) 'The West Indian domestic scheme in Canada', *Social and Economic Studies*, 17(1): 83–91.

Heyes, C.J. (2006) 'Foucault goes to Weight Watchers', *Hypatia*, 21(2): 126–49.

Hicks, P. (2008) *Social policy in Canada – Looking back, looking ahead*, School of Policy Studies Working Paper No. 46, Available from: www.queensu.ca/sps/sites/webpublish.queensu.ca.spswww/files/files/Publications/workingpapers/46-Hicks.pdf [Accessed 22 October 2019].

Hill, S.A. (2004) *Black intimacies: A gender perspective on families and relationships*, Walnut Creek, CA: Rowman and Littlefield.

Hochschild, A.R. (2009) 'Love and gold', *S&F Online*, 8(1): 35–46.

Hoffman, D.M. (2010) 'Risky investments: Parenting and the production of the "resilient child"', *Health, Risk & Society*, 12(4): 385–94.

Hoffman, D.M. (2013) 'Power struggles: The paradoxes of emotion and control among child-centered mothers in the privileged United States', *ETHOS*, 41(1): 75–97.

hooks, b. (2007) 'Revolutionary parenting', in A. O'Reilly (ed) *Maternal theory: Essential readings*, Toronto, ON: Demeter Press, pp. 145–56.

Howard, E. (2014) 'Coroner raises concerns over baby slings after boy suffocates', *The Guardian*, [online] 4 April, Available from: www.theguardian.com/lifeandstyle/2014/apr/04/coroner-raises-concerns-over-baby-slings-after-boy-suffocates [Accessed 22 October 2019].

Jamieson, S. (2017) 'Health tourism warning as NHS chases £350,000 bill from Nigerian woman who gave birth in a British hospital', *The Telegraph*, [online] 16 January, Available from: www.telegraph.co.uk/news/2017/01/16/health-tourism-warning-nhs-chases-350000-bill-nigerian-woman [Accessed 22 October 2019].

Jasen, P. (1997) 'Race, culture, and the colonization of childbirth in northern Canada', *Social History of Medicine*, 10(3): 383–400.

Jenner, E. (2014) 'The perils of attachment parenting', *The Atlantic*, [online] 10 August, Available from: www.theatlantic.com/health/archive/2014/08/the-perils-of-attachment-parenting/375198 [Accessed 22 October 2019].

Jenson, J. (2004) 'Changing the paradigm: Family responsibility or investing in children', *The Canadian Journal of Sociology*, 29(2): 169–92.

Jordan-Zachery, J.S. (2009) *Black women, cultural images, and social policy*, New York, NY: Routledge.

Kandaswamy, P. (2008) 'State austerity and the racial politics of same-sex marriage in the US', *Sexualities*, 11(6): 706–25.

Kapoor, N. (2013) 'The advancement of racial neoliberalism in Britain', *Ethnic and Racial Studies*, 36(6): 1028–46.

Kellymom (2019) 'Co-sleeping and bed-sharing', *Kellymom*, [Blog] 21 May, Available from: http://kellymom.com/parenting/nighttime/cosleeping [Accessed 22 October 2019].

Kershaw, P. (2005) *Carefair: Rethinking the responsibilities and rights of citizenship*, Vancouver, BC: UBC Press.

Knaak, S.J. (2005) 'Breast-feeding, bottle-feeding and Dr Spock: The shifting context of choice', *Canadian Review of Sociology and Anthropology*, 42(2): 197–216.

Knaak, S.J. (2010) 'Contextualising risk, constructing choice: Breastfeeding and good mothering in risk society', *Health, Risk & Society*, 12(2): 345–55.

Koshy, S. (2013) 'Neoliberal family matters', *American Literary History*, 25(2): 1–37.

Kukla, R. (2006) 'Ethics and ideology in breastfeeding advocacy campaigns', *Hypatia*, 21(1): 157–81.

Kukla, R. (2008) 'Measuring mothering', *International Journal of Feminist Approaches to Bioethics*, 1(1): 67–90.

La Leche League Canada (nd) 'About LLLC', La Leche League Canada, [online], Available from: www.lllc.ca/about-lllc [Accessed 23 October 2019].

Lareau, A. (2011) *Unequal childhoods: Class, race, and family life* (2nd edn), Berkeley, CA: University of California Press.

Larner, W. (2000) 'Neo-liberalism: Policy, ideology, governmentality', *Studies in Political Economy*, 63: 5–25.

Lawson, E. (2002) 'Images in black: Black women, media and the mythology of an orderly society', in N.N. Wane, K. Deliovsky and E. Lawson (eds) *Back to the drawing board: African-Canadian feminisms*, Toronto, ON: Sumach Press, pp. 199–223.

Lawson, E. (2013) 'The gendered working lives of seven Jamaican women in Canada: A story about "here" and "there" in a transnational economy', *Feminist Formations*, 25(1): 138–56.

Lawson, E. (2018) 'Bereaved black mothers and maternal activism in the racial state', *Feminist Studies*, 44(3): 713–35.

Lee, E.J. (2008) 'Living with risk in the age of "intensive motherhood": Maternal identity and infant feeding', *Health, Risk & Society*, 10(5): 467–77.

Lee, E.J. (2014) 'Introduction', in E. Lee, J. Bristow, C. Faircloth and J. Macvarish (eds) *Parenting culture studies*, Basingstoke: Palgrave Macmillan, pp. 1–22.

Lee, E.J. and Jackson, E. (2002) 'The pregnant body', in M. Evans and E.J. Lee (eds) *Real bodies: A sociological introduction*, Basingstoke: Palgrave, pp. 115–32.

Lee, R. (2018) *The ethics and politics of breastfeeding: Power, pleasure, poetics*, Toronto: ON: University of Toronto Press.

Lentin, A. and Titley, G. (2011) *The crises of multiculturalism: Racism in a neoliberal age*, London: Zed Books.

Lero, D.S. (2015) 'Current stats on paternity leave and fathers' use of parental leave and income support in Canada and Québec', Centre for Families, Work & Well-being, University of Guelph brief, [online], Available from: www.worklifecanada.ca/cms/resources/ files/731/CURRENT_STATS_ON_PATERNITY_LEAVE_ AND_FATHERS.pdf [Accessed 22 October 2019].

Lewis, G. (2000) *'Race', gender, social welfare: Encounters in a postcolonial society*, Cambridge: Polity Press.

Liss, M. and Erchull, M.J. (2012) 'Feminism and attachment parenting: Attitudes, stereotypes and misconceptions', *Sex Roles*, 67: 131–42.

Litt, J.S. (2000) *Medicalized motherhood: Perspectives from the lives of African-American and Jewish women*, New Brunswick, NJ: Rutgers University Press.

Lowe, P., Lee, E. and Macvarish, J. (2015) 'Biologising parenting: Neuroscience discourse, English social and public health policy and understandings of the child', *Sociology of Health & Illness*, 37(2): 198–211.

Lullaby Trust (2019) 'New survey shows 40% of parents are not co-sleeping safely', Lullaby Trust, [online], Available from: www.lullabytrust.org.uk/new-survey-shows-40-of-parents-are-not-co-sleeping-safely [Accessed 23 October 2019].

Macdonald, C. (2009) 'What's culture got to do with it? Mothering ideologies as barrier to gender equality', in J.C. Gornick and M.K. Meyers (eds) *Gender equality: Transforming family divisions of labor*, New York, NY: Verso Press, pp. 411–34.

MacLeavy, J. (2011) 'A "new politics" of austerity, workfare and gender? The UK coalition government's welfare reform proposals', *Cambridge Journal of Regions, Economy and Society*, 4(3): 355–67.

Mama, A. (1997) 'Black women, the economic crisis and the British state', in H.S. Mirza (ed) *Black British feminism: A reader*, London: Routledge, pp. 36–41.

Manuel, T. and Zambrana, R.E. (2009) 'Exploring the intersections of race, ethnicity, and class on maternity leave decisions: Implications for public policy', in B.T. Dill and R.E. Zambrana (eds) *Emerging intersections: Race, class, and gender in theory, policy, and practice*, New Brunswick, NJ: Rutgers University Press, pp. 123–49.

Marshall, K. (2008) 'Fathers' use of paid parental leave', *Statistics Canada*, [online], Available from: www.statcan.gc.ca/pub/75-001-x/2008106/article/10639-eng.htm [Accessed 22 October 2019].

Massaquoi, N. (2004) 'An African child becomes a black Canadian feminist: Oscillating identities in the black diaspora', *Canadian Woman Studies*, 23(2): 140–44.

Massaquoi, N. (2007) 'Future imaginings of black feminist thought', in N. Massaquoi and N.N. Wane (eds) *Theorizing empowerment: Canadian perspectives on black feminist thought*, Toronto, ON: INANNA Publications and Education Inc, pp. 5–24.

Maylor, U. and Williams, K. (2011) 'Challenges in theorizing "Black middle-class" women: Education, experience and authenticity', *Gender and Education*, 23(3): 345–56.

McAndrew, F., Thompson, J., Fellows, L., Large, A., Speed, M. and Renfrew, M.J. (2012) 'Infant feeding survey – UK, 2010', NHS, [online], Available from: https://webarchive.nationalarchives.gov.uk/20180321190208/http://digital.nhs.uk/catalogue/PUB08694 [Accessed 22 October 2019].

McCain, M.N. and Mustard, J.F. (1999) *Reversing the real brain drain: Early years study final report*, Final report of the Early Years Study, Toronto: Government of Ontario, Available from www.oise.utoronto.ca/guestid/humandevelopment/UserFiles/File/Early_Years_Study_1.pdf [Accessed 22 October 2019].

McDonald, K.B. (1997) 'Black activist mothering: A historical intersection of race, gender, and class', *Gender & Society*, 11(6): 773–95.

McKay, L. and Doucet, A. (2010) ' "Without taking away her leave": A Canadian case study of couples' decisions on fathers' use of paid parental leave', *Fathering*, 8(3): 300–20.

McKay, L., Mathieu, S. and Doucet, A. (2016) 'Parental-leave rich and parental-leave poor: Inequality in Canadian labour market based leave policies', *Journal of Industrial Relations*, 58(4): 543–62.

McKittrick, K. (2002) ' "Their blood is there, and they can't throw it out": Honouring black Canadian geographies', *TOPIA*, 7: 27–37.

McKittrick, K. (2006) 'Nothing's shocking: Black Canada', in *Demonic grounds: Black women and the cartographies of struggle*, Minneapolis, MN: University of Minnesota Press, pp. 91–119.

McKittrick, K. (2013) 'Plantation futures', *Small Axe* 17(3): 1–15.

McRobbie, A. (2013) 'Feminism, the family and the new "mediated" materialism', *New Formations*, 80–81: 119–37.

Morris, T. and Schulman, M. (2014) 'Race inequality in epidural use and regional anesthesia failure in labor and birth: An examination of women's experiences', *Sexual & Reproductive Healthcare*, 5: 188–94.

Morrissey, M.E. and Kimball, K.Y. (2017) '#SpoiledMilk: Blacktavists, visibility, and the exploitation of the black breast', *Women's Studies in Communication*, 40(1): 48–66.

Mullings, L. (2000) 'African-American women making themselves: Notes on the role of black feminist research', *Souls*, 2(4): 18–29.

Murphy, E. (2003) 'Expertise and forms of knowledge in the government of families', *Sociological Review*, 51(4): 433–62.

Murray, J., Majeed, A., Khan, M.S., Lee, J.T. and Nelson, P. (2011) 'Use of the NHS Choices website for primary care consultations: Results from online and general practice surveys', *Journal of the Royal Society of Medicine*, 2(56): 1–25.

Nathoo, T. and Ostry, A. (2009) *The one best way? Breastfeeding history, politics, and policy in Canada*, Waterloo, ON: Wilfrid Laurier University Press.

Nelson, C. (2017) 'Modern racism in Canada has deep colonial roots', *Huffington Post Canada*, [online] 20 February, Available from: http://www.huffingtonpost.ca/charmaine-nelson/modern-racism-canada_b_14821958.html?ncid=engmodushpmg00000004 [Accessed 23 October 2019].

Nestel, S. (2006) *Obstructed labour: Race and gender in the re-emergence of midwifery*, Vancouver, BC: UBC Press.

NHS (National Health Service) (2017) 'Benefits of breastfeeding', NHS, [online], Available from: www.nhs.uk/conditions/pregnancy-and-baby/benefits-breastfeeding [Accessed 23 October 2019].

NHS Choices (2009) 'NHS Choices annual report 2009', NHS, [online] 26 June, Available from: www.nhs.uk/aboutNHSChoices/Documents/2009/AnnualReporNHSChoices09.pdf [Accessed 23 October 2019].

NICE (National Institute for Health and Care Excellence) (2006/2015) 'Postnatal care up to 8 weeks after birth', NICE, [online], Available from: www.nice.org.uk/guidance/cg37/chapter/1-Recommendations [Accessed 23 October 2019].

Nicholson, B. and Parker, L. (nd) 'FAQ', *Attached at the Heart*, [Blog], Available from http://attachedattheheart.attachmentparenting.org/faq [Accessed 23 October 2019].

Norwood, C. (2013) 'Perspective in Africana feminism: Exploring expressions of black feminism/womanism in the African diaspora', *Sociology Compass*, 7(3): 225–36.

O'Brien, M. and Koslowski, A. (2016) 'United Kingdom country note', in A. Koslowski, S. Blum and P. Moss (eds) *12th International Review of Leave Policies and Research 2016*, [online], Available from: https://www.leavenetwork.org/annual-review-reports/archive-reviews [Accessed 23 October 2019].

O'Brien, M., Aldrich, M., Connolly, S., Cook, R. and Speight, S. (2017) *Inequalities in access to paid maternity and paternity leave and flexible work*, London: UCL Grand Challenges Report.

O'Brien, M. and Twamley, K. (2017) 'Fathers taking leave alone in the UK: A gift exchange between mother and father?', in M. O'Brien and K. Walls (eds) *Comparative perspectives on work-life balance and gender equality*, Life Course Research and Social Policies 6: 163–81.

O'Reilly, A. (2004) 'Introduction', in A. O'Reilly (ed) *Mother outlaws: Theories and practices of empowered mothering*, Toronto, ON: Women's Press, pp. 1–30.

Orloff, A.S. (2006) 'From maternalism to "employment for all": State policies to promote women's employment across the affluent democracies', in J.D. Levy (ed) *The state after statism: New state activities in the age of liberalization*, Cambridge, MA: Harvard University Press, pp. 230–68.

Owens, J. (2018) 'Women are overburdened with their families "mental loads"', *Slate*, [online] 2 March, Available from: https://slate.com/human-interest/2018/03/women-are-overburdened-with-their-families-mental-loads.html [Accessed 18 October 2019].

Page, R.M. (2015) *Clear blue water? The Conservative Party and the welfare state since 1940*, Bristol: Policy Press.

Perry, K.H. (2015) *London is the place for me: Black Britons, citizenship, and the politics of race*, New York, NY: Oxford University Press.

Peterson, A. and Lupton, D. (1996) *The new public health: Health and self in the age of risk*, London: SAGE Publications.

PHAC (Public Health Agency of Canada) (2009) '10 great reasons to breastfeed', Public Health Agency of Canada, [online], Available from: www.canada.ca/en/public-health/services/health-promotion/childhood-adolescence/stages-childhood/infancy-birth-two-years/breastfeeding-infant-nutrition/10-great-reasons-breastfeed-your-baby.html [Accessed 16 July 2020].

PHAC (2010/2014) 'Safe sleep for your baby', Public Health Agency of Canada, [online], Available from: www.canada.ca/en/public-health/services/health-promotion/childhood-adolescence/stages-childhood/infancy-birth-two-years/safe-sleep/safe-sleep-your-baby-brochure.html [Accessed 23 October 2019].

PHAC (2011) 'Joint statement on safe sleep: Preventing sudden infant deaths in Canada', Public Health Agency of Canada, [online], Available from: www.canada.ca/content/dam/phac-aspc/migration/phac-aspc/hp-ps/dca-dea/stages-etapes/childhood-enfance_0-2/sids/pdf/jsss-ecss2011-eng.pdf [Accessed 23 October 2019].

PHAC (2014) 'Breastfeeding your baby', Public Health Agency of Canada, [online], Available from: www.canada.ca/en/public-health/services/health-promotion/childhood-adolescence/stages-childhood/infancy-birth-two-years/breastfeeding-infant-nutrition.html [Accessed 23 October 2019].

Phipps, A. (2014) *The politics of the body: Gender in a neoliberal and neoconservative age*, Cambridge: Polity Press.

Phoenix, A. (1990) 'Black women and the maternity services', in J. Garcia, R. Kilpatrick and M. Richards (eds) *The politics of maternity care: Services for childbearing women in twentieth century Britain*, Oxford: Clarendon Press, pp. 274–99.

Phoenix, A. (1996) 'Social constructions of lone motherhood: A case of competing discourses', in E.B. Silva (ed) *Good enough mothering? Feminist perspectives on lone mothering*, London: Routledge, pp. 175–90.

Plumming, K. (2000) 'From nursing outposts to contemporary midwifery in 20th century Canada', *Journal of Midwifery & Women's Health*, 45(2): 169–75.

Polzer, J. and Power, E. (2016) 'Introduction: The governance of health in neoliberal societies', in J. Polzer and E. Power (eds) *Neoliberal governance and health: Duties, risks and vulnerabilities*, Montreal, QC and Kingston, ON: McGill-Queen's University Press, pp. 3–42.

Power, E.M. (2005) 'The unfreedom of being other: Canadian lone mothers' experiences of poverty and "life on the cheque"', *Sociology*, 39(4): 643–60.

Ray, R., Gornick, J.C. and Schmitt, J. (2010) 'Who cares? Assessing generosity and gender equality in parental leave policy designs in 21 countries', *Journal of European Social Policy*, 20(3): 196–216.

Reich, J.A. (2014) 'Neoliberal mothering and vaccine refusal: Imagined gated communities and the privilege of choice', *Gender & Society*, 28(5): 679–704.

Renfrew, M.J., Fox-Rushby, J., Pokhrel, S., Dodds, R., Quigley, M., Duffy, S., McCormick, F., Trueman, P. and Williams, A. (2012) 'Preventing disease and saving resources: The potential contribution of increasing breastfeeding rates in the UK', UNICEF UK, [online], Available from www.unicef.org.uk/babyfriendly/about/preventing-disease-and-saving-resources/preventing_disease_saving_resources [Accessed 23 October 2019].

Reynolds, T. (1997) '(Mis)representing the black (super)woman', in H.S. Mirza (ed) *Black British feminism: A reader*, London: Routledge, pp. 97–112.

Reynolds, T. (2001) 'Black mothering, paid work and identity', *Ethnic and Racial Studies*, 24(6): 1046–64.

Reynolds, T. (2002) 'Re-thinking a black feminist standpoint', *Ethnic and Racial Studies*, 25(4): 591–606.

Reynolds, T. (2005) *Caribbean mothers: Identity and experience in the U.K.*, London: Tufnell Press.

Reynolds, T. (2016) 'Black mammy and company: Exploring constructions of black womanhood in Britain', in F. Stella, Y. Taylor, T. Reynolds and A. Rogers (eds) *Sexuality, citizenship and belonging: Trans-national and intersectional perspectives*, New York, NY: Routledge, pp. 95–111.

Rhee, J. (2013) 'The neoliberal racial project: The tiger mother and governmentality', *Educational Theory*, 63(6): 561–80.

Roberts, D.E (1991) 'Punishing drug addicts who have babies: Women of color, equality and the right of privacy', *Harvard Law Review*, 104(7): 1419–82.

Roberts, D.E. (1993) 'Racism and patriarchy and the meaning of motherhood', *American University Journal of Gender and the Law*, 1(1): 1–38.

Roberts, D.E. (1995) 'Race, gender, and the value of mothers' work', *Social Politics*, 2(2): 195–207.

Roberts, D.E. (1997a) 'Unshackling black motherhood', *Michigan Law Review*, 95(4): 938–64.

Roberts, D.E. (1997b) *Killing the black body: Race, reproduction, and one meaning of liberty*, New York, NY: Pantheon Books.

Roberts, D.J. and Mahtani, M. (2010) 'Neoliberalizing race, racing neoliberalism: Placing "race" in neoliberal discourses', *Antipode*, 42(2): 248–57.

Romagnoli, A. and Wall, G. (2012) ' "I know I'm a good mom": Young, low-income mothers' experiences with risk perception, intensive parenting ideology and parenting education programmes', *Health, Risk & Society*, 14(3): 273–89.

Rose, N. (1999) *Powers of freedom: Reframing political thought*, Cambridge: Cambridge University Press.

Ruckert, A. and Labonté, R. (2016) 'The first federal budget under Prime Minister Justin Trudeau: Addressing social determinants of health?', *Canadian Journal of Public Health*, 107(2): 212–14.

Ruhm, C.J. (2000) 'Parental leave and child health', *Journal of Health Economics*, 19: 931–60.

Russell, N.U. (2015) 'Babywearing in the age of the internet', *Journal of Family Issues*, 36(6): 1130–53.

Sa'ar, A. (2005) 'Postcolonial feminism, the politics of identification, and the liberal bargain', *Gender & Society*, 19(5): 680–700.

Samantrai, R. (2002) *AlterNatives: Black feminism in the postimperial nation*, Stanford, CA: Stanford University Press.

Sears, W. and Sears, M. (1993) *The baby book: Everything you need to know about your baby – from birth to age two*, Boston, MA: Little, Brown and Company.

Sears, W. and Sears, M. (2001) *The attachment parenting book: A commonsense guide to understanding and nurturing your baby*, New York, NY: Little, Brown and Company.

Shirani, F., Henwood, K. and Coltart, C. (2012) 'Meeting the challenges of intensive parenting culture: Gender, risk management and the moral parent', *Sociology*, 46(1): 25–40.

Shome, R. (2011) ' "Global motherhood": The transnational intimacies of white femininity', *Critical Studies in Media Communication*, 28(5): 388–406.

Silva, J.M. (2019) 'Using qualitative methods to uncover the hidden mechanisms of poverty and inequality', *American Family Diaries: Can ethnographic research help shape public policy?*, Washington, DC: American Enterprise Institute.

Símonardóttir, S. (2016) 'Constructing the attached mother in the "world's most feminist country"', *Women's Studies International Forum*, 56: 103–12.

Spence, L.K. (2012) 'The neoliberal turn in black politics', *Souls*, 14(3–4): 139–59.

Springer, K. (2007) 'Divas, evil black bitches, and bitter black women: African American women in postfeminist and post-civil-rights popular culture', in Y. Tasker and D. Negra (eds) *Interrogating postfeminism: Gender and the politics of popular culture*, Durham, NC: Duke University Press, pp. 249–76.

Squires, C.R. (2010) 'Running through the trenches: Or, an introduction to the undead culture wars and dead serious identity politics', *Journal of Communication Inquiry*, 34(3): 211–14.

Stephens, J. (2011) *Confronting postmaternal thinking: Feminism, memory, and care*, New York, NY: Columbia University Press.

Stone, P.K. (2009) 'A history of Western medicine, labor, and birth', in H. Seline and P.K. Stone (eds) *Childbirth across cultures: Ideas and practices of pregnancy, childbirth and the postpartum*, New York, NY: Springer, pp. 41–53.

Szalinski, C. (2019) 'A history of cribs and other brilliant and bizarre inventions for getting babies to sleep', *Smithsonian.com*, [online] 9 May, Available from: www.smithsonianmag.com/innovation/history-cribs-other-brilliant-bizarre-inventions-getting-babies-to-sleep-180972138 [Accessed 18 October 2019].

Taylor, U. (1998) 'The historical evolution of black feminist theory and praxis', *Journal of Black Studies*, 29(2): 234–53.

Teasley, M. and Ikard, D. (2010) 'Barack Obama and the politics of race: The myth of postracism in America', *Journal of Black Studies*, 40(3): 411–25.

Tomori, C. (2014) *Nighttime breastfeeding: An American cultural dilemma*, New York, NY: Berghahn Books.

Twamley, K. and Schober, P. (2019) 'Shared parental leave: Exploring variations in attitudes, eligibility, knowledge and take-up intentions of expectant mothers in London', *Journal of Social Policy*, 48(2): 387–407.

Tyler, I. (2008) 'Chav mum chav scum', *Feminist Media Studies*, 8(1): 17–34.

Tyler, I. (2010) 'Designed to fail: A biopolitics of British citizenship', *Citizenship Studies*, 14(1), 61–74.

Tyler, I. (2011) 'Pregnant beauty: Maternal femininities under neoliberalism', in R. Gill and C. Scharff (eds) *New femininities: Postfeminism, neoliberalism and subjectivity*, London: Palgrave, pp. 21–36.

Tyler, I. (2013) 'Naked protest: The maternal politics of citizenship and revolt', *Citizenship Studies*, 17(2): 211–26.

UK Sling Consortium (nd) 'The T.I.C.K.S rule for safe babywearing', [online], Available from: http://babyslingsafety.co.uk [Accessed 25 October 2019].

UNICEF (United Nations Children's Fund) (2017) 'Improving breastfeeding, complementary foods and feeding practices', UNICEF UK, [online], Available from: www.unicef.org/nutrition/index_breastfeeding.html [Accessed 23 October 2019].

UNICEF and WHO (World Health Organization) (2018) 'Enabling women to breastfeed through better policies and programmes: Global breastfeeding scorecard 2018', World Health Organization, [online], Available from: www.who.int/nutrition/publications/infantfeeding/global-bf-scorecard-2018/en [Accessed 23 October 2019].

Vincent, C., Rollock, N., Ball, S. and Gillborn, D. (2012) Raising middle-class black children: Parenting priorities, actions and strategies, *Sociology*, 47(3): 427–42.

Wacquant, L. (2012) 'Three steps to a historical anthropology of actually existing neoliberalism', *Social Anthropology*, 20(1): 66–79.

Walcott, R. (2003) *Black like who?: Writing black Canada* (2nd edn, revised), Toronto, ON: Insomniac Press.

Wall, G. (2001) 'Moral constructions of motherhood in breastfeeding discourse', *Gender & Society*, 15(4): 592–610.

Wall, G. (2004) 'Is your child's brain potential maximized? Mothering in an age of new brain research', *Atlantis*, 28(2): 41–9.

Walshe, S. (2014) 'The heir, the judge and the homeless mom: America's prison bias for the 1%', *The Guardian*, [online] 2 April, Available from: www.theguardian.com/commentisfree/2014/apr/02/dupont-heir-homeless-mom-america-prison-bias [Accessed 23 October 2019].

Wane, N.N. (2002) 'Black-Canadian feminist thought: Drawing on the experiences of my sisters', in N.N. Wane, K. Deliovsky and E. Lawson (eds) *Back to the drawing board: African-Canadian feminisms*, Toronto, ON: Sumach Press, pp. 29–53.

Wane, N.N. (2009) 'Black Canadian feminist thought: Perspectives on equity and diversity in the academy', *Race Ethnicity and Education*, 12(1): 65–77.

Wane, N.N., Deliovsky, K. and Lawson, E. (2002) 'Introduction', in N.N. Wane, K. Deliovsky and E. Lawson (eds) *Back to the drawing board: African-Canadian feminisms*, Toronto, ON: Sumach Press, pp. 13–26.

Ward, J.R. (2015) 'Introduction: The real scandal – portrayals of black women in reality TV', in J.R. Ward (ed) *Real sister: Stereotypes, respectability, and black women in reality TV*, New Brunswick, NJ: Rutgers University Press, pp. 1–15.

Warren, A.J. (2001) 'The mom who invented the Snugli', *CBS*, [online] 6 March, Available from: www.cbsnews.com/news/the-mom-who-invented-the-snugli [Accessed 18 October 2019].

Webster, W. (1998) *Imagining home: Gender, 'race' and national identity, 1945–64*, London: UCL Press.

Weeks, C. (2010) 'Why aren't more women breastfeeding?', *The Globe and Mail*, [online] 11 July, Available from: https://beta.theglobeandmail.com/life/why-arent-more-women-breastfeeding/article561821/?ref=http://www.theglobeandmail.com& [Accessed 23 October 2019].

Weiner, L.Y. (1997) 'Reconstructing motherhood: The La Leche League in postwar America', in R.D. Apple and J. Golden (eds) *Mothers & motherhood: Readings in American history*, Columbus, OH: Ohio State University Press, pp. 362–88.

West, E. with Knight, R.J. (2017) 'Mothers' milk: Slavery, wet-nursing, and black and white women in the antebellum South', *The Journal of Southern History*, 83(1): 37–68.

Wilkie, L.A. (2003) *The archaeology of mothering: An African-American midwife's tale*, New York, NY: Routledge.

Wolf, J.B. (2011) *Is breast best? Taking on the breastfeeding experts and the new high stakes of motherhood*, New York, NY: New York University Press.

Women's Budget Group (2016) 'A cumulative gender impact assessment of ten years of austerity policies', Women's Budget Group, [online], Available from: https://wbg.org.uk/wp-content/uploads/2016/03/De_HenauReed_WBG_GIAtaxben_briefing_2016_03_06.pdf [Accessed 23 October 2019].

Wren-Lewis, S. (2019) 'The promised Tory tax cuts will only mean austerity in the long run', *The Guardian*, [online] 5 September, Available from: www.theguardian.com/commentisfree/2019/sep/05/tory-spending-increases-tax-cuts-austerity-economic-stimulus-boris-johnson-sajid-javid [Accessed 23 October 2019].

Index

Notes: AP is used as an abbreviation of attachment parenting. *Italic* page numbers indicate Figures and Tables.

www.ingramcontent.com/pod-product-compliance
Lightning Source LLC
Chambersburg PA
CBHW070925030426
42336CB00014BA/2537